THE OUTDOOR TRAVELER'S GUIDE
AUSTRALIA

BY GERRY ELLIS AND SHARON COHEN
WITH RESEARCH BY MARK C. KESTIGIAN

PHOTOGRAPHS BY

GERRY ELLIS

STEWART, TABORI & CHANG
NEW YORK

Library of Congress Cataloging-in-Publication Data

Ellis, Gerry.
    Australia.

    (The Outdoor traveler's guide)
    Includes index.
    1. Australia – Description and travel – 1981 –
– Guide-books.   2. Outdoor recreation – Australia –
Guide-books.   3. National parks and reserves –
Australia – Guide-books.   I. Cohen, Sharon (Sharon
Anne) II. Kestigian, Mark. III. Title. IV. Series.
DU105.2.E45   1988   919.4'0463   87-33586
ISBN 1-55670-019-9

Published in 1988 by Stewart, Tabori & Chang, Inc.,
740 Broadway, New York, NY 10003
Distributed by Workman Publishing,
708 Broadway, New York, NY 10003

Design: J. C. Suarès, Jeff Batzli
Maps: Guenter Vollath

Printed in Japan.

Frontispiece: Maria Island, Tasmania.

F O R E W O R D

THE NATURAL HERITAGE of Australia is dramatically unlike that of any other in the world. We have long felt the responsibility to help preserve this heritage for future generations, and our vast tracts of protected land attest to this. A strong conservationist impulse has permitted the survival of several endangered species and has ensured the protection of many other natural treasures.

We are proud to support Stewart, Tabori & Chang in the creation of THE OUTDOOR TRAVELER'S GUIDE TO AUSTRALIA, a book that makes two important contributions. First, Gerry Ellis captures our most prized natural treasures as few photographers have before. Second, the book conveys an enthusiasm for adventure and discovery that is very much in the Australian spirit. We believe this book will help us share our natural resources with interested and respectful travelers from all over the world.

Ansett.  Tourism Australia    *THE AUSTRALIAN AIRLINE*

Ross Alexander	Bill Baker	Peter N. Roennfeldt
Public Affairs Executive	Area Manager,	Sales Development Director,
Ansett, Australia	Los Angeles	The Americas
	Tourism Australia	Qantas Airways Limited

C O N T E N T S

Eddystone coastline in Mount William National Park, Tasmania.

AUSTRALIA

```
0                    400 Mi
0                    400 Km
```

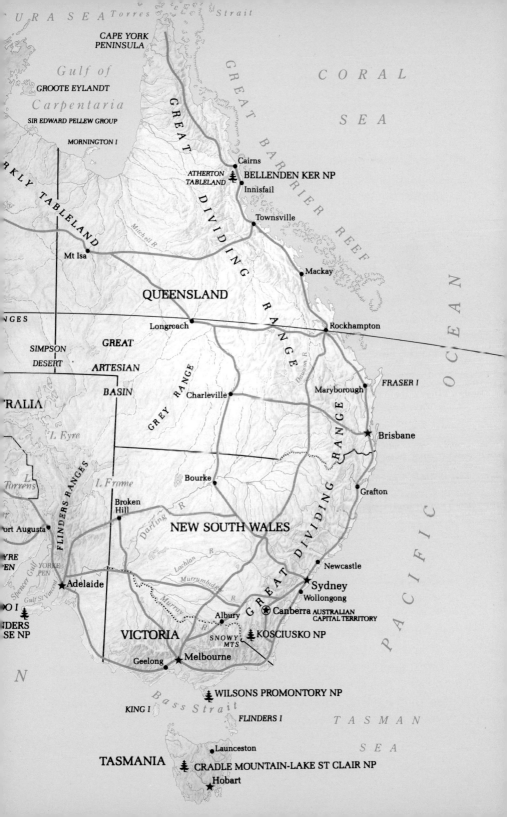

ACKNOWLEDGMENTS

WE WOULD LIKE TO ACKNOWLEDGE the vital help and support that many people provided us during the completion of this book. We are indebted to more people than could be named here, but extend our appreciation to all, both named and unnamed.

A special thanks to the countless men and women in the Australian National Park system who provided not only unending guidance, information, and good cheer but who were also willing to open their hearts and homes to us. Much of their work often goes unrecognized. It is our hope that the beauty and quality of this book will reflect our appreciation.

Tourism Australia was instrumental in transforming a fledgling idea into reality. We received help, cooperation, and blessings from both the New York and the Sydney offices, which served as our main communication channel as well as our major source of guidance for the two years of this project. Our gratitude to Bill Baker in Los Angeles and Peggy Bendel in New York can never be great enough. Thanks to John Rowe, John King, Wayne Storey, and Donna Smail in Sydney, and to Alan Drew in the Los Angeles office.

And a special debt is owed to Gemma Tisdell, without whose patience, caring, and ceaseless dedication this book might never have been.

A warm thanks to Neil Travers, Wayne Stenning, and Joan Exeter of Ansett Airlines.

Grateful acknowledgment to Peter Roennfeldt and Peter Schaap of Qantas Airways.

Special thanks go to Avis Australia.

Photographic assistance, even when it required rising before dawn or working through the night, was selflessly given by Jeff Foster and Richard Ellis.

Thanks to the staff at Stewart, Tabori & Chang, whose tremendous support, encouragement, and direction was uncompromising in changing this dream into a reality. And a special thanks to our editor, Maureen Graney, whose tireless devotion to even the smallest of details was appreciated and admired.

We would also like to acknowledge the grateful assistance of the following: Gary Bell, Lance Bennett, Chris Boylan, Sharon Chambers, David Douglas, Geoff Doyle, Chris Eden, Ray & Millie Ellis, Deb Foster, Tony Gander, Mike Gillam, Graz, Ian Hall, Peter Hornsby, Kay Hoskings, Michael Hutchins, Bob Jenkins, Dean Lee, Fiona Marr, Frank McFayden, Tracy McGregor, Mike Osmond, Tom Perrigo, Craig Saunders, Barbara Spence, Wayne Stenning.

Last but certainly not least we wish to thank the people of Australia. During the two years we and our associates spent in Australia, they never ceased to ease our work with their smiles, warm g'days, and genuine friendship.

We were fortunate in being able to draw upon a wealth of information currently available on Australian natural history. Though we do not cite individual references in the text, the following should be cited as invaluable in our preparation of this book. However, the responsibility for the interpretation of their work remains with us. In addition to serving as an acknowledgment, this list also provides useful suggestions for further reading.

Andrews, Phil. *Tasmania's Native Mammals*. Hobart: Tasmanian Museum and Art Gallery, 1981.

Archer, Michael, Gordon C. Grigg, and Dr. Tim F. Flannery. *The Kangaroo*. McMahons Point, NSW: Weldons, 1985.

Blombery, Alec M. *What Wildflower is That?* Sydney: Paul Hamlyn, 1972.

Breeden, Stanley, and Kay Breeden. *Australia's Far North*. Sydney: Collins, 1982.

Breeden, Stanley, and Kay Breeden. *Australia's Southeast*. Sydney: Collins, 1982.

Breeden, Stanley, and Kay Breeden. *Tropical Queensland*. Sydney: Collins, 1982.

Breeden, Stanley, and Kay Breeden. *Wildlife of Eastern Australia*. New York: Taplinger, 1973.

Coggers, H. G. *Reptiles and Amphibians of Australia*. Sydney: Reed, 1975.

Complete Book of Australian Birds. Sydney: Reader's Digest, 1976.

Frith, Clifford, and Dawn Clifford. *Australia's Tropical Rainforest Life*. Paluma via Townsville, QLD: Tropical Australia Graphics, 1986.

Great Barrier Reef. Sydney: Reader's Digest, 1984.

Isaacs, Jennifer. *Australia's Living Heritage.* Sydney: Landsdowne, 1984.

National Parks of New South Wales. Sydney: Gregory's, 1984.

Native Plants of Australia. Kensington, NSW: Bay Books, 1986.

Pizzey, Graham. *A Field Guide to the Birds of Australia.* Sydney: Collins, 1980.

Raymond, Robert. *Discover Australia's National Parks.* Melbourne: Macmillan, 1985.

Strahan, Ronald, ed. *Complete Book of Australian Mammals.* London: Angus & Robertson, 1983.

Wild Australia. Sydney: Reader's Digest, 1984.

– GERRY ELLIS AND SHARON COHEN

THE PUBLISHER AND EDITOR would like to thank the many people whose generosity and accessibility ensured a high standard of accuracy in this volume.

Two individuals provided invaluable guidance in the completion of the Tasmania chapter: Prof. Christopher Eastoe, a Tasmanian geologist working at the University of Arizona, and Jayne Wells, botanist, Western Tasmania Wilderness World Heritage Area.

The following people gave us essential advice on specific chapters. In New South Wales, Berkeley Wiles, New South Wales National Parks and Wildlife Service. In Victoria, Hazel Berry and Ian Weir, Victorian Tourism Commission. In Tasmania, Shane Hunniford and Craig Macaulay. In South Australia, Robert B. Jenkins, South Australian Department of Tourism. In Western Australia, Henry Kujda, Western Australia Tourism Commission, and John Hunter, National Parks Authority of Western Australia. In the Northern Territory, Charles Blackwell (of the Los Angeles office) and Barb Johnston, Northern Territory Tourist Commission, and Andrea Schulzer and R. E. Fox, Conservation Commission of the Northern Territory. In Queensland, Patricia Geale and Cherryl Stanbridge, Queensland Tourist & Travel Corporation; Stan Wilcox, Department of the Arts,

National Parks, and Sport; and Don Marshall, Queensland National Park & Wildlife Office. In the Great Barrier Reef, Jean Dartnall.

A number of scientists at the American Museum of Natural History in New York graciously agreed to review the vignettes about animals. They are: Dr. Timothy J. McCarthy, Department of Mammalogy; Jay Pitocchelli, Department of Ornithology; Dr. C. L. Smith, Department of Ichthyology; and Dr. Richard G. Zweifel, Department of Herpetology.

Dr. J. G. West, Australian Botanical Liaison Officer, Royal Botanic Gardens at Kew, London, reviewed the vignettes about plants.

Dr. Stephen Cairns and Dr. Frederick Bayer in the Department of Invertebrate Zoology at the Smithsonian Institution helped us review a number of our Great Barrier Reef photographs.

Many thanks also go to Moira Duggan.

We are grateful to all of these individuals for their professionalism and their interest in this project.

Ayers Rock, Northern Territory.

NEW SOUTH WALES

Sydney Harbour National Park
Ku-ring-gai Chase National Park
Royal National Park
Blue Mountains National Park
Lord Howe Island
Border Ranges National Park
Barrington Tops National Park
Kosciusko National Park
Ben Boyd National Park
Yuraygir National Park
Warrumbungle National Park
Kinchega National Park
Mungo National Park
Sturt National Park

Every available space in Border Ranges National Park is lush and green. This area, which becomes Lamington National Park over the Queensland border, supports a rich variety of wildlife: one fourth of all Australian bird species have been seen here.

Kosciusko National Park encompasses the largest protected alpine area in Australia.

FOR MANY VISITORS, New South Wales is the gateway to Australia. As one arrives in the state's metropolitan hub, Sydney, one's first impressions of the continent "down under" begin to take shape. Unfortunately, many travelers to New South Wales venture little farther than Sydney's sprawling city limits. Boarding a jet bound for the red center or the Great Barrier Reef, they fly over many national and state parks. Quintessential Australian creatures – the kangaroo, koala, sulphur-crested cockatoo, and wallaby – all reside a mere hour's drive from Sydney in three of Australia's most popular parks: Blue Mountains, Ku-ring-gai Chase, and Royal.

Eastern New South Wales is dominated by the Great Dividing Range, an ancient eroded range of uplifted sandstone and granite pockmarked by intrusions of volcanic basalt. Along the range, between the Queensland and Victoria borders, environments contrast dramatically. At Barrington Tops, for example, snow is not uncommon on the high plateaus, while in the valley below a subtropical rain forest sustains relic Antarctic vegetation. The mountains form a weather barrier, trapping moisture in the coastal

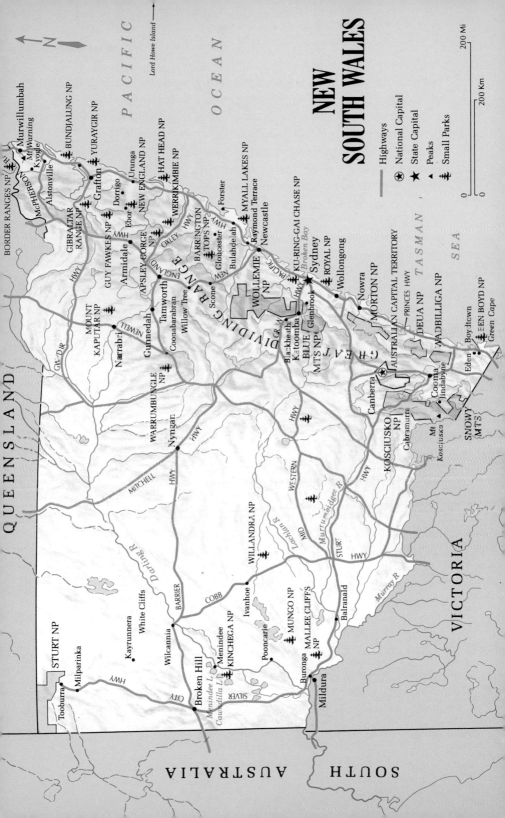

regions and leaving the western part of the state an endless expanse of farmland and scrub, largely deprived of rain.

New South Wales has a long tradition of protecting its wilderness in national parks. Royal National Park was established in 1879, becoming only the second declared national park in the world (Yellowstone in the United States, a year earlier, was the first). Five years later, "a national park for North Sydney" was created, which later was named Ku-ring-gai Chase. This tradition of concern for the natural heritage of New South Wales continues today; the state has sixty-six national parks, twenty state recreation areas, and more than 170 nature reserves.

SYDNEY HARBOUR NATIONAL PARK

Sydney Harbour National Park,
Greycliffe House, Vaucluse, NSW
2030, or call (02) 337 5511.

Visitors come to Sydney Harbour National Park for its spectacular views of the harbor and as a place of retreat within the confines of the city. Formerly a military installation, the land within the park was opened to the public in 1975. Old fortifications still loom protectively on the headlands which, from their height of 300 ft/90 m, give an excellent view of the entire harbor.

The soil is nutrient-poor, and, except in selected areas, most of the vegetation has been cleared. The salt sea wind has stunted much of the hardier vegetation: dwarf eucalyptus trees grow on Grotto Point, and small patches of forest grow at Dobroyd Head and Bradleys Head. The verdant areas support a variety of plants and shrubs, including bottlebrush, she-oaks, wattles, spider flowers, yellow pea flowers, and several species of native orchids. The park is especially lush with wildflowers from July through October.

Occasionally, possums may be spotted here. Much more common are lizards and several species of native birds, especially honey eaters and tawny frogmouths.

Aboriginal rock engravings are found at Grotto Point and elsewhere in the park.

KU-RING-GAI CHASE NATIONAL PARK

New South Wales National Parks
and Wildlife Service District Office,

Bobbin Head, Turramurra, NSW
2074, or call (02) 457 9322.

Named for the Guringai tribe that originally inhabited the area, this small park, only 15.5 mi/25 km north of Sydney, offers city dwellers a ready escape. There are walking trails and picnic areas, beautiful quiet beaches, and some exceptional viewing areas, especially at West Head.

Oils evaporating from blue gum trees are responsible for the early morning blue haze of Ku-Ring-Gai Chase National Park.

This frog of the Litoria species is found in rain forests throughout New South Wales. Known as a tree frog, its long fingers enable it to climb trees if necessary, but it prefers to spend most of its time on the ground.

Rising above Broken Bay, the park's slopes support an array of vegetation even though the soil is fairly low in nutrients. Originally an extensive delta, the area was flooded by the sea more than 200 million years ago and then covered by layers of sand. The underlying Hawkesbury sandstone began pushing upward 50 million years ago, leaving deep gorges and valleys. The area was brought to its present state just 10,000 years ago, when sea levels began rising and the valleys surrounding the uplifted sections were flooded. Several areas, such as Lion Island, were left isolated, and a number of waterways were created.

From July through October a host of wildflowers—including banksias, grevilleas, waratahs, hakeas, boronias, and pea flowers—blooms throughout the park. Angophoras, she-oaks, eucalypts, turpentines, wattles, and other tree varieties line the slopes and inland waterways.

The vegetation attracts many insects and birds such as honey eaters, kookaburras, lyrebirds, and an assortment of parrots including the sulphur-crested cockatoo. The park provides an ideal environment for possums, swamp wallabies, and echidnas. There are lizards, too, notably the huge lace monitors. Tortoises, frogs, and an occasional snake may also be seen.

SHORT-BEAKED ECHIDNA
Tachyglossus aculeatus

The echidna belongs to the remarkable group of mammals called monotremes, egg-laying mammals. It possesses attributes of mammals—fur and mammary glands—yet it reproduces by laying an egg which it incubates for about ten days and carries in a temporary abdominal pouch until spines develop on the baby's back and sides.

The sharp spines that cover the echidna's body deter predators, with the exception of an occasional dingo. When threatened, the echidna will either roll into a tight ball or dig down into the soil. Its spines enable it to wedge itself into hollow logs and rock crevices where it can hide during the day or for as long as necessary.

It eats termites and ants, catching them with a sticky tongue that can be extended as far as 7 in/18 cm. It can fast for days during a downpour or other unfavorable situation. The echidna is also called the spiny anteater.

ROYAL NATIONAL PARK

New South Wales National Parks and Wildlife Service District Office, P.O. Box 44, Sutherland, NSW 2232, or call (02) 521 2230. Bush camping is permitted in the park, but permits must be obtained first.

When National Park was established in 1879, it was managed by a trust that was continually in search of money for park maintenance. It succumbed many times to pressures by timber companies seeking to log the white turpentine trees and several varieties of strong eucalypts that covered the area. This practice was halted finally in 1922 by the State Crown Solicitor, but parts of National Park, which became Royal National Park in 1955 after a visit by Queen Elizabeth II, still reflect an uncertain understanding of what a national

park should represent. In some places, the human presence is strongly felt: there are paved walkways, well-manicured lawns, and ornamental trees. But other parts of the park retain some of the original natural splendor of the landscape, and the wilderness is returning in some places.

The park, only 20 mi/32 km south of Sydney, is composed of deeply etched sandstone ridges covered with heath and cut by deep creeks and gullies. The cliffs facing the Pacific Ocean are constantly being reshaped by the waves. There is little vegetation along the shore, but plant life abounds on the inland slopes and deep gullies of the park, especially along the Hacking River.

Several of the beaches along the coast of Royal National Park are excellent for surfing. Freshwater swimming holes, such as the popular Flat Rock Crystal Pool, dot the inland areas of the park. Wattamolla Cove offers excellent swimming, fishing, scuba diving, and snorkeling. It was called Providential Cove by its discoverers, George Bass and Matthew Flinders, who used its sheltered waters to escape a raging storm, but later its Aboriginal name was reinstated.

The park was inhabited originally by the Dharawal people. An Aboriginal tribe that lived in the area for centuries, the Dharawal fell victim to the diseases brought by the European settlers. Evidence of their occupation can be seen at Curracurrang, Jibbon, Marley Head, and several other areas in the park.

WILDLIFE

The many flowers that blossom in this park attract a great variety of insects and some nectar-feeding birds, such as honey eaters and wattlebirds. Many other birds are found in the park, but they are more elusive. Satin bowerbirds are a rare but welcome find, especially if you are lucky enough to spot a male strutting in his bower, awaiting the attentions of a prospective mate. Lyrebirds, with their long, lyre-shaped tailfeathers, sing out loudly, and pied currawongs may be seen flying overhead. Other birds that may be sighted include

The brilliant colors of the flowering banksia attract many birds and insects. Growing up to 16 ft/5 m tall, the spikes of this shrub's conspicuous flowers grow to about 3 in/8 cm long.

BRUSH-TAILED POSSUMS
Trichosurus spp.

Brush-tailed possums are the most commonly seen mammals in Australia. They are found in most wooded and forested areas and are extremely widespread because of their ability to adapt to different habitats and their rapid reproductive cycle (they breed once or twice a year and have a brief gestation period of about seventeen days).

There are three main species generally recognized in Australia: common brush-tailed (*T. vulpecula*), mountain brush-tailed (*T. caninus*), and northern brush-tailed (*T. arnhemensis*). While there are differences in their color and fur, all three share certain characteristics. All are nocturnal and spend most of their existence in trees. They eat a variety of foods including eucalyptus leaves, young shoots, fruits, flowers, seeds, bark, insects, and, in some cases, small animals such as young birds.

These possums have an elaborate method for defending their territory

by means of scent markings. They have a number of different scent-producing glands, especially in the chest region, to accomplish this.

the wonga pigeon, gray butcher-bird, and eastern whipbird. The male whipbird calls out with a long whistled whipcrack and the female answers with a few chirps.

Most of the mammals at Royal National Park are nocturnal and therefore rarely seen; occasionally a swamp wallaby or an echidna may be sighted near dusk. Night brings out a variety of small animals – ring-tailed and brush-tailed possums, southern bush rats, swamp rats, New Holland mice, and the tiny, mouse-like antechinus – in search of food.

VEGETATION

The moist areas of the park support tall turpentines, coachwood trees, and fig trees. A tall open forest grows in the gullies and lower slopes, where the soil is more fertile. Varieties here include black-butts, Sydney blue gums, and hibbertia shrubs as well as an under-story of forest oak, hop bush, and black wattle. On the valley slopes near the Hacking River, a low subtropical rain forest has a brilliant array of flowering shrubs, including bright orange parrot peas; grass-like gymea lilies with showy red flowers atop 13-ft/4-m stems; and conspicuous orange and red banksias.

The heath on the exposed parts of the park is covered with wild-flowers from August through October. The species include the gee-bung, with its tiny yellow flowers; several varieties of flowering peas; mallee banksia; and needlebush.

BLUE MOUNTAINS NATIONAL PARK

New South Wales National Parks and Wildlife Service District Office, P.O. Box 43, Blackheath, NSW 2785, or call (047) 87 8877 (northern part of park, open seven days), or (047) 39 2950 (southern part of park, week-ends only).

The magnificent Blue Mountains National Park lies only 62 mi/ 100 km west of Sydney and totals 585,459 acres/236,932 hectares. It offers some of the most spectacular mountain scenery on earth. A deep blue haze – an optical effect created by oils evaporating from the gums – lingers over the mountains, especially in the morning when the sun first appears.

Raised from a coastal plain more than 1 million years ago, the Blue Mountains are not actually mountains, but are rather the elevated remains of a vast plateau that at places is over 1,968 ft/600 m thick. The hard layers of sandstone are all that is left of the sediments deposited when the area was part of a large river system. Now

Pages 26 and 27: This rock formation, called the Three Sisters, is found in the greater southern section of Blue Mountains National Park. Best viewed from the Echo Point Lookout, about 3 mi/5 km from the center of Katoomba, the Three Sisters is a favorite among the many shapes eroded from the plateau.

undercut and split by rivers, the plateau is still being eaten away by erosion; huge boulders and small rock slides are ever plunging into the rivers.

The sandy soil of the plateau is not very fertile, but it does support wildflowers. A greater variety of vegetation grows in the sheltered gullies and valleys surrounding the plateau and along its riverbanks.

The park is divided into three sections: the north, south, and greater southern sections. North and south are divided by the Great Western Highway, and the newest area, the greater southern section, extends 242,158 acres/87,253 hectares south of Katoomba to the Wombeyan Caves. Largely a wilderness section with few roads, it offers fine opportunities for bushwalking and camping.

Glenbrook, the southern section of the park from Glenbrook to Wentworth Falls to Erskine Creek, is known for its rock swimming pools, teeming waterfalls, and picnic and camping areas.

Grose Valley, the northern section of the park, covers the area from the highway to the Wollangambe Wilderness. The Grose Valley is an impressive sight, with its sheer walls smoothed by the Grose River. It is accessible but still wild, and visitors must descend on foot, via sometimes steep paths, to get to the valley floor. Here they find lush grasses and ferns, as well as peppermint, scribbly gums, black and white ash, and stunted mallees. Plants of particular interest include insect-eating sundew plants, several varieties of colorful boronias, and the magnificent scarlet waratah, the state flower.

Many birds are found here, including lyrebirds, wrens, honey eaters, tawny frogmouths, and parrots. Few mammals are seen during the day, but kangaroos and wallabies can often be spotted at dusk.

BUSHWALKING

Bushwalking is exciting and rewarding in Grose Valley because of the magnificent views of the gorges and a fine waterfall. Visitors are advised to boil any water before drinking it: the area has not completely escaped the effects of civilization.

Grand Canyon to Neates Glen. Although not recommended for the elderly or for young children, this is one of the most popular bushwalking trails in the northern sector of Blue Mountains National Park. It is a three- to four-hour hike that winds through thickly for-

TAWNY FROGMOUTH
Podargus strigoides

If you were to approach a tawny frogmouth during the day you might think it was a piece of wood; at night you might take it for an owl. But, of course, the tawny frogmouth is neither.

The tawny frogmouth, a member of the nightjar family, is named for its broad, hooked bill that makes it look as if it had an endless mouth; the bird resembles an owl in that it has large round gleaming yellow eyes. Known also as the *mopoke*, it is widespread in timbered country and occurs also in some suburban and city parks. It eats many creatures that are found typically on road surfaces, such as insects, lizards, and other small vertebrates, and consequently many of these birds are killed by motor vehicles.

What makes the frogmouth especially interesting is the way it camouflages itself during the daytime or when it is alarmed. It narrows its big yellow eyes to mere slits and raises its head and bill skyward. Its

usually fluffy feathers become compressed. In this position it looks like a piece of dead wood and is able to fool most of its predators.

ested gray-barked sassafras, giant ferns, and patches of moist green rain forest. More open areas along the trail reveal clusters of banksias, Sydney golden wattles, and she-oaks.

Red Hands Cave Nature Trail. This three-hour trip in the Glenbrook area goes by several early Aboriginal art sites where hand stencils decorate cavern walls. The walk also features beautiful floral displays and many lizard species, such as jacky lizards, skinks, and goannas.

Narrow Neck to Mt. Solitary. There are several starting points to this all-day hike in the greater southern section, the least arduous being a ride on the scenic railway at Katoomba down to the Federal Pass; one then walks to the higher rocky remains known as the Ruined Castle. The ascent of Mt. Solitary from the Ruined Castle is quite steep and should be attempted only by experienced bushwalkers. Those who attain the summit enjoy the panoramic views of the park.

LORD HOWE ISLAND

The Administrative Officer, Lord Howe Island, NSW 2898, or call (065) 63 2066.

No camping is allowed on the island, but tourist accommodations are available. The island is reached via regular charter planes from Sydney, Port Macquarie, Brisbane, and Norfolk Island.

A luxuriant, crescent-shaped island, Lord Howe lies 436 mi/702 km northeast of Sydney. Approximately 17.7 mi/11 km long and 1.75 mi/2.8 km at its widest point, Lord Howe is believed to be the remnant of a volcano formed in a series of eruptions that ended 6.4 million years ago.

Two peaks dominate the island: Mt. Gower (3,090 ft/942 m) and Mt. Lidgbird (2,743 ft/836 m), named for the island's discoverer, Henry Lidgbird Ball. The island is flanked on its western side by the most southerly-occurring coral-reef formation in the world. The reef is spectacular and has been allowed to grow unhindered by human intervention for centuries.

Lord Howe Island is one of the few places in Australia where European settlers did not impose themselves. It did not fall victim to timber companies or have large tracts of its land turned over to livestock. Instead, it was used for the cultivation of kentia palms, a valuable export, and as a station to provide food and supplies to whaling ships.

The island is remarkable in that it demonstrates a transition between an algal and a coral-reef system. And–despite damage

Dense vegetation dominates Mt. Lidgbird but does not obstruct the view of Lord Howe Island's Mt. Gower or the island's coral reef.

done in earlier years by free-ranging pigs and goats and by invading ants—its ecosystem remains largely intact. Lord Howe is now on the World Heritage List, and its inhabitants and environment are protected from commercialization.

What all this means for the visitor is a guarantee of an ideal island experience. The beaches glisten in the sun and stretch endlessly along the coast. Small bays guard tranquil swimming waters, while open beaches, such as that at Blinky Point, provide perfect waves for the novice surfer.

The coral reef is exciting to explore, both above and below water. Glass-bottomed boats carry visitors on ninety-minute tours that reveal the splendors of the coral. The waters surrounding Lord Howe are alive with more than 440 species of multicolored fish and a diverse assortment of coral species. Scuba diving is particularly rewarding here. At Neds Beach, the fish are so tame that they will eat from your hand.

While snorkeling and scuba diving are favorite activities, the visitor on Lord Howe Island has many more to choose from. The warm weather and cool tropical breezes allow for many types of outdoor activities, including swimming, boating, fishing, and bushwalking. Boats are available to provide sightseeing tours around the island, as well as for fishing and scuba diving.

WILDLIFE

Besides the great variety of fish species that inhabit the island's waters, Lord Howe supports a large population of birdlife. Parts of the island, together with Admiralty Island off its northwest shore, serve as breeding sanctuaries for pelagic (ocean-dwelling) birds and some birds indigenous to the island.

Muttonbirds, or shearwaters, are the most popular residents, usually seen returning to their colonies at night. Boobies and gannets, with their clearly defined faces and soft, downy chicks, enjoy the plentiful supply of fish, as do the terns and tropic birds. The population of the Lord Howe wood hen, a flightless brown bird that was nearly extinct until islanders and conservation officials jointly began a captive breeding program, has increased steadily.

Each species of brightly colored angelfish has its own unique pattern, which enables members to identify each other easily during breeding season.

VEGETATION

The island is covered with luxuriant vegetation on its sand-covered shores and high mountain peaks. Everything benefits from the cool breeze off the ocean, the plentiful supply of freshwater creeks and streams, and the abundant rainfall. The climate and rich soil are ideal for growing kentia palms, the second largest industry on the island, after tourism. Three other palm species grow on the island: the curly, umbrella, and little mountain palms.

An unusual tree to be seen here is the banyan fig tree, whose roots fall to the forest floor from high branches and then grow to a thickness rivaling that of the tree trunk. The trees cover a large area of ground, appearing both eerie and imposing. Screw pines, or pandanus, which grow along creeks, also have a system of prop roots that helps them survive the harsh winds and downpours.

Flowers grow profusely throughout the island and coastal heath. Some varieties found here are bush orchids, mountain roses, white mountain daisies, and wedding lilies. The pumpkin tree, which blooms from October to April, sports large orange blossoms.

BORDER RANGES NATIONAL PARK

New South Wales National Parks and Wildlife District Office, P.O. Box 91, Alstonville, NSW 2477, or call (066) 28 1177.

The park is 18.6 mi/30 km west of Murwillumbah. Motel accommodations are available nearby, and bush camping is permitted.

Resting on the northern border of New South Wales, this superb park is a continuation of Queensland's Lamington National Park and represents a further preservation of the extremely rich vegetation of the McPherson Range. When the area was declared a national park in 1983, logging operations were halted abruptly, and the giant blackbutt trees were granted immunity from destruction.

Border Ranges National Park is made up of three distinct regions, each offering the visitor a different park experience. For the hardiest of visitors, the Mt. Lindesay-Levers Plateau section in the west is extremely rugged and untamed. There are no roads for conventional vehicles here, no picnic areas, and no nearby information centers. The terrain is difficult to traverse, and the rain forest is thick

The scarlet leaves of poinsettia trees pepper the rain forest at Border Ranges. Facing page: The crimson rosella searches for fruit and seeds among high forest branches.

with prickly vines, mosquitoes, and leeches. There probably is no area in New South Wales that better demonstrates what this region was like before European settlement.

For those equally adventurous though less inclined toward rugged bushwalking, the eastern or Tweed Range area of the park is an ideal destination. This section is accessible by most vehicles. A beautiful 37-mi/60-km scenic drive, which one should begin at Lillian Rock, takes visitors out of the park and into Mt. Warning National Park for a ride around the rim of the Mt. Warning crater. Far-reaching vistas and magnificent scenery open out at many points along the

way. Several walking trails explore this section, which contains steep waterfalls and rushing streams.

The third, central part of the park is called the Lions Road section. This road is part of the scenic route between northern New South Wales and Brisbane, Queensland. There are several picnic areas along the way where visitors can stop and enjoy the scenery.

Mt. Warning is an important landmark and can be seen for miles. It is visible to ships far out at sea and was used as a marker by many explorers, most notably Captain James Cook, for judging the location of hazardous reefs.

Geology

The entire region was formed more than 20 million years ago, when constant action from a ring of volcanoes etched the landscape. Rivers, streams, and waterfalls contributed to the scenery by sculpting the volcanic rock. Mt. Warning stood at the center of this activity and still stands as one of the most impressive land masses in the region.

Wildlife and Vegetation

The extremely fertile volcanic soil and the abundant rainfall provide perfect conditions for a luxuriant subtropical rain forest. In the higher regions of the park, these conditions support a cool temperate rain forest of Antarctic beech.

Because of its ideal climate, available water supply, and abundance of vegetation, everywhere one looks—from high in the trees, to the banks of the streams, to the small water holes—bird life abounds. An observant bird watcher might sight seventy or more species in a single day. The most popular birds are the several varieties of parrots, seen plucking at seeds in the trees. Also common are kookaburras boldly calling to their mates and competitors, brush turkeys foraging on the ground, wrens flickering incessantly from bush to bush, and lyrebirds with their magnificent tails and loud, screeching voices.

An interesting animal found in the Border Ranges is the tiger quoll. The appearance of this little spotted creature belies its ferocious nature. A carnivorous marsupial, the quoll will shout with an explosive call when alarmed. Usually found combing the forest floor for food, it is an adept climber and may often be sighted in trees. Although basically nocturnal, it can sometimes be seen basking in the sun during the day.

Other mammals of the Border Ranges include the small furry potoroos, brush-tailed and ring-tailed possums, bandicoots, marsupial mice, and echidnas.

The very steep waterfalls in Border Ranges National Park drop from the Caldera Rim into the valley, forming streams that flow into the Tweed or Richmond rivers. Moss, lichen, and other vegetation grow on the rocks that line the falls.

Bandicoots, sometimes seen scurrying across roads at Barrington Tops National Park, are active at dusk as they search for insects, fallen fruit, and grass seeds in areas of low growth.

BARRINGTON TOPS NATIONAL PARK

New South Wales National Parks and Wildlife Service District Office, P.O. Box 270, Raymond Terrace, NSW 2324, or call (049) 87 3108.

The park is 23.6 mi/38 km west of Gloucester. Camping facilities are available in the park, in addition to camping and accommodations in nearby Gloucester, Dungog, and Scone.

A thick layer of cool mist enshrouds the two linked plateaus of Barrington Tops National Park. Side by side, these masses of granodiorite rock serve as the catchment area for the Hunter and Murray rivers. The deep gullies and ravines below the plateau eagerly drink up the teeming waterfalls from above and support a community of Antarctic beech. Farther down in the valley, below the cliff line, the warm climate and constant moisture sustain a subtropical rain forest of moss-covered trees complete with a host of colorful birds – lyrebirds, brush turkeys, parrots, and a few species of bowerbirds.

Formed from volcanic activity that forced granodiorite up through joints in folded sedimentary rock, the Barrington Tops are a delight to bushwalkers. The varying altitudes and excellent soil conditions are able to support a great variety of vegetation that includes snow gums, peat bogs, and grasslands, and the great height of the plateaus (5,085 ft/1,550 m) provides breathtaking vistas. The area is deluged often, and snowfall is common in the winter months of July and August.

The park's mammals include eastern gray kangaroos, wombats, possums, and marsupial mice. Present, too, but rarely seen are bandicoots and spotted quolls.

KOSCIUSKO NATIONAL PARK

Kosciusko National Park, Private Bag, Cooma, NSW 2630, or call (064) 56 2102.

Cabins are available, and camping is permitted, but not within 1.25 mi/ 2 km of public roads or facilities. A license is required for fishing. Some roads into the park may be closed in July and August; check with the park rangers before setting out.

Embracing the most extensive alpine region in all of Australia, Kosciusko is also one of the largest parks in the world, covering an area of 1,598,517 acres/646,911 hectares. Its northern section is only 12.4 mi/20 km from the capital in Canberra, and its southern section borders Victoria. With several peaks exceeding 6,500 ft/2,000 m in elevation, the park is the birthplace of many of the major rivers on the eastern coast of Australia, including the Snowy, Murray, Murrumbidgee, Tumut, and Eucumbene. It is also a major source for water and power in eastern Australia.

Snow usually covers much of this lofty region; it is not unusual for a sudden snowstorm to blanket the area, even during the summer month of December. An impressive array of alpine vegetation, including ribbon gums and hardy snow gums, grows on mountain slopes cut by ambling streams and trickling waterfalls. In heavy snowfalls, the snow gums stand out proudly, their trunks, stripped of bark, showing red and their branches edged with enduring green leathery leaves.

The high mountain slopes of the park, topped by Mt. Kosciusko at 7,310 ft/2,228 m, attract thousands of skiers each winter. Many view Kosciusko National Park as the best ski area in all of Australia, offering challenges to both downhill and cross-country skiers. There are several resorts catering to skiers, but the demand for accommodations far exceeds their availability.

Kosciusko has much more to offer visitors than excellent skiing, however. In the summer, the park's altitude provides a cooling antidote to the heat of the Australian sun. After the major winter thaw, the alpine meadows blaze forth in a sea of brightly colored wildflowers, including buttercups, snow daisies, and mountain gentians. Streams that flow after the winter thaw encourage a lively cluster of vegetation along their banks.

Lakes in the park were formed millions of years ago when glaciers carved natural reservoirs in the valley and rainfall filled them in. Today in these quiet pools trout fishing is superb. Lake Cootapatamba, 656 ft/200 m below the summit of Mt. Kosciusko, is one of the highest lakes in the world.

Winter in Kosciusko National Park attracts skiers from every state on the continent. Close to Canberra and Sydney, it offers the best slopes and terrain for skiing in Australia.

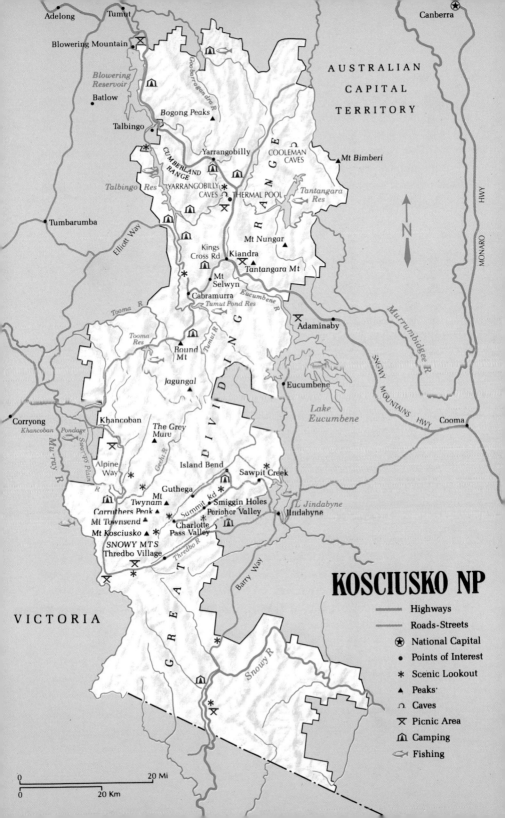

Adelong
Tumut
Canberra

Blowering Mountain
Blowering Reservoir
Batlow
Bogong Peaks
Talbingo

AUSTRALIAN
CAPITAL
TERRITORY

CUMBERLAND RANGE
Yarrangobilly
COOLEMAN CAVES
Mt Bimberi

Talbingo Res
YARRANGOBILLY CAVES
THERMAL POOL
Tantangara Res

Tumbarumba

Elliot Way

Mt Nungar

Kings Cross Rd
Kiandra
Tantangara Mt

Mt Selwyn
Cabramurra
Tumut Pond Res

Tooma R

Tooma Res
Round Mt

Eucumbene R

Adaminaby

Jagungal

Tumut R

GREAT DIVIDING RANGE

Lake Eucumbene

Eucumbene

Corryong
Khancoban
Khancoban Pondage
The Grey Mare
Island Bend
Sawpit Creek

SNOWY MOUNTAINS HWY

Cooma

Swampy Plain R

Murray R

Alpine Way

Geehi R

Guthega
Summit Rd
Smiggin Holes
Perisher Valley
Jindabyne
L Jindabyne

Mt Twynam
Carruthers Peak
Mt Townsend
Mt Kosciusko
Charlotte Pass Valley

SNOWY MTS
Thredbo Village

Thredbo R

Barry Way

VICTORIA

Snowy R

Murrumbidgee R

MONARO HWY

N

KOSCIUSKO NP

Highways
Roads-Streets
⍟ National Capital
• Points of Interest
∗ Scenic Lookout
▲ Peaks
∩ Caves
⋈ Picnic Area
⌂ Camping
🐟 Fishing

0   20 Mi
0   20 Km

Bushwalking is challenging, and many enjoy walking to the top of Mt. Kosciusko, a 12.4-mi/20-km round trip. Visitors are cautioned to carry warm clothing, since snowstorms can occur suddenly at any time of the year.

The Yarrangobilly Caves include four well-lit caves that are open for public viewing. The thermal pools in the caves maintain a fairly constant temperature of 80° F/26° C, and visitors are allowed to bathe in their soothing waters.

BEN BOYD NATIONAL PARK

New South Wales National Parks and Wildlife Service District Office, P.O. Box 186, Eden, NSW 2551, or call (064) 96 1434.
No camping is permitted in the northern section of the park, but it is permitted in the southern section. No camping is allowed within ½ mi/1 km of roads or picnic areas.

Ben Boyd National Park flanks Twofold Bay on the north and south. It is named for Benjamin Boyd, who tried to found here a city to rival Sydney. Instead, an abandoned village and the relic of a lighthouse are all that remain of Boyd's dream. The land, however, has been put to productive use as one of New South Wales' finest national parks.

The southernmost coastal park in the state, it encompasses long undulating beaches, multicolored promontories, cool dark caves, expanses of heath, and tall eucalypt woodlands. Within a day's drive of Sydney, Ben Boyd delights visitors whether their search is for bushwalking, fishing, swimming, or beautiful views.

The scenery at Ben Boyd is remarkable for its reddish-brown and white cliffs and headlands. The coloration was caused by the leaching of iron deposits that lay on the surface of the clay soils. The process is most evident at the Quoraburagun Pinnacles, where the difference between the iron-rich and iron-poor clays is marked by a distinct line separating red and white sections. The cliffs occur mostly in the northern section of the park and are reserved for day visiting only. Magnificent vistas await those who make the rigorous climb to the top.

The southern section of the park contains rolling stretches of heath filled with coastal vegetation that includes tall orange and red banksias, red-bellied native fuchsias, and showy woody hakeas.

Bordering the heath is a large woodland forest of angophoras and tall eucalyptus trees, including red bloodwoods and silvertop ash. Bushwalking and bird watching here are excellent. You might spot a yellow-tailed black cockatoo high among the trees or hear a lyrebird calling out to its mate. The rare ground parrot finds the heath ideally suited for its particular needs, while the water and beaches draw white-breasted sea-eagles in search of prey.

The area is home to a wide range of mammals, including gray kangaroos, swamp wallabies, wombats, and occasionally the rare yellow-bellied glider, which is found only in tall eucalypt forests with high rainfall on the eastern coast of Australia. The loudest and largest of the gliders, the yellow-bellied is distinguished by its long, fluffy tail.

An Australasian gannet stands proudly by her fluffy chick, which has grown to almost adult size. Found on land only when breeding, gannets are superbly graceful fliers.

YURAYGIR NATIONAL PARK

Senior Ranger, Grafton District, National Parks and Wildlife Service, State Office Block, Grafton, NSW 2460, or call (066) 42 0613. This park, 24 mi/39 km south of Grafton, has excellent camping facilities within its boundaries. Accommodations outside the park include motels, camping reserves, and camper vehicle parks.

Yuraygir is one of the most beautiful coastal parks in all of Australia, with more than 25 mi/40 km of sweeping coastline, cozy isolated beaches, and towering dunes. It is known especially for its wide choice of water activities. You can surf off its coast, fish or canoe on either of its two major rivers, or cool off in its refreshing waters.

The park was named after the Yuraygir Aborigines who once lived in the region. At many sites there are shells and sacred and mythological artifacts that give evidence of their habitation. The Europeans who first settled the area harvested the timber, clearing the land for farming. Beekeeping was a major source of income for many of the farmers.

The Wooli and Sandon rivers divide the park into three sections: a northern section that is mostly coastal; a central section of heath and dunes bordered by paperbark trees and carpeted with epacris and pultenaea flowers; and a southern section consisting of high dunes, jutting headlands, and secluded beaches. Throughout the park, small pools and ponds are favorite drinking spots for wildlife. Many wading birds, including egrets and ibises, frequent these water holes, as do goannas and other lizards.

Caution should be exercised when exploring the heath, since the dense vegetation affords excellent protection and camouflage for snakes. Many of Australia's snakes are poisonous; a few, like the brown snake and the myall, or curl, snake, can inflict painful and sometimes fatal bites. Watch for snakes under the brush and keep your feet and calves protected with heavy boots when you walk through the scrub. Generally, snakes avoid contact with humans, but a snake is likely to bite if it is stepped on.

Friendlier animals that may be sighted in the park include eastern gray kangaroos, swamp wallabies, and an occasional wombat. Wedge-tailed eagles are a common sight overhead.

Since swamp wallabies breed throughout the year they will often be seen with joeys.

WARRUMBUNGLE NATIONAL PARK

P.O. Box 39, Coonabarabran, NSW 2357, or call (068) 42 1311.

Several campsites are available throughout the park.

Jutting out of the dry northeastern plains of New South Wales, the Warrumbungles loom over the surrounding countryside. At one time a place of tremendous volcanic activity, all that remains are the plugs of trachyte that halted 5 million years of geologic unrest. The layers of volcanic ash and cinder bombs have since eroded away, leaving only these sentinels of peace and tranquility.

WILDLIFE AND VEGETATION

Warrumbungle National Park exemplifies two very different climatic conditions. In the north and west, where very little rain falls, plains support a community of water-conserving plants and trees, including several varieties of eucalypts. In the south and east, moist, rich soils and sheltered gorges sustain a more varied vegetation. Tall white box trees dominate the fertile southwestern slopes of the Warrumbungles, appearing as a carpet of green surrounding the rocky pinnacles. On the sharp outcrops of the peaks grow narrow-leaf ironbarks and black and white cypress gums, which can survive in the nutrient-poor soil there.

Throughout the park there are patches of heath overlying sandstone. With the coming of spring, the heath plants–irises, peas, heaths, and more than twenty-five species of wattles–burst into flower bringing swaths of purple, pink, yellow, and white to the area.

While many visitors come to the park for its flowers and scenic vistas, thousands more come to view its wildlife and to take up the many challenges it presents for rock climbers. Bird watchers take note: more than 170 species of birds have been sighted here; a third of all of Australia's cockatoo and parrot species occur in the area, including the red-winged parrot, a stunning bird clad in green and blue and named for the red patches that flash when it spreads its wings.

The area harbors gray kangaroos, wallaroos, and swamp and red-necked wallabies. There are koalas, too, which may be spotted high

SULPHUR-CRESTED COCKATOO
Cacatus galerita

The sulphur-crested cockatoo is probably the most popular of all Australian parrots. It is found in most parts of northern and eastern Australia wherever there are trees. Its diet consists of native seeds, berries, and insects and their larvae. The damage it does to wheat crops has made it a target for many farmers.

The cockatoos have avoided complete destruction by their cooperative system of self-defense. While thousands of cockatoos are feeding on the open plains, several individual birds stand by as sentinels, alert for approaching danger. As soon as one of them gives off the shriek of

alarm, the whole flock immediately takes off. Because of this behavior, the word *cockatoo* has come to mean "sentinel" to Australians.

in the eucalyptus trees. Overhead, in search of small game or carrion, the soaring wedge-tailed eagle is a common sight.

BUSHWALKING AND CLIMBING

The Warrumbungles are a favorite venue for serious rock climbers. A popular ascent is the Belougery Spire, whose sheer rock face tops 330 ft/100 m. Permits are required for climbing all of the formations, and climbers should check with rangers before attempting any ascent.

Several bushwalks are available throughout the park, the most popular being the walk to Grand High Tops. This 6.5-mi/10.5-km round trip takes a whole day, beginning at Camp Pincham. Along the way, the trail takes you near many volcanic plugs of the Warrumbungles, through areas of dense forests and cool babbling streams, and to scenic lookouts of the entire park.

KINCHEGA NATIONAL PARK

Superintendent, Broken Hill District, P.O. Box 454, Broken Hill, NSW 2880, or call (080) 88 0253.

Excellent campsites are available. A license is required for fishing, and a permit for boating.

The far-western region of New South Wales is not on most visitors' must-see list. For the average traveler, Kinchega, as well as the other relatively new national parks, Mungo and Sturt, offer few enticements for packing up and driving 600 mi/1,000 km or more across uneventful, arid landscape. Time and a hardy spirit are the key ingredients for enjoying and appreciating these unique wilderness areas.

The beauty of the far-western parks is subtle for most of the year but overwhelming just after the rains of July through September. While temperatures are cool and days cloudy and damp on the coast, warm winds blow across the desert in the west, skies are a cloudless blue, and nights are crisp under a matchless spectacle of stars.

It rains only about 8.5 in/216 mm per year at Kinchega, and the rain comes in bursts, not steadily throughout the year. But the rains in the Great Dividing Range 600 mi/1,000 km to the northwest affect this region, as tributaries on its western slopes collect the runoff and join to flood the Darling River. In the heart of the parched western scrub, the Darling suddenly leaves its confines and spreads out into the dry lake bed at Menindee. Eventually the winter runoff submerges nearby Emu Lake and Cawndilla Lake as well, before finding its way back into the channel of the Darling River.

It only takes a few days for the now-brimming dry lakes of Kinchega National Park to become a mecca for thousands of migratory wetland birds. As vast numbers of ducks, waders, herons, swans, pelicans, geese, and ibises return to rookery and nesting sites, the shallow lakes become one of the primary breeding refuges in Australia. Mobs of red kangaroos and emus also come to the life-giving waters.

River red gums and coolibahs grace the banks of the lakes, while blue bush and prickly wattle dot the surrounding red sand plains.

Efforts to retain some of the water in the lakes include a system of dams, but the best time to visit the park remains the floodtime of August and September.

Clockwise from top left: Australian magpie; pied heron; red-breasted goose (introduced from the U.S.S.R.); black duck.

MUNGO NATIONAL PARK

New South Wales National Parks and Wildlife Service District Office, P.O. Box 318, Buronga, NSW 2648, or call (050) 23 1278.

The park is 68 mi/110 km northeast of Mildura. Self-contained camping is permitted, but visitors must check with rangers first.

Mungo National Park, once a series of freshwater lakes along Willandra Creek, is now filled with large and small dry lake beds that have been stabilized by mallee vegetation. Here one feels transported to the world as it was 35,000 years ago.

The entire Willandra drainage system has preserved both the landforms and environmental conditions from the last ice age. Fossil

FERAL ANIMALS

In settling the untamed land of Australia, Europeans wrought profound and often destructive environmental changes. Vegetation was uprooted for agriculture, and forests were cut down by timber companies. Aborigines suffered from the diseases the Europeans brought with them and from the displacement of their communities. Wildlife suffered from the destruction of habitats, but many species were particularly affected by domestic animals that escaped from European households and reverted to wild, or feral, ways in the Australian outback.

Feral donkey.

The stronger introduced animals managed to survive off the available vegetation and thus occupied the ecological niches of endemic animals. Some endemic animals, like the rabbit-eared bilby, survived annihilation by moving on to more arid regions. But many other native species could not make the environmental transition and so became extinct.

Bird and reptile populations were decimated by feral cats and foxes. Feral donkeys and horses (the so-called brumbies) still ravage grasslands and destroy the surface habitats of smaller mammals. Feral goats are known for denuding areas of all vegetation, and even feral chickens and rabbits run wild in some areas.

remains discovered by anthropologists have revealed a culture of finely featured and lightly built people who lived in this area for over 10,000 years. They cremated their dead, ground flour, and cooked fish, mammals, and emu eggs. Their remains are so well preserved that the area has been included on the World Heritage List since 1981. (The burial sites cannot be visited, except by special permission from the Aboriginal Land Council.) Mungo was once a sheep station, and the vegetation was destroyed by grazing animals but has been recovering since the area was declared a national park.

Like the other dry lake beds around it, the dry bed of Lake Mungo is bordered by high lunettes – sand dunes hardened by salty clay – that sometimes reach a height of 80 ft/24 m. These forms are finely etched and sculpted and support minimal vegetation. The lunette at Lake Mungo was named Walls of China by some early Chinese laborers.

Mungo is one of the newest national parks in Australia and is extremely rewarding for those interested in Australia's earliest inhabitants. Because summers are extremely hot in this barren landscape, it is best to visit in the winter, from July to September.

STURT NATIONAL PARK

New South Wales National Parks and Wildlife Service District Office, c/o P.O. Tibooburra, NSW 2880, or call (080) 91 3308.

The park is 211 mi/340 km north of Broken Hill. Self-contained camping is permitted, but travelers must carry extra water, fuel, and spare parts, and contact the park rangers before camping. There are hotels at Tibooburra and Milparinka.

Sturt National Park is in the northwest corner of New South Wales, about 620 mi/1,000 km from Sydney. This is "jump up" country, where vast, stone-strewn plains give way suddenly to isolated, flat-topped mountains. Sturt National Park was named after the Australian explorer Charles Sturt, who set out in 1845, during one of the worst droughts ever to occur on the continent, in search of a mythical inland sea. Originally the site of several sheep stations, the area was reclaimed in 1972, and its native grasses have since regenerated from the destruction caused by grazing.

Sturt National Park is not the ideal destination for the visitor with limited time and resources. The park is isolated, and its few

DINGO
Canis familiaris

Other than humans, the introduced dingoes are now the most powerful predators in Australia. Looking like a short-haired, sandy-colored (or sometimes black) wolf, the dingo is found in the scrub and semidesert environments of Australia, excluding Tasmania. It is thought that this dog was brought to Australia from Asia more than 8,000 years ago by Aborigines.

At first the dingoes subsisted mainly on large kangaroos, which they hunted in packs. After the more easily caught rabbits were introduced by the Europeans, however, dingoes became solitary hunters.

Besides rabbits, dingoes eat small marsupials, birds, and reptiles. Contrary to belief, only about 2 percent of their prey consists of livestock. This fact did not stop the construction of the longest fence in the world in eastern Australia to prevent the dingo from preying on livestock.

---

roads and tracks become flooded during heavy rains. But for those who want to experience Australia's outback as it appeared to the first European explorers, Sturt is very alluring, indeed. It is especially glorious to visit after the rains, when temporary lakes and water holes fill to their capacity and attract a variety of bird life. Plants and flowers sprout from seeds that have been lying dormant, awaiting the rains. One of the most spectacular plants blooming here is the Sturt's desert pea. The flower has irregularly shaped black and scarlet petals surrounded by gray-green, silken-haired leaves.

Sturt's best-known inhabitants are its red kangaroos, much at home in the dry conditions and native grasses of the park. Emus also are found here, along with wedge-tailed eagles, nankeen kestrels, and lizards such as shingle-backs and bearded dragons.

Bearded dragons, found throughout all but the northern regions of Australia, will puff out their bodies and inflate their beards when alarmed. Their color—gray, brown, or yellow—varies with the environment in which they live.

VICTORIA

Grampians National Park
Wyperfeld National Park
Hattah-Kulkyne National Park
Mount Eccles National Park
Tower Hill State Game Reserve
Port Campbell National Park
Phillip Island
Wilsons Promontory National Park
Lakes National Park
Croajingolong National Park
Mount Buffalo National Park
Bogong National Park
Snowy River National Park

Plummeting several hundred feet, magnificent Erskine Falls and the surrounding fern forest epitomize the rain-forest beauty of the Otway Ranges, located west of Melbourne along the coast.

Victoria is Australia's smallest and southernmost state. Its 87,876 sq mi/227,600 sq km contain a magnificent diversity of environments and wildlife species. In proportion to its size it has a longer seashore than any other state, and its coastal scenery is superb. Although it is Australia's most populous state, Victoria has ensured the protection of its natural environment by designating nearly one-third of its Crown land to state and national parks and other nature reserves.

In eastern Victoria, the Great Dividing Range rambles across the New South Wales border, creating the region of the Bogong High Plains with a cluster of peaks reaching 6,371 ft/1,986 m at the highest. The Great Dividing Range terminates at the Grampians, an isolated uplift near the South Australian border. Vaulting out of the dry, west Victorian farmlands, the Grampians' green hillsides of eucalypts, fern gullies, and sandstone promontories are a refuge for dozens of plant and animal species.

Parts of Victoria, such as Port Campbell National Park and the Grampians, are geological wonders, demonstrating the sculptural power of erosion in some of the earth's most ancient land areas.

Rolling wheatfields dominate the arid landscape of western Victoria, once blanketed by dense tangles of mallee scrub.

Other parts of Victoria are extremely fragile and subtly beautiful, especially the endangered mallee country of the Wyperfeld and Hattah-Kulkyne national parks.

The alpine and subalpine areas of Australia are very different from similarly classified regions elsewhere in the world. The land is considerably flatter and receives far less snow than European or North American counterparts. There is no permafrost and, except in isolated gullies and sun-sheltered ridge faces, snow seldom accumulates deeper than a few feet, nor does it usually remain longer than one or two months. As a consequence, few plants or animals in the Australian alpine need to survive long torpor periods or undergo hibernation.

For years, the Victorian alpine has drawn considerable attention centering on issues of conservation. Cattlemen have utilized the idyllic alpine herb fields to graze their cattle for nearly a century and a half, and in consequence much damage has been done to certain fragile environments found in the high country. While the cattlemen, with their legendary status, are under no threat of displacement, it is hoped that nonrenewal of grazing leases by the

Surf pounds rugged sections of the Victorian coastline near Port Campbell National Park.

government may help safeguard sensitive areas from total devastation. There is very little alpine and subalpine country remaining in Victoria; less than 870 sq mi/2,254 sq km qualify for inclusion as true high-country environment.

Victoria offers its visitors a wealth of natural attractions, each in close proximity to major townships and facilities. Wilsons Promontory National Park, for example, hosts a wonderful collection of wild creatures, including koalas, wombats, cockatoos, parrots, and kangaroos. It also contains outstanding coastal scenery and excellent walking tracks. Yet, despite their attractiveness, many areas of "the Prom" are virtually untouched and unseen by the more than 1 million visitors who come to it annually from Melbourne, the state's metropolitan hub.

Victoria is a confluence of differing landscapes and weather patterns. In western Victoria, hot winds from South Australia meet with icy breezes from Antarctica. Near Mount Buffalo National Park, these colliding moist and dry air masses build into tremendous storm clouds. In summer, heavy rains accompany lightning. In winter, thick blankets of snow fall across the Victorian alpine.

GRAMPIANS NATIONAL PARK

Department of Conservation, Forests and Lands, 23 Patrick Street, Stawell, VIC 3380, or call (053) 58 1588.

Bush camping is permitted throughout the park except in water-catchment areas and the Wonder-land Range. Campground facilities are available at Zumstein and Halls Gap. Campgrounds with pit toilets and fresh water only are located at Glenisla, near Lake Wartook, and along the Wannon River below Mt. Frederick and Mt. Burchell.

West of Melbourne, the Western Highway passes through a monotonous rolling countryside of sheep and wheat farms until it approaches the little town of Ararat. To the west of Ararat, the landscape makes a radical departure from the fields of grain and river red gums, climbing over 3,000 ft/910 m in a gigantic swell of eucalypt-covered sandstone called the Grampian Ranges. Until 1984, the Grampians were state forest opened to limited forestry and grazing. Today, these gorges, summits, and dense forests make up the 412,657-acre/167,000-hectare Grampians National Park.

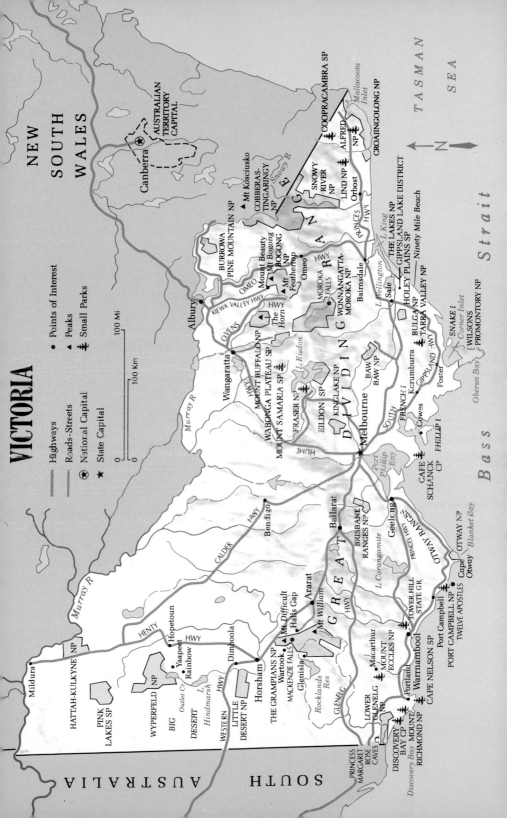

Grampians National Park is the largest in Victoria. On the western slope of the Victoria Range, open eucalypt forests grow below the face of the quartzose sandstone escarpment. Peregrine falcons nesting in secluded overhangs and crevices high above the forest canopy send out piercing cries that can be heard for miles across the valley. Fern gullies survive in the shaded ravines on the eastern slopes of the Serra Range. Storms that build up along the summits of the Grampians drop most of their rain along the Serra Range and Mt. William.

The Grampians are considered the westernmost heights of the Great Dividing Range. Surrounded by farmland, the Grampians create a biological refuge for a great number and variety of plants and animals. From the air, the park looks like a north–south elongated horseshoe closed at the top by Mt. Difficult and sided by the Victoria Range on the west and the Serra Range and Mt. William Range on the east. The interior of the horseshoe, between the ranges, is called Victoria Valley.

Creeks flow all year throughout the Grampians, but four main watercourses gather most of the precipitation: Fyans Creek, Wannon River, Glenelg River, and MacKenzie River. The Glenelg is a vital source of irrigation for hundreds of farms and ranches in southwestern Victoria. Near the coast, the Glenelg cuts deep gorges in the limestone of Lower Glenelg National Park.

The MacKenzie River draws its water from Lake Wartook, the largest reservoir in the Grampians. The MacKenzie travels the shortest distance within the park yet offers the most spectacular scenery along its course as it cuts through sandstone and cascades over a 300-ft/90-m wall of black volcanic stone at Broken Falls.

The view at the Halls Gap entrance of the Grampians National Park is of massive walls of pink and beige sandstone vaulting above the dry eucalypt forest. This brief but magnificent ridge of tilted earth forms the Wonderland Range, created, as was most of the area, from an uplifting of the earth that occurred 250 to 300 million years ago. Since that time, the ranges of quartzose sandstone have endured folding, tilting, and constant erosion. Several natural stone sculptures still bear the nicknames early visitors gave them: Lady's Hat, Fallen Giant, Mushroom Rock, Grand Canyon, and Elephant's Hide.

Flooded gums tower over 80 ft/24 m into the clear Grampians sky.

Along the 62-mi/100-km length of the Grampians, the geology of the ranges departs occasionally from the general scene of ridges and walls of sandstone. In the Grand Canyon, for example, formations of deeply etched sandstone have been worn down by rain and chemical action to the shape of pudding mounds.

Near the easternmost extension, Mt. William rises to 3,832 ft/ 1,168 m, dominating the Grampians and offering breathtaking vistas of the flat countryside to the east. Mt. William's summit is often capped in thick gray clouds. Despite its relatively low altitude, snow is not uncommon on its slopes; there can be light dustings as late as November.

The protection afforded by caves and large overhangs throughout the Grampians, along with the abundance of wildlife and vegetation, made the ranges an ideal home for several local Aboriginal tribes. More than 80 percent of the Aboriginal rock art in the state of Victoria is found in the Grampians. On the western side of Victoria Range near Glenisla, a well posted trail leads from the campground to one of the richest displays of rock art. At another site, on the undersurface of Flat Rock Shelter, you can see red ocher handprints and a curious collection of short lines, roughly the size of a finger.

VEGETATION

The hillsides and valleys of the Grampians are dominated by woodlands and open sclerophyll forest. Composed chiefly of several eucalypt species and acacias, sclerophyll forests form on the moist easterly slopes of Serra Range. Here the canopy can extend 130 ft/ 40 m above the forest floor. In places eucalypts such as messmate-stringybark prevent light from penetrating. As a result, the understory in some areas—for example, the southern road around Wonderland Range—is a lush mixture of rain-forest ferns in the deeper gullies and a profusion of flowering herbaceous plants throughout.

Near the crest of the ranges, drier eucalypt forests of stringybark and scribbly gum take over. Here the forest is shorter and more open overall. The full sunlight fosters an abundance of flowering shrubs and small annuals, although the variety of species in this

The delicate blossoms of the black anther lily are common in the Grampians' springtime bloom of wildflowers.

area is severely limited by the mineral-poor soil. Wattles of yellow and white and the comb-shaped banksia blossoms are prominent. In unexposed sandstone crevices, where seeping water maintains dampness most of the year, the carnivorous sundew plant flourishes. Consuming insects to supplement its mineral intake, the sundew can grow in otherwise inadequate conditions.

On a few of the higher slopes, the spaces between granite and sandstone outcrops harbor a wind-dwarfed variety of eucalypt and an extensive highland heath. These highlands, especially in the area of Mt. William, are the focus of considerable attention in late September and October each season. The floral display throughout the Grampians is regarded as one of the most spectacular in Australia; only the Stirling Range of Western Australia compares. More than a thousand species of flowering plants, shrubs, and trees enliven the scene, most putting forth their pistils and petals within a brief two-week span. The result is a feast of color and a thick perfuming of the highland air. A dozen varieties of the pea family paint the open country in shades of gold, pink, and orange. The peas, together with bright lemon-colored guinea flowers and yellow-white wattles, predominate among the flowers that bloom in the ranges each season.

Wattles are among the more abundant flowers in the Victorian bush, especially in the Grampians.

In addition to the bounty of native flowers, numerous introduced species also add to the eruption of floral color in early September.

WILDLIFE

As an island of forests, open bush, and flowers, the Grampians attract a great many birds and animals. For many species, the mixed environments of the ranges are but a seasonal home. More than 200 species of birds find the area a perfect place to spend the spring and summer months, nesting and rearing their young. Other animals, such as the brush-tailed rock wallaby, are relatively rare, being isolated by the surrounding lowlands.

The Grampians are a bird watcher's delight. In the two hours it takes to drive through the ranges from Halls Gap to Zumstein, the traveler passes through at least a half-dozen different environments, each hosting its own special complement of birds.

Near the Halls Gap camping facility, the valley floor is overshadowed by towering flooded gums. Here, long-billed corellas barnstorm among the treetops, screeching and squawking. Restless flycatchers and willy-wagtails flit between nearby perches, snatching an assortment of aerial insects. The characteristic sounds of the laughing kookaburras begin echoing through the area as the evening sun throws its last golden rays on the summit of Wonderland Range.

LAUGHING KOOKABURRA
Dacelo gigas

The most famous of all the Australian birds, the kookaburra is a difficult bird to miss. It announces its presence at the crack of dawn with a loud, long hoot that breaks into raucous laughter. When two kookaburras are competing for territory, the noise can seem endless.

Found in woods, parks, and gardens, the kookaburra is welcomed because it kills rats, mice, and snakes. It sometimes will dive into shallow water after its prey or while bathing.

The kookaburra has a long life span—sometimes more than twenty years—and a consequently lower birth rate. The young remain with their parents for three to four years. These young "auxiliary" birds aid in territorial defense and in the raising of later offspring.

On the other side of the range, magnificent yellow-tailed black cockatoos dot the tops of giant manna gums. The dry eucalypt forest below comes alive with wrens, honey eaters, and whistlers, all vying for sticks, grasses, spider webs, and assorted other nest-building materials in the warm November sun.

Near the crest of the Wonderlands, the road forks to the south (left) and northeast (right). In gullies to the south, patches of rain forest attract the white-browed scrub wren and the gray fantail. Above, on a drier slope, a pair of gang-gang cockatoos may be spotted investigating a fire-ravaged gum. With its deep gray body and scarlet head, the gang-gang is a striking member of the cockatoo family.

A dramatic change accompanies the MacKenzie River as it flows down the Mt. Difficult escarpment. On the western slopes of the Grampians, the air is dry and the forest is open with little undergrowth. This is perfect habitat for the eastern gray kangaroo. In and around the Zumstein campground, a mob of thirty to forty eastern grays lounge about as if the campground were built for their con-

KOALA
Phascolarctos cinereus

The cuddly koala is a favorite among young and old alike, and a "must see" for many visitors to Australia. The only arboreal marsupial with no visible tail, it uses its strong claws to climb slowly through the eucalyptus trees that it inhabits. Living mainly on eucalyptus leaves, it combs the tops of trees at night in search of food. Although the fibrous eucalyptus leaves are toxic to most animals, the koala is able to eat them —except for the young leaves—by virtue of an elaborate digestive system that includes cheek pouches and an elongated cecum.

Koalas are found in eucalypt forests and woodlands of eastern Australia, usually sleeping in the fork of a tree. A koala may descend to the ground either to eat earth to supplement its diet with calcium and other minerals or to travel from tree to tree.

venience. Laughing kookaburras, which nest in the area, may swoop by at any moment and snatch food from a barbecue or picnic table.

Grampians National Park is one of the best places in Australia for observing koalas in the wild. Often they are more easily heard than seen. Midway up the Mt. William Range, look for dark gray koalas wedged in the forks of manna gum and blue gum trees. Koalas also feed on swamp gums and on noneucalypt plants.

BUSHWALKING

Mt. Rosea. Take Dunkeld Road 4.7 mi/7.5 km and turn right up Silverband Road. Walk by Silverband Falls and Delleys Dell to Mt. Rosea picnic ground. Allow about four hours for the round trip of 3.7 mi/6 km to the summit, which is the highest point in the Serra Range, with panoramic views in all directions. Be prepared for some sections of steep, rough, rocky track.

Stony Creek–Grand Canyon Trail. Take Peuckers Track (between Stony Creek and the tennis courts) past Venus Bath to Wonderland

Turntable. Continue through the Grand Canyon and Silent Street to the Pinnacle, a distance of about 3 mi/4.8 km from the starting point. The track then winds down past Ralph and Mackeys peaks to the parking area. Allow four to six hours for the 5-mi/8-km round trip. The trail is rated fairly difficult due to its steepness and the rough, rocky track in some sections.

Emus patrol the dry eucalypt forest for the small rodents and reptiles that make up much of their diet.

Mt. William. From Halls Gap, take Dunkeld Road 8 mi/13 km to the left turn, then another 6.2 mi/10 km to the Turntable. Allow one hour for the walk to the summit of the park's highest peak; it is a steep but relatively easy climb.

WYPERFELD NATIONAL PARK

Ranger-in-Charge, Wyperfeld National Park, RMB 1465, Yaapeet, VIC 3424, or call (053) 95 7221. The park maintains a fine campground with fresh water, toilets, cold showers, and fire pits (visitors should bring gas stoves since bans on open fires often apply). There is a per-night fee for camping. Nearest facilities are 13.7 mi/22 km away at Yaapeet; overnight accommodations may be had at Rainbow and Hopetoun. The summer months here are extremely hot.

Wyperfeld National Park beckons in the distance like a wilderness mirage, its gray-green expanse of mallee scrub appearing on the horizon like a giant pan of water on a plain of golden beige wheat. At a point nearly 280 mi/450 km northwest of Melbourne the road leaves behind the seemingly endless wheatlands and breaks the surface of the mirage.

Wyperfeld protects the largest mallee forest in Australia. An Aboriginal word that has been adopted into scientific usage, *mallee* describes the multiple-stemmed growth characteristic of some two dozen eucalypt species found in this dry country. Mallee once covered much of western Victoria north into New South Wales and west into South Australia.

Pressure from conservationists who visited the region near the turn of the century convinced government officials that much of the area's mallee vegetation and associated wildlife would face certain destruction unless preservation legislation was quickly enacted. By 1900, almost 9,600 acres/3,888 hectares had been set aside for eventual national-park status. Today, what remains of the mallee and its associated wildlife exists in a series of parks exemplified by the 247,100 acres/100,000 hectares of Wyperfeld National Park.

In Wyperfeld the effects of drought are notable, like the aftermath of fire in most other national parks. Heavy rainfall, the kind that causes lowlands to flood and waterways such as Outlet Creek to flow, has occurred here only three times in this century (1918, 1952, 1975).

Wyperfeld contains numerous shallow lakes that are connected by Outlet Creek. Lake Brambruk, north of the campground, is the

The echidna's elongated proboscis is keenly sensitive to smells, allowing it to search through leaf litter and soils for the tiny insects and grubs on which it feeds.

park's largest lake but, like a half-dozen smaller lakes, it is mostly a shallow dry pan. After one of the rare heavy rains the overflow into Outlet Creek may flood the tiny lakes for a year or more.

While the water in some of the lakes is less than 3 ft/1 m deep, it is enough to lure dozens of wading-bird species such as avocets and stilts. The waters of the creek saturate the adjacent earth enough to encourage black box trees and river red gums to put forth new growth.

VEGETATION

Hundreds of black box trees make up the forest in the vicinity of Outlet Creek. Farther inside the park, the forest shifts to native pines, callitris, and scattered large river red gums. The dark green bushy branches of the callitris and the giant trunks and open tops of the gums provide ample food and shade for the numerous species of parrots that feed in the park.

The dominant vegetation and feature of Wyperfeld, however, is mallee. Its tangled branches grow everywhere except on the crests of sand dunes and other areas of heath growth.

Mallee gives the appearance of treetops branching out just above the ground with their trunks buried below. This is somewhat close to the truth. Branches and stems part from one another at a point near the ground originating from a large rootstock that has little or no intermediate trunk. With each branch and its crown of leaves diverging from the rest, the mallee takes on an umbrella shape. Closely and evenly spaced, the trees of the mallee forest form one continuous canopy across much of the park.

The western mallee country of Wyperfeld National Park is a harsh environment where aridity, strong winds, and fire from dry lightning storms ravage the landscape. Not only has mallee adapted to these conditions, it even flourishes in this unforgiving land. Although many trees, such as callitris, can withstand long droughts, few can tolerate the brush fires touched off by lightning in this corner of Victoria.

Mallee has evolved to respond to severe and repeated burnings. The oily stems and leaves are highly combustible. Fires therefore race across the mallee canopy at an incredible speed, and after the

MALLEE FOWL
Leipoa ocellata

The mallee fowl – or native pheasant – is a large bird found primarily near mallee and other scrubs, particularly where there is sandy soil. It spends its days in the cool shade, roosting in nearby eucalypt trees. It eats the seeds and fruit from shrubs as well as the insects that abound in the mallee.

What is most unusual about mallee fowl is the mound the birds build to house their eggs, a structure up to 20 ft/6 m in diameter and about 3 ft/1 m high composed of soil, leaves, twigs, bark, and vegetation. The males work on it daily, uncovering the top of the mound to check the temperature within. The decaying vegetation give off a natural warmth upon which the mallee fowl depend to incubate their eggs. When it reaches about 100° F/37.7° C, the female lays sixteen to thirty-three eggs inside a hole in the mound about 18 in/46 cm deep; she may take a week to seventeen days to lay all her eggs. Then, each day, the males dig to within a couple of inches of the eggs to allow the sun to warm them. These attentions continue until the eggs are hatched.

---

fire all that remains are charred black stems smoldering in the desert sun. Below ground, however, the insulated roots are left virtually unscathed. Within a few weeks, new stems and shoots spring forth.

Mallee responds in much the same manner if it is broken or cut. The mallee's regenerative ability was a severe trial for farmers as they struggled to clear the land outside the park earlier in this century.

On sand dunes, the mallee yields to heath plants that are better adapted for survival in poor, sandy soil. Spring is an especially beautiful time in Wyperfeld, as the plants of the heath – banksias, tea trees, grevilleas, myrtle, and hakeas – erupt with wonderfully shaped blossoms, their colors and scents attracting scores of insects and nectar-feeding birds. The normally naked earth near the heath also sprouts a number of showy orchids, daisies, and other flowers.

Many unusual forms of vegetation grow here, such as the stone-making fungus, which, like all fungi, capitalizes on rotting matter for its livelihood. Aboveground, this caramel-colored toadstool looks innocent, scarcely rising above the level of the sand. Below sand level, however, is an ever-expanding network of sticky strands that radiates in all directions, entrapping grains of sand to form a stone-like ball.

WILDLIFE

The amount of animal activity one encounters at Wyperfeld varies greatly depending upon the time of day. At midday all is quiet as nearly every creature seeks refuge from the scorching sun. But from late afternoon through the early hours of morning, Wyperfeld is a different world. A drive along the Black Flat Lake road reveals the park's visible and abundant wildlife.

The park's two dominant creatures are the 6-ft-/1.8-m-tall emu and the black-faced mallee kangaroo, a large subspecies of the gray kangaroo. October and November are perfect times to watch the flightless emu lead its black-and-white-striped chicks on a feeding stroll through the paddocks near the campground. Emus are common throughout the park. They are not tame, however, nor are they inclined to beg from visitors as happens in other parks, and as a result they are much more in harmony with the beauty of the mallee wilderness.

The black-faced mallee kangaroos, like the emus of Wyperfeld, also are untamed. A short way from the campground, the Black Flat Lake road dips through a large grassy paddock surrounded by dense eucalypt forest. The cool air and fading light of evening draw dozens of these kangaroos into the opening to feed, the joeys cajoling one another into spirited play. Wyperfeld National Park is one of the best places in Australia for watching large mobs of kangaroos living in a natural state.

Numerous species of birds inhabit Wyperfeld. The plentiful numbers of parrots and parrot-like species make the park one of the prime bird-watching spots in the arid southeast of Australia. An average

The inquisitive stares of the black-faced mallee kangaroo dot the evening landscape of Wyperfeld National Park.

day's viewing might include galahs, the yellow-fronted regent parrot, the red-rumped parrot, the blue-winged parrot, the mallee ring-necked parrot, the purple-crowned lorikeet, long-billed and little corellas, budgerigars, and the splendid pink cockatoo. Robins, honey eaters, and wrens also shelter and forage in the mallee.

The most unusual bird in the park is the mallee fowl, remarkable for its nesting behaviors. Wyperfeld is one of the last wild strongholds of this species, and December through April is the best time to observe the bird's activities. There are mallee fowl mounds located throughout the park and most are in use year-round. Rangers at the information center are helpful in giving directions to an active mallee fowl mound.

HATTAH-KULKYNE NATIONAL PARK

Department of Conservation, Forests and Lands, 250 Victoria Parade, East Melbourne, VIC 3002, or call (03) 651 4011. Hattah-Kulkyne is best visited between March and November when temperatures remain bearable. Camping is permitted in the park, and all facilities are available at nearby Ouyen.

Wedged into the northwest corner of Victoria, 310 mi/500 km from Melbourne, Hattah-Kulkyne borders the mighty Murray River. The attractiveness of the park depends largely on the amount of rainfall it receives. During most of the year there is very little rainfall and near-drought conditions can continue for years.

But when the Murray River is running high, flooding spills over into the park, filling the dry lake beds that dot the mallee-dominated landscape. When water is plentiful, Hattah-Kulkyne erupts with

bird life, and the park offers one of the most magnificent waterfowl spectacles to be seen anywhere in southeast Australia.

When water is available, the mallee scrubland of the area is capable of supporting an amazingly rich and varied population of plants and animals. The Latjilatji Aborigines realized the area's worth and hunted here during flood seasons. The names of lakes in the park reflect the Aboriginal influence – Hattah, Bulla, Arawak, Tullamook, and Nip Nip. The only physical remains of the Latjilatji are a scattering of shells and bones in the charred soil and the scarred trunks of gum trees from which bark was stripped to make canoes.

European settlers were indiscriminate in their use of the fragile land, and destruction started soon after the area was leased for farming in 1840. Overgrazing and foraging by a very large rabbit population denuded the landscape, and devastating soil erosion followed.

Although exposed parts look dead, vital sections of the mallee tree thrive underground. Facing page: Mallee eucalypts are scattered throughout Hattah-Kulkyne.

In establishing the area as a national park, there were many problems to be solved. A major obstacle was a surplus of feral pigs and goats. These pests are still present in the park, but their numbers have been reduced to the point where native vegetation is once again able to flourish.

WILDLIFE AND VEGETATION

Most of the park is covered with mallee scrub and dry sand ridges. Desert wildflowers, wattles, ham-and-egg daisies, climbing clematis, and ground orchids all add flecks of color to the stark mallee backdrop. Flowering species are especially prominent in areas where forests of casuarina, acacia, and white cypress pine have been logged for timber and sheep farming.

What makes this arid area unique, however, is the number of exotic waterfowl it attracts when the lake beds fill with runoff from the Murray River. More than 200 bird species have been sighted in the park, including the white-bellied sea eagle. Normally the sea eagle is sighted near ocean or marine environments, but these birds often follow rivers upstream from the coast, along with egrets, black swans, ibises, darters, pelicans, and several varieties of ducks.

The region in and around Hattah-Kulkyne National Park is an outstanding kangaroo habitat, the only place in Australia where all major species of kangaroo can be spotted—eastern and western grays, reds, and euros.

MOUNT ECCLES NATIONAL PARK

Mount Eccles National Park, RMB
1160, Macarthur, VIC 3286, or call
(055) 76 1014.

In this part of Victoria, volcanic eruptions that began about 20,000 years ago formed Mt. Eccles, a series of craters, and an extensive lava flow. The last-known eruption was only 7,000 years ago, and because the blast was so recent many of the area's features remain largely unchanged by weathering and erosion.

Mt. Eccles is a mound of scoria, a lightweight rock full of gas holes

Able to soar through the air up to 164 ft/50 m, sugar gliders, smallest of the glider family, spread the thick membranous skin beneath their fur and leap from tree to tree.

that formed when molten lava was thrown explosively into the air. The largest of the craters contains Lake Surprise, a stretch of water nearly 0.5 mi/1 km long and 600 ft/182 m wide. This lake is always cool and fresh, being fed by underground springs.

Running from the north of Lake Surprise is a lava canal, a long depression formed by lava as it flowed back to the crater. At a point near the beginning of the canal, there is an impressive lava cave. An incline leads to its black-walled interior, where solidified drips of lava hang from the arched roof.

There are panoramic views from the lip of the crater. Graded tracks run around Lake Surprise, along the crater rim, and down to the lava canal. There are several short walks. These include: a crater-rim nature walk that takes only an hour; a forty-five-minute hike around Lake Surprise; and a two-hour walk along the canal for a look at the lava flow. Mt. Eccles is fun to explore in a long day or to use as a wilderness stopover when traveling from the Great Ocean Road east to Adelaide or north to Grampians National Park.

TOWER HILL STATE GAME RESERVE

Department of Conservation, Forests and Lands, 250 Victoria Parade, East Melbourne, VIC 3002, or call (03) 651 4011. Access to Tower Hill State Game Reserve is from the Princes Highway 9.3 mi/15 km west of Warrnambool. A drive through the reserve can take less than thirty minutes. If staying nearby in Warrnambool or Port Fairy (there is no camping in the reserve), visit Tower Hill early in the morning for excellent viewing of waterfowl.

Tower Hill State Game Reserve sits among rolling farmlands that meet the sea some 170 mi/275 km west of Melbourne. Tower Hill itself is a significant geological feature. It consists of a volcanic crater rimmed by beds of volcanic ash. The floor of the crater contains subsidiary volcanic cones surrounded by shallow lakes.

Very little of this countryside resembles the wilderness found by the European settlers. The country was considered too valuable and rich a resource to waste on native eucalypt and coastal heath. Intense burning and cutting swept away the wild vegetation and with it went dozens of animal species. The 1,500 acres/609 hectares of Tower Hill were no exception to the cultivating frenzy of the late 1800s. The forests at the center of the great crater were stripped bare as grazing sheep and cattle reduced the two hills to barren knobs. Erosion cut deep grooves into the hillsides and sediments began to fill the lake. The profusion of wildlife that had inhabited the crater disappeared, and local residents took to using the lake as a dump. Since water for local wells originated from the lake, the people were poisoning their own water reservoir.

The early 1960s saw a surge of public interest in Tower Hill. The trend of neglect was reversed, and solicitations were made to gain protection for the area. Today Tower Hill attests to a rare effort in conservation and reclamation. The reforestation project has returned the central hills of the crater to a state very similar to that lost for over a century. Several species of native wildlife have been reintroduced (koala, emu, ring-tailed and brush-tailed possums, sugar glider), and more than 200 species of birds migrate in and out of the reserve. Sightings of the musk duck are a special treat during November and December.

During the approaching summer these fledgling nankeen kestrels will remain with their parents and learn to hunt for themselves.

PORT CAMPBELL NATIONAL PARK

Port Campbell National Park, Tregea Street, Port Campbell, VIC 3269, or call (055) 98 6382. The township of Port Campbell, which divides the park at the mouth of the Campbell Creek, houses the park's visitors' center and camping facility. The township also offers complete facilities for travelers.

The deeply eroded cliffs of Port Campbell National Park make this stretch of coastline an unforgettable spectacle. Often violent, always relentless, the Southern Ocean is constantly at work shaping and reshaping the sandstone and limestone cliffs. Today, spires and headlands that stood against the ocean less than a quarter century ago no longer exist. Their colossal forms have simply eroded into billions of grains of sand.

The park is a narrow 19-mi/30-km length of southern Victoria coast, bordered on the land by the Great Ocean Road; in many places the roadway comes within a few steps of the cliff edge. Despite the efforts of rangers to protect the park from the ravages of the sea, Port Campbell is disappearing at a rapid rate. With each surging wave, another thin layer washes from the existing cliffs and the 4,324-acre/ 1,750 hectare park shrinks yet more. Eventually even the Great Ocean Road will have to be rerouted before it plunges into the sea.

Port Campbell National Park presents visitors with views both awesome and accessible. The coast drive from the park's eastern entrance at the Twelve Apostles to its western border at Curdies Inlet passes more than a dozen major wave-carved geologic formations, many of them combining grottoes, arches, and precipitous walls.

The Twelve Apostles are, aside from Ayers Rock, the most famous natural features in Australia. These wedge-like stone stacks rise from the sea within a few hundred feet of the shore. Many of them still host coastal heath plants, relics of the pillars' recent attachment to the land.

About 3.5 mi/6 km west of the Apostles is a cluster of interesting

Port Campbell National Park contains the most breathtaking coastal scenery in Australia, and the Twelve Apostles are its highlight.
Pages 86 and 87: Twenty thousand years of wind and surf have etched deep into the sand and limestone cliffs to create Lock Ard Gorge.

formations – Blowhole, Broken Head, Mutton Bird Island, and Lock Ard Gorge. The last of these is named after the worst shipwreck on the Port Campbell coast, the 1878 sinking of the *Lock Ard*. Out of fifty-four passengers, only a boy and girl survived the disaster.

Along the western section of the park, turnoffs lead to two fascinating sculptures – the Arch and, a short distance farther, London Bridge. A collection of historic photos at the visitors' center shows the evolution of the London Bridge. The giant archway has been cut from a solid peninsula in only a few decades.

The cliffs of limestone and sandstone currently being carved along the Port Campbell coast were deposited as seabed 20 to 25 million years ago, when sea levels stood approximately 330 ft/100 m higher than at present. As the continental land mass rose and as sea levels dropped in response to increased polar ice formation, the thick shelf

Many sculptured headlands and inlets await discovery along the coastline of Port Campbell National Park. These formations are just west of London Bridge.

of sediments, mud, seashells, limestone, and sand became the new coastline. With strong winds whipping up thunderous waves in the Southern Ocean, the new coastline quickly began to erode.

The sculptures we see today are harder sediments that are more resistant to weathering. The sea has bypassed the pillars and begun work on the cliffs. In time even the stately Apostles will fall victim to the relentless sea.

PHILLIP ISLAND

A ferry service runs from Stoney Point to Cowes across Western Port Bay. At San Remo on the mainland, a vehicle bridge connects with Phillip Island at Newhaven.

Phillip Island, only 77 mi/124 km from Melbourne, is noted for its variety. Its rocky headlands are prime habitats for an abundance of wildlife. Its southern coast borders the Bass Strait, where pounding waves are a surfer's delight. Its northern coast, in contrast, abuts the more tranquil waters of a bay, which it shares with French Island. These calmer waters are excellent for swimming, yachting, and other water sports. Cowes, on the northern shore, is a popular resort area.

Discovered in 1798 by George Bass, the island has undergone several name changes over the years. George Bass and later James Grant of HMS *Lady Nelson* described the highest point at Cape Woolami (356 ft/108.5 m) as looking like a snapper's head. The island was thus called Snapper Island. Later it became Grant Island, then Phillip Island in honor of Governor Phillip.

It gained the distinction of being the first area in Victoria to be cultivated, rewarding early farmers with good crops of wheat, vegetables, fruit, rice, and coffee.

Today Phillip Island is best known for its wildlife, particularly its little, or fairy, penguins. Visitors gather each night on Summerland Beach to watch the penguins return from their daily fishing forays. The spectacle lasts for almost an hour as hundreds of the creatures come waddling from the waters of the Bass Strait and quickly scurry to their families bearing food from the sea.

FAIRY PENGUIN
Eudyptula minor

The little penguin–popularly known as the fairy penguin–is the only resident penguin in Australia. Found on the coast of southern Australia and its offshore islands, it spends its days swimming and fishing in the oceans, bays, and jetties near its rookeries, coming ashore in the evening to avoid predators.

Like its penguin cousins, the fairy penguin is more adept at moving in the water than on land. It can swim at speeds of up to 1,000 ft/300 m per minute, but it must assume a slow rocking motion when it walks on land. When speed is necessary, it will sometimes slide on its belly down sand dunes into the water.

The fairy penguin is a social bird, often living in rookeries of hundreds; sometimes, however, an isolated pair makes its home in a rock cavity or under vegetation. The nest consists of a burrow in the sand, up to 4 ft/ 1.2 m long, lined with sticks, seaweed, and thistle stems.

Some people know this bird by the name *southern blue penguin*.

Off the southwest tip of Phillip Island, a rocky island called the Nobbies is home to a noisy colony of seals during breeding season. More than 5,000 fur seals gather there, and though the area is restricted, much can be seen by telescope from nearby headlands.

There are also several koala reserves on Phillip Island where visitors can come quite near the unwary marsupials. They are found generally in the isolated clumps of eucalypts that dot the island.

Bird life thrives on the island, on both the northern and southern coasts. On the calmer northern side, fishing is popular among humans and birds alike. It is common to see pelicans, ibises, royal spoonbills, swans, and gulls all vying for the same catch. Muttonbird rookeries also are numerous on the sandy coasts of the island.

WILSONS PROMONTORY NATIONAL PARK

Park Office, Wilsons Promontory National Park, Tidal River via Foster, VIC 3960, or call (056).80 8358.

Although the park is extremely popular, measures are taken to lessen the impact of visitors on the environment. Rangers limit the number of people allowed on specific trails, and permits are issued at the visitors' center to ensure that the overnight camping areas do not become crowded. The cabins are rented on a lottery basis from October to March, the busy season.

Rangers lead daytime nature walks and popular nighttime spotlight tours to view nocturnal wildlife. The visitors' center is extremely well equipped, with excellent reference materials, films, and slide presentations. The accommodation center at Tidal River contains more than 500 camping and parking sites as well as the cabins and a lodge.

Travelers who have time to visit only one park in Victoria would do well to choose Wilsons Promontory, perhaps the most popular national park in Australia. Combining many elements of other national parks, "the Prom" incorporates temperate rain forests, towering eucalypt forests, grasslands, swamps, coastal salt marshes, and isolated inlets and beaches. There are high mountain slopes to climb and fern gullies in the valleys to explore. The open heaths are often ablaze with wildflowers. In the north, sand dunes undulate along isolated beaches, a far different picture from the granite cliffs and boulder-strewn beaches of the southern tip.

Occupying the southernmost tip of mainland Australia, Wilsons Promontory is only 143 mi/230 km southeast of Melbourne. The area was once part of a land bridge that connected Tasmania and Victoria. As sea levels rose, the promontory was isolated from the mainland. Over time enough sand collected to fill in the gap between the Prom and the Victorian coast. This sandy connection is called Yanakie Isthmus.

Wilsons Promontory is a mass of granite, 18.6 mi/30 km long and 12.4 mi/20 km wide. Most visitors are surprised by the height of the park's major peaks. Six of them exceed 1,640 ft/500 m, and the highest, Mount Latrobe, reaches 2,474 ft/754 m.

WILDLIFE

The wildlife of Wilsons Promontory is as diverse as the park's geographical regions. Your walk through the eucalypt forest in the early morning will be greeted by the raucous cry of laughing kookaburras. If you are there in autumn, you will see large flocks of rainbow lorikeets flying overhead and chattering among the treetops as they settle to feed. Brilliant flame robins also inhabit this eucalypt woodland, and small groups of them will be seen on the wing in search of small insects.

You will almost certainly spot a furry koala in the fork of a manna gum tree, eating the last bite of a leaf before it settles to sleep away the day. The koalas and many of the other larger creatures at the Prom can often be approached. Indeed, the voracious emus can be nuisances in their quest for a meal. Children, especially, enjoy wombat-spotting at night by torchlight. Large mobs of gray kangaroos and emus can be seen at most times of the day along the grasslands of the Yanakie Isthmus.

The brightly colored rainbow lorikeet is often seen (and heard) foraging among the treetops, sometimes in groups up to several hundred, throughout coastal Victoria.

WOMBATS
Vombatus and *Lasiorhinus*

The furry wombat resembles a small, lumbering bear. Its closest marsupial relative is the koala, but unlike the koala it cannot climb trees nor is it as visible or as well known as its cousin.

There are three species of wombats: the southern hairy-nosed (*L. latifons,* found in central South Australia); the northern hairy-nosed (*L. krefftii,* found in mideastern Queensland); and the common wombat (*V. ursinus,* found in southeastern Australia). The two hairy-nosed species are plains dwellers and are very well adapted to the drier habitats: they experience a minimal loss of water and heat and have a low nitrogen requirement, which allows them to live off food of poor quality. The common wombat lives in forests and is less efficient at conserving water.

Working their short, powerful legs and long, strong claws, wombats dig very long, elaborate burrows that may be home to one, two, or three wombats. They often visit other burrows during the night as they forage for grass and the succulent roots of shrubs and trees. They also emerge during the day in the cooler wintertime.

VEGETATION

The vegetation at Wilsons Promontory is incredibly varied. Eucalypts are the dominant trees. Tall mountain ash, usually found in the more temperate regions of Australia, line the slopes along the coast. In the temperate rain forest of the eastern slopes, these trees can grow as high as 200 ft/61 m. The light is poor in the understory of the rain forest and the ground is always wet. Fallen leaves decay quickly here, and ferns and other epiphytes grow in abundance. Casuarinas, with their dark bark and delicate feather leaves, are pretty accents to the stately mountain ash, whose bark cascades off in long, thin strings.

The exposed slopes are dry woodlands with very little growth on the forest floor. Leaf-fall carpets the ground and is slow to decay. The trees are not as tall as those in the rain forests, but their branches spread farther because of the available light.

Bordering the dry woodlands are expanses of heath covered with wildflowers that include several species of the brightly colored banksia and many varieties of the pea family including bush peas, parrot peas, and bitter peas. Their rosy red and pink bushes are a splendid complement to the overpowering banksias.

First-time visitors are always amazed to find mangrove trees lining Corner Inlet near the coast. This is the southernmost region in the world in which one can find mangroves. The trees once thrived throughout this coastal area when saltwater marshes were more widespread. The Prom's small grove is all that remains of this once-flourishing population.

BUSHWALKING

Lilly Pilly Gully Nature Walk. A 3-mi/5-km trip, it begins at the Lilly Pilly parking area near Tidal River and takes you through flowering heathland and rain forests graced with ancient tree ferns and bubbling streams. Koalas may be seen in forks of eucalyptus trees along the way. The walk takes approximately two to three hours.

Mt. Oberon Nature Walk. This walk begins from the Mt. Oberon parking area located southeast of Tidal River. The 2-mi/3.2-km trail

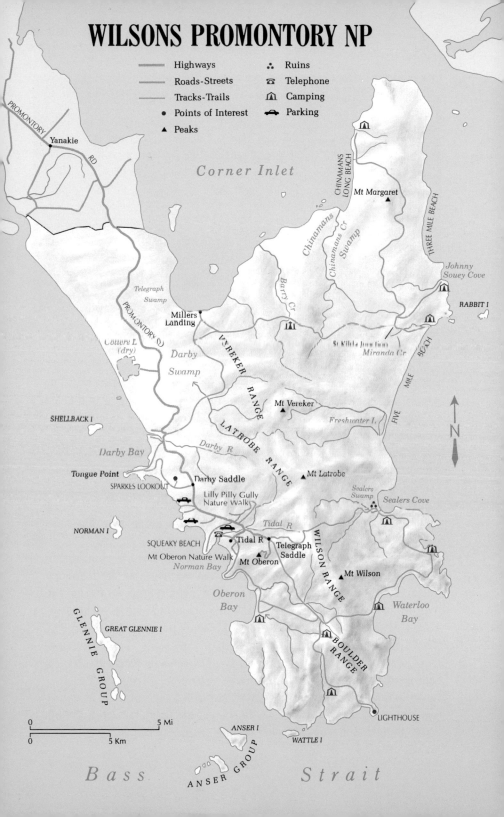

Fern fronds are part of the coastal undergrowth near Five-Mile Beach in Wilson's Promontory National Park.

goes from temperate rain forest to higher eucalypt woodlands. The round trip takes approximately two hours and follows a moderate to steep grade.

Sealer's Cove. One of the most popular walks at the Prom, this trail starts at the Mt. Oberon parking area and slowly winds east through a series of slopes of the Mt. Wilson Range. Further along, the 6-mi/9.6-km trail descends to Sealer's Swamp and then enters a lush, tree-fern gully region before winding up at the secluded Sealer's Cove. Fresh water can be obtained along this five-hour round-trip hike.

Wilsons Prom offers several overnight hikes. You are required to register at the visitors' center before leaving. Both of the following hikes start at the Millers Landing road, which is signposted from the main road between the entrance to the park and Tidal River Resort.

Five-Mile Beach. This 10.7-mi/17.2-km walk passes through Barry's Creek campsite, Chinaman's Creek picnic area, St. Kilda Junction, and Corner Inlet before ending at Five-Mile Beach. Corner Inlet is a sheltered bay and a haven for many sea birds. Five-Mile Beach is raw and unspoiled, and a constant mist bathes the visitor. The camping area is at the north end of the beach at Miranda Creek. Fresh water is available from a spring on the creek's north side.

Johnny Souey Cove. Those preferring to head north can take the left-hand fork at St. Kilda Junction and proceed toward Mt. Margaret for 0.33 mi/0.5 km. Here a steep track branches to the right, leading to the magnificent and secluded Johnny Souey Cove. The distance is about 3 mi/4.7 km from St. Kilda Junction and takes about two hours each way.

LAKES NATIONAL PARK

Lakes National Park, Department of Conservation, Forests and Lands, Central Gippsland Region, Traralgon, VIC, or call (051) 74 6166.

There are overnight accommodations at Loch Sport as well as camping facilities at Point Wilson.

Only 199 mi/320 km east of Melbourne, Lakes National Park is part of the Gippsland Lake District, thought by many to be Victoria's finest holiday area. The numerous lakes of the district are actually one continuous waterway, formed when coastal lagoons became lakes after sea levels rose 10,000 years ago. The lakes were closed off by frontal dunes as waves deposited material to form a great sand barrier, today called Ninety-Mile Beach. Vegetation and coastal heath secured the sand and ensured protection from the sea. The largest lakes include Wellington, King, Victoria, Tyers, Reeve, and Coleman. The lakes form Australia's largest inland waterway. Lakes Entrance, cut in 1889, connects the lakes to the sea. Cruises are available and are the best way to view the whole lake region.

At the center of all the lakes stands Lakes National Park, a 5,930-acre/2,400-hectare park that can be reached by road or by a jetty at Point Wilson. Spermwhale Head, one of the major attractions of the park, was at one time an isolated and little-known vacation retreat. It is a thickly wooded area that attracts many forms of wildlife including swamp wallabies, wombats, ring-tailed and pygmy possums, and echidnas. A population of at least fifty eastern gray kangaroos lives near the campsite at Point Wilson.

The sheltered waters of the park attract a variety of bird life, and bird watchers are well rewarded for journeying here. Permanent hides at Lake Killarney allow visitors to observe water birds such as black swans, pelicans, grebes, ducks, and cormorants as they go about their daily habits undisturbed by human intrusion.

With an abundance of water nearby, the park is able to support a diverse assortment of plant species. Flowers in the winter and spring—July through October—include the strangely shaped and multicolored ground orchids, orange and golden wattles, and pink- and white-flowered tea trees. Other vegetation includes manna and red gums, peppermint trees, paperbarks, she-oaks, and box trees.

RIVER RED GUM
Eucalyptus camaldulensis

The river red gum, the most widely distributed of all eucalypts, grows throughout mainland Australia. It is found predominantly in low-lying areas, including the flood plains of most creeks and rivers, and in seasonal watercourses of the arid and semiarid regions. Growing to heights of 125 ft/38 m, its trunk and leaves are home to many animals. Insects and birds are especially attracted to the tree because it produces copious amounts of nectar.

An adaptable tree, it has the ability to grow new bark to replace any slight injury. During times of drought, it has been known to drop whole branches suddenly to the ground.

River red gums have played a role in two major Australian historical events. Burke, Wills, and King, the intrepid explorers, chose a river red gum tree in Menindee National Park in New South Wales as their departure point on their way to Cooper Creek. The "Separation Tree," where citizens of Melbourne gathered to hear the proclamation of the separation of Victoria and New South Wales, also was a river red gum.

CROAJINGOLONG NATIONAL PARK

Department of Conservation,
Forests and Lands, Orbost Region,
Orbost, VIC, or call (051) 54 1393.

Croajingolong National Park covers a 62-mi/100-km stretch of coast east of Melbourne, the northernmost area of Victoria that borders the sea. Because of its location, the park offers visitors Victoria's mildest year-round climate. This 212,506-acre/86,000-hectare park was created in 1979 as a combination of two older parks, James Cook and Mallacoota Inlet.

Since most of the park borders the sea, its coastline is constantly changing as the pounding surf erodes the rocky shores. With strong winds moving the dunes, the scattered spinifex plants must struggle to remain in place. Inlets and estuaries are formed by the enclosing movement of sand, then breached by the sea during violent storms.

Scrubs and heath plants grow wild in the sand, while inland the area's steep slopes and ridges support dry woodlands. Flowers and mountain gums grow on the riverbanks.

Beaches here are usually deserted and tranquil, their sands stretching for miles with nothing to block the view. Thousands of birds inhabit the shores and the vegetation on the heath. Some of the species, like the eastern bristle-bird, are extremely rare. The bristle-birds live in the dense heath, moving about rodent-like as they search for food on the ground. Rarely are they seen flying. Their colors match the brown and beige tones of the heath and make them difficult to spot.

Even though the area is so much influenced by water, parts of Croajingolong are subject to frequent dry electrical storms in the summertime. Many of the plants that grow here are superbly adapted to survive drought and fire, especially the eucalypt varieties.

Visitors come to Croajingolong not only for its mild climate but also for its variety. Mallacoota Inlet hosts a fine boating and fishing resort and other areas offer excellent fishing, sailing, canoeing, swimming, and enjoyable bushwalking trails. These walks take visitors through dry eucalypt forest, over coastal heaths and dunes, and through steep forested ridges and gullies.

MOUNT BUFFALO NATIONAL PARK

Department of Conservation, Forests and Lands, Northeast Region, Wangaratta, VIC, or call (060) 242 788.

Many visitors come to Mount Buffalo National Park during the winter months to ski cross-country; others prefer to visit during November through May, when the flowers are blooming and the hiking is extremely rewarding. There is an area with good facilities for camping and camper-vehicle parking located near Lake Catani, which also has a lodge and guesthouse nearby.

Rising over 3,280 ft/1,000 m above the Ovens Valley, the Buffalo Plateau was the first ski area to be developed in Victoria. It was first sighted and named in 1824 but was not scaled until 1854. Its dark walls, looming straight up from the ground, are indeed forbidding obstacles. At 1,427 ft/435 m, its straight rock face is the longest in all of Australia, a challenge to be taken up by only the most expert climbers.

The plateau, covering an area 6.2 mi/10 km long and 4.3 mi/7 km wide, features excellent walking and skiing trails. It is called Mt. Buffalo because of its resemblance in profile to a buffalo; The Horn at the southern end of the plateau is likened to the buffalo's head. Topping 5,642 ft/1,720 m, The Horn is the highest point in the park.

GEOLOGY

At one time, this area of Victoria was covered by a layer of sedimentary rock left by receding seas millions of years ago. An immense column of molten rock forced its way up from below but did not break through the surface. Instead, it cooled and formed a granite plug. Over time, erosion wore away the sedimentary rock and revealed the harder granite, which now exists as Mt. Buffalo Plateau.

WILDLIFE

The lyrebird is the best known of all the birds in the park. Generally unafraid of visitors, lyrebirds often are seen near campgrounds and picnic areas. The large songbird (up to 40 in/1 m) is a favorite of

The sheer eastern wall of The Gorge, in the heart of Buffalo National Park, falls 1,427 ft/ 435 m. It is the longest straight-faced rock climb on the Australian continent.

visitors, who marvel as the male sends out his resounding song and lifts high his brilliant white train of feathers to catch the attention of a nearby female. Males visit display mounds daily during the breeding season, singing and showing off their tailfeathers.

Gang-gang cockatoos are seen here often, quietly eating seeds in the trees overhead. The males, with their gray bodies and bright orange red heads, show up easily among the branches.

Because it is fairly cool in the park year-round, wombats can be seen quite often during the day. Black-tailed wallabies and sugar gliders may be glimpsed at dusk.

VEGETATION

The vegetation in Mount Buffalo National Park is extremely varied and well defined according to the elevation at which it grows. The highest levels of the park support a true alpine vegetation of snow gums and bright white mountain gums with an understory of alpine shrubs. They grow in every available rock cleft and crevice, where they are protected from the strong winds.

Vegetation at the bottom of the slopes is composed of thick wet forests of peppermint gums, manna gums, silver wattles, and blackwoods. Peppermint gums are replaced by alpine ash and snow gums in higher elevations. Subalpine flowers color the plains and the fringes of the woodlands. Golden paper daisies carpet this region, while purple mountain gentians bedeck the higher slopes. Other flowers include the buffalo sallow wattle and weeping sallee.

BUSHWALKING

There are more than 44 mi/70 km of walking trails throughout the park. Some of these include:

Eurobin Falls. This 1-mi/1.6-km trail located near the park's entrance takes you past several waterfalls surrounded by large white manna gums and lush tree ferns.

The Monolith. The trail begins opposite the RCA shelter next to Reservoir Road and takes about an hour to complete. The view

Rollasons Falls cascades through several types of forests, including wet sclerophyll, until it reaches Buffalo Creek.

from atop this granite mass takes in much of the neighboring landscape, including Lake Catani.

The Cathedral and The Hump. Beginning from The Cathedral picnic area, located in the south-central part of the park, follow the signposted track to The Cathedral. A longer trail to the left leads to the top of The Hump. The walk takes only about an hour to finish. Huge clusters of Bogong moths, inactive during the day, are a feature of this area during the warm summer months.

The Horn. This half-hour trip starts near the lookout hut at the parking area of The Horn. Although a steeper track than many of the others, it rewards those who attempt it with vistas from the park's tallest peak.

Mt. McLeod. This extended walk starts from the parking area at The Reservoir, located in the west-central part of the park. The 12.4-mi/20-km trail features outstanding wildflower displays beginning at the end of December. It also provides many long-range views of the park. It takes about six hours to complete.

BOGONG NATIONAL PARK

Department of Conservation, Forests and Lands, Northeast Region, VIC, or call (060) 242 788.

In the spring and summer months, there is bushwalking on the excellent walking trails, as well as horseback riding, mountaineering, fishing (license required), and sailing on the Rocky River Dam. Camping is available throughout the park; however, no camping is allowed within 660 ft/ 200 m of roads or within 99 ft/30 m of streams.

In the winter months there is cross-country skiing in the Bogong High Plains and Bogong National Park. The resorts at Falls Creek and Mt. Hotham also offer downhill skiing.

Towering high above the surrounding plains, Bogong National Park (200,151 acres/81,000 hectares) encompasses eleven of the twelve highest peaks in Victoria. Among the highest are Mt. Bogong at 6,516 ft/1,986 m, Mt. Feathertop at 6,306 ft/1,932 m, and Mt. Hotham at 6,109 ft/1,862 m. Caves are scattered about the area and in some of these live the famous Bogong moths, which cluster in the thousands on cave walls during the daytime and take wing at night to feed. At one time Aborigines frequented this area in search of moths as food.

The area's climate is changeable and relatively cool. Gale-force winds are not uncommon, and sometimes thick fogs roll in, reducing visibility to zero. The western slopes and high plains receive the most rainfall, and it is not unusual for a snowstorm to strike without warning. Visitors to the area are cautioned to bring warm clothing and to be prepared for these sudden changes.

The mountains were formed from volcanic activity; basalt columns still line several of the slopes. At the Ruined Castle, the columns have split and cracked and look like giant stepping-stones. The extreme temperatures and climatic conditions have sculpted the mountains and flattened areas into tablelands that are now prime venues for cross-country skiers.

Alpine wildflowers, able to withstand the harsh winds and precipitation, adorn most of the mountain slopes from October through March, spring and summer. Bright yellow alpine daisies and lilac-colored hairy cut-leaf daisies are two daisy varieties that thrive here. Snow gums and mountain gums fill the woodlands, while alpine ash grow in the lower forests.

The plentiful wildlife of the Bogong includes wombats, eastern gray kangaroos, swamp wallabies, and the tiny mountain pygmy

Daisies dominate the summer alpine of Bogong National Park. The area's vegetation was once threatened by the overgrazing of cattle.

Looking out from the Bogong Plateau over the Murray River and into New South Wales, one sees a series of ridges. Most distant are the Suggan Buggan Range and the Charcoal Range.

possums, which are known to hibernate in the winter. Kookaburras sing out from lower branches of trees and crimson rosellas and king parrots eat seeds in the treetops. Brown falcons soar overhead, and black-and-white pied currawongs hop from the trees to the ground in their ceaseless search for food. In all, about 150 bird species have been recorded in the park.

SNOWY RIVER NATIONAL PARK

Department of Conservation, Forests and Lands, Bairnsdale   Region, Bairnsdale, VIC, or call (051) 52 6211.

At first daylight in Snowy River National Park, a thick blue mist rising from thousands of eucalypt trees brightens in the morning sun and lifts gently off the mountain ridges that line the Snowy River. Mobs of rock wallabies prepare to settle down for the day among the cool rock crevices.

The Snowy River, for which this park is named, rushes through the narrow gorges and out to the Tasman Sea. From its source at Mt. Kosciusko in New South Wales, the river winds southeast and then abruptly west before heading south into Victoria.

The Snowy River now is well contained, except for times when heavy rainfall causes a sudden rise in the water level. At one time, the river was prone to flooding but it has been diverted and its flow regulated in several areas, and flooding is no longer a problem.

The Snowy River National Park, 280 mi/450 km east of Melbourne, is a 358,295-acre/145,000-hectare park that features the Snowy River, several gorges, rain-forest gullies, and mountain ridges peaking at 2,300 ft/700 m. The western side of the park is made up of limestone caves and uneven molten-rock slabs that are reminders of the area's geological past—the caves from the time when the land was completely submerged by water, and the molten slabs from a period of volcanic activity.

The Snowy River continues to make changes in the geology of the region as it flows through gorges and carves away at their walls. Smooth boulders, strewn helter-skelter in the waters, are constantly being shifted by the pressure of the flow.

Snowy River gained national notoriety from the poem "The Man from Snowy River," written by the famous balladeer, Banjo Patterson, who also wrote "Waltzing Matilda." Patterson's poem romanticized the early stockmen who grazed their cattle by this river. The situation is different today, as environmentalists seek to have the practice of grazing stopped. They claim that the cattle have already caused significant damage to the environment.

Snowy River National Park offers visitors the chance to see myriad flowers, including Snowy River daisies, rock guinea flowers, buttercups, and river beard heath. For most visitors, however, the attraction is the magnificent adventure of canoeing the river, navigating around its obstacles, and exploring gorges that can be reached only via the river.

Hardy bushwalkers can explore the river shores on foot, but they must be prepared for some rough going. South along the Snowy Valley, for example, the river becomes wedged between towering rock walls at Tulloch Ard Gorge, and the only way walkers can get through the gorge is to swim.

There are less strenuous trails that fan out from the Buchan-Jindabyne Road. These take hikers through lightly timbered ridges, past teeming waterfalls, and over tranquil streams to vistas of incredible beauty.

TASMANIA

Cradle Mountain-Lake St. Clair
National Park

Franklin-Lower Gordon Rivers
National Park

South West National Park

Mount Field National Park

Walls of Jerusalem National Park

Tasmanian Caves

Rocky Cape National Park

Maria Island National Park

Freycinet National Park

Ben Lomond National Park

Mount William National Park

From the lichen-covered dolerite pillars of Cradle Mountain there is a clear view across Cradle Mountain National Park to Barn Bluff.

TASMANIA HAS THE MOST DRAMATIC landscape to be seen anywhere in Australia. Etched from rock squeezed between Antarctica and Australia, the island seems to vault out of the surrounding icy waters on pillars of erosion-resistant dolerite stone. From any vantage point, one sees its landscape climbing upward until the loftiest peaks are lost in cloud.

The seasons are more distinct in Tasmania than on the mainland, though Tasmania's weather changes are often unpredictable. Often, when the sun is shining on the eastern coast, rain or snow is falling on the western peaks. The state is susceptible to long wet spells and wintry storms at any time of year, with some areas receiving 200 in/508 cm of rain annually, more than ten times the average for many mainland areas. Trails in the western region are wet year-round and so saturated that bushwalkers often say it is like walking on giant sponges. Strong winds blowing from Antarctica reach Tasmania uninterrupted. A westerly or southwesterly wind almost guarantees bad weather, while northerly breezes mean mild, temperate days ahead.

Tasmania is the only state in Australia where autumn brings a dramatic display of foliage, as the deciduous beech, or tanglefoot (*Nothofagus gunnii*), paints the mountain slopes in shades of crimson and gold. In spring most flowering plants of the east coast

Remnants of Aboriginal tools and piles of discarded shells can be found along the northern beaches of Mount Williams National Park.

bloom, including countless varieties of orchids that grow in the understory of the eucalypt forests. On the long summer days of December and January, the sun rises early and sets late. The air is crisp in the mornings and warm in the afternoons along the eastern seashore. In the mountains, where the summer sun dries the moorlands between thunderstorms, the climate is more humid. Although it can snow in Tasmania in any season – even in summer in the higher elevations – snow is expected on the moorlands in winter (late June and July). For the adventurous, this is the time to don cross-country skis and glide into a pristine world few visitors ever see.

GEOLOGY

Two hundred million years ago, Tasmania and mainland Australia, New Zealand, South America, India, Africa, and Antarctica were all joined in a supercontinent that geologists call Gondwanaland. Since that time, the supercontinent has split into fragments and oceans have formed in the still-widening fissures. What was Tasmania's neighboring land mass to the west and south is now part of Antarctica.

As Gondwanaland was beginning to fragment, molten dolerite welled up into the top of the crust. In Tasmania, this happened 165 million years ago. Before it could reach the surface, the dolerite spread into vast horizontal sheets, forcing apart layers of sedimentary rock. When it solidified, the dolerite formed a rock much harder than the sedimentary layers. Gradual wearing away of these rocks over millions of years left the dolerite as flat, erosion-resistant caps on many of Tasmania's highest peaks.

Much of Tasmania's current landscape dates to the last ice age, only 20,000 years ago. As the ice sheets melted, they scoured the terrain, and previously created mountain ranges were redefined and reshaped. Lakes formed as receding glaciers scooped out bedrock and glacial deposits acted as natural dams.

WILDLIFE

There are few established limits or boundaries for the wildlife of Tasmania. Much of the state's topography remains in a natural condition, and the rest is cultivated in field crops and orchards. En route to a park, you may see creatures wandering through the countryside as if the landscape had never changed. Wombats waddle on the roads, Bennett's wallabies race through paddocks, and green parrots feast in apple orchards.

Usually thought of as mainland curiosities, the two Australian monotremes (mammals that lay eggs), the platypus and echidna, are glimpsed far more often in Tasmania than visitors might expect. Platypuses frequently inhabit the lowland streams and subalpine lakes of the southwest, while the habitat of echidnas encompasses all but the mountain and rain-forest regions.

More than 200 bird species are at home in Tasmania's temperate climate. They include wedge-tailed eagles (one of the world's larger birds of prey), black cockatoos, green rosellas, and the tiny and rare forty-spotted pardalote. Three snakes inhabit Tasmania: the tiger snake, copperhead, and white-lipped whipsnake. The state's most unusual inhabitant is surely the Tasmanian mountain shrimp, which has remained unaltered for at least 200 million years. Several species of freshwater crayfish, or yabbies, also share these alpine waterways.

VEGETATION

There are approximately nineteen species of eucalyptus trees in Tasmania. In dry regions and in cool high-altitude areas one sees open dry eucalypt forests, the dominant species depending on environmental factors. Wet eucalypt forests occur mostly in western Tasmania, where the dominant tree is often the Smithton peppermint.

Cool temperate rain forests occur throughout Tasmania, except on the east coast, where they are largely excluded. These green forests have great variety, ranging from park-like and ferny to tangled and scrubby, although the myrtle beech is a dominant species in all types.

At higher elevation Tasmania possesses some of the finest alpine landscape in Australia, a mosaic of shrubs, mosses, bogs, and lower-growing trees.

Twenty percent of Tasmania's vegetation is low tussock moorland dominated by button grass in association with other sedge and cord-rush species. A range of other low-growing environments – coastal heaths, grasslands, and wetlands – completes the picture of the Tasmanian landscape.

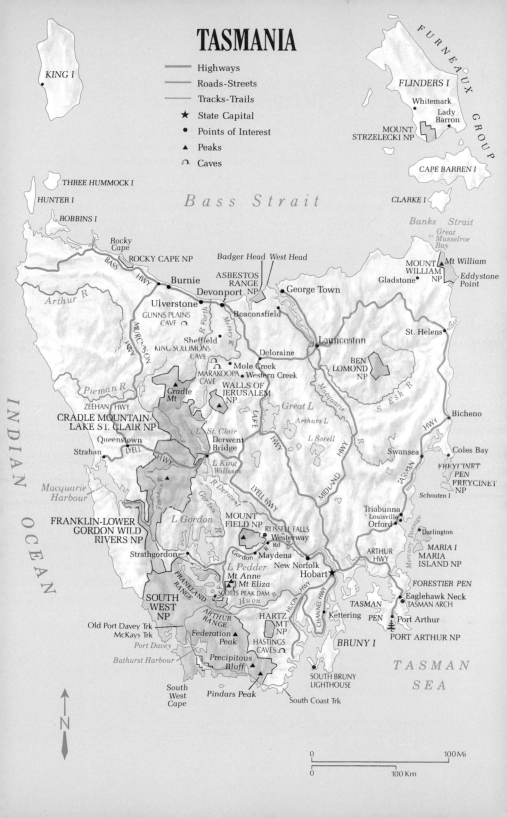

TASMANIA

Highways
Roads-Streets
Tracks-Trails
★ State Capital
● Points of Interest
▲ Peaks
⋂ Caves

KING I

F U R N E A U X   G R O U P

FLINDERS I

Whitemark
Lady Barron

MOUNT STRZELECKI NP

CAPE BARREN I

THREE HUMMOCK I

HUNTER I

ROBBINS I

Bass Strait

CLARKE I

Banks Strait

Great Musselroe Bay

Rocky Cape
ROCKY CAPE NP

Badger Head   West Head

MOUNT WILLIAM NP   Mt William
Eddystone Point

BASS HWY
Burnie
Devonport
ASBESTOS RANGE NP

George Town

Gladstone

Arthur R

Ulverstone
GUNNS PLAINS CAVE ⋂

Beaconsfield

Launceston

St. Helens

MURCHISON HWY

Sheffield
KING SOLOMONS CAVE ⋂

Deloraine

BEN LOMOND NP

R Forth   *Mersey R*

Pieman R

Cradle Mt

MARAKOOPA CAVE ⋂
Mole Creek
Western Creek

WALLS OF JERUSALEM NP

Great L

S Esk R

Macquarie R

Bicheno

ZEEHAN HWY

CRADLE MOUNTAIN-LAKE ST. CLAIR NP

Queenstown

Strahan

LYELL HWY

L. St. Clair

Derwent Bridge

LAKE HWY

Arthurs L

L Sorell

Swansea

Coles Bay

FREYCINET PEN
FREYCINET NP

Schouten I

▲

L King William

▲

Macquarie Harbour

FRANKLIN-LOWER GORDON WILD RIVERS NP

Franklin R

R Derwent

LYELL HWY

MIDLAND HWY

L Gordon

Gordon R

MOUNT FIELD NP
RUSSELL FALLS ●
Westerway
Rd

Triabunna
Louisville
Orford

Darlington

MARIA I
MARIA ISLAND NP

Strathgordon

Gordon R
Maydena

New Norfolk

ARTHUR HWY

Mercury Passage

FRANKLAND RANGE

L Pedder
Mt Anne ▲
▲ Mt Eliza
SCOTTS PEAK DAM

Hobart ★

Huon R

FORESTIER PEN

Eaglehawk Neck
TASMAN ARCH

SOUTH WEST NP

ARTHUR RANGE

Huon

HARTZ MT NP

CHANNEL HWY

Kettering

TASMAN PEN

Port Arthur
PORT ARTHUR NP

Old Port Davey Trk
McKays Trk

Port Davey

Federation ▲
Peak

HASTINGS CAVES ⋂

HUON HWY

BRUNY I

TASMAN SEA

Bathurst Harbour

Precipitous Bluff ▲

South West Cape

Pindars Peak ▲

South Coast Trk

SOUTH BRUNY LIGHTHOUSE

INDIAN OCEAN

N

0   100 Mi
0   100 Km

CRADLE MOUNTAIN–LAKE ST. CLAIR NATIONAL PARK

The Ranger, Cradle Mountain via Sheffield, TAS 7306, or call (003) 63 5187. The Ranger, Lake St. Clair via Derwent Bridge, TAS 7465, or call (002) 89 1115.

The park is accessible by roads from both the north and south. Cradle Mountain entrance is 53 mi/ 85 km from the northern coast town of Devonport. Lake St. Clair, Cynthia Bay, is accessible via the Lyell Highway. Both ends of the park are serviced by bus: the north end from Launceston, and the south end from the state capital, Hobart. Fuel, food, and accommodations (by advance reservation) are available at nearby kiosks and lodges.

There are huts at both ends of the park; ones with amenities such as electricity, a stove, and mattresses are available on a rental basis. Huts along the alpine trail are available on a first-come, first-served basis and they are often overcrowded, especially during bad weather. If you are planning a trek across the park, you will be wise to carry your own tent and other camping gear.

Cradle Mountain and Lake St. Clair encompass a huge expanse of subalpine and alpine moorlands as well as important vestiges of cool temperate rain forest. Since its discovery by Europeans at the turn of the twentieth century, the area has become a mecca for alpine climbing and bushwalking enthusiasts. During summer the park is Tasmania's most popular outdoor destination. Cradle Mountain, to the north, is a spectacular peak of weathered dolerite columns, often shrouded in clouds and mist. The 5,069-ft/1,545-m peak draws storms like a weather magnet – all too often to the frustration of hikers and day visitors.

At the opposite end of the park, 50 mi/80 km to the south, lies Lake St. Clair, a classic example of glacial gouging, formed as sheets of ice moving between mountain ranges scooped deeper scars into the mountain landscape. The basins thus created filled quickly with melting glacial runoff and rainwater.

Between the park's two landmarks lies some of Tasmania's most beautiful topography, comprising rugged mountain slopes, wild open grassland, lush rain forest, dense eucalypt forests, countless lakes, and long sweeping waterfalls.

The slopes of Cradle Mountain are covered with vegetation.

The waratah's beautiful red flowers manage to grow among boulders in areas where there is sufficient rainfall. The word waratah is an Aboriginal word meaning "seen from afar."

All bushwalkers, whether visiting for an afternoon or a week, should be prepared for sudden changes in weather, especially in the higher elevations. It is not unusual for a snowfall or hail storm to blow over Cradle Mountain in two hours' time during the middle of the summer. Like all of the Tasmanian mountain parks, Cradle Mountain-Lake St. Clair can be extremely hazardous for the visitor who disregards warnings to be prepared.

HISTORY

"This must be a national park for all time. It is magnificent. Everyone should know about it, and come and enjoy it." So proclaimed Gustav Weindorfer, an Austrian-born diplomat who moved to Tasmania at the turn of the century and eventually became the founder of the park. Weindorfer was so taken by this area that he built a chalet from local timber in 1912, naming it Waldheim, or "forest home." Ten years later, the area was proclaimed a national park. Waldheim, now restored, stands at the beginning of the walk from Cradle Mountain to Lake St. Clair. Its owner died in 1932 and was buried on the valley slope in sight of the mountains he loved.

Many Europeans had visited the area prior to Weindorfer, but unlike the Austrian, who wished to preserve it for future generations, they thought only of what they could extract from the land. Prospectors, cattlemen, hunters, and woodsmen all carved their niches in the region, leveling large sections of the park's endemic trees and plants. While it is somewhat easier to traverse the park's rugged landscape today than when explorers trekked through during the early part of the nineteenth century, the words of the first man to climb Cradle Mountain, Englishman Henry Hellyer, still carry some meaning for those who have hiked across the park: "We were often obliged to be walking upon these never dry slippery branches covered with moss . . . which being in many instances rotten occasioned as many awkward falls and tore our clothes to rags."

GEOLOGY

The oldest rocks in Cradle Mountain-Lake St. Clair are Precambrian sedimentary rocks at least 700 million years old. These were folded and metamorphosed, in large part prior to 600 million years ago. Then, 300 million years ago, glaciers scoured the area, leaving behind sedimentary rocks. These flat-lying rocks were intruded by dolerite 165 million years ago. All of these rocks were uplifted and eroded, and were particularly deeply eroded by ice sheets about 20,000 years ago. The ice also scoured out the park's many lakes and tarns (small mountain lakes) from the bedrock. Lake St. Clair, for instance, lies in a valley 700 ft/213 m deep carved by a large glacier that formed at the confluence of smaller glaciers from the north.

WILDLIFE

The entire range of Tasmanian wildlife resides in the park. Few bushwalkers pass through the park without seeing common brush-tailed possums (which can be unrelenting in their pursuit of food carried by backpackers), wombats, friendly Tasmanian pademelons, and perhaps a Tasmanian devil or two.

Whether you begin your exploration in the north or south, you are bound to be greeted by a band of Bennett's wallabies, good-natured kangaroo cousins that graciously pose for snapshots in exchange for

TASMANIAN PADEMELON
Thylogale billardierii

The shy Tasmanian pademelon, also called the rufous wallaby or red-bellied pademelon, spends its days hiding in low scrub and dense vegetation. It is known for the well-defined, tunnel-like runways it forms in the thick underbrush and for its strong forepaws, which it uses to hold food, manipulate herbage in its mouth, and dig out vegetation from the snow.

It emerges at night from its hiding places to feed on grasses, herbs, and some browse from the tops of woody plants, but it never ventures too far out into open areas. When alarmed, it thumps the ground loudly with its foot.

Because of its palatable flesh and its thick red fur, the Tasmanian pad-emelon became a prime target for the Europeans who viewed its meat as a delicacy and its pelts as a potential source of profit.

---

a morsel or two of fresh vegetables. Feeding wallabies is permitted in the park, but rangers ask that visitors refrain from feeding them anything other than fresh fruits and vegetables.

VEGETATION

The alpine and subalpine moorlands that cover large areas of the park are home to many of the endemic plants of Tasmania. These include creeping pine trees and the Tasmanian deciduous beech, the state's only deciduous native tree. The dominant tree species in the higher elevations is the Tasmanian snow gum.

One species found at higher elevations is the cushion plant, which thrives in the harsh alpine areas of the park. It is a flat, rounded mound, up to 40 in/1 m across, consisting of a network of branches and coarse leaves so dense that the plant appears to be a solid mass.

Many other small plants and insects take advantage of the cushion plant's remarkable defense against the elements by using it as a base from which to grow. Tiny carnivorous sundew plants commonly are seen dotting the cushion plant's surface. Alpine botanists have compared the ecosystem surrounding this plant to that of a coral reef.

Autumn on the slopes of Cradle Mountain brings a spectacle in shades of orange, gold, crimson, and brown as the deciduous beech trees prepare for winter. Their tiny 0.8-in/2-cm leaves fall like confetti during late April as winter winds start to howl through the alpine, stripping branches. The vivid display is not confined to the Cradle Mountain area of Tasmania, but this northern section of the park offers easy access and a wealth of walking tracks with panoramic views.

At lower altitudes, where montane grasslands flourish in the deeper soil, one sees all the colors of the spectrum—the greens and soft browns of the rain forests, the bright red of the waratah in bloom, the gaily painted yellows and purples of assorted mountain

An extremely ancient tree, the nothofagus, or beech tree, is abundant on Tasmania, growing on mountainsides and in less likely places, such as on the underside of waterfalls.

flowers. In more fertile wet sites a major timber species is the swamp gum (*Eucalyptus regnans*, known in Victoria as "stringy bark"). It is the tallest flowering tree in the world, reaching heights in excess of 315 ft/96 m, and is distinctive also for the way its outer layers peel away like shedding skin.

BUSHWALKING

The Overland Trail. Completion of this 50-mi/80-km walk is a prized accomplishment among bushwalkers. The walk can be done in five days, but a walk of six to eight days allows time for some of the trail's outstanding side trips. The trail is well marked, and good maps are available that detail campsites along the way.

Most bushwalkers start from the northern end of the park. After a brief trek across open grassland, they find themselves hiking up Cradle Plateau, past Crater Lake or Lake Dove. Many stop the first night at Waterfall Valley, about 6 mi/10 km along the trail.

Beyond the undulating grasslands you will pass by Lake Windermere, about 4.3 mi/7 km from Waterfall Valley. Midway along the Overland Trail is the heart of the mountain country. Many visitors take an extra day here to climb one of the nearby peaks, including Mount Pelion West, Mount Oakleigh, or Mount Ossa.

Southward the trail wanders 5 mi/8 km through rain forest and scrub to Kia Ora hut. The track in this section climbs continually to cross the high Pelion Gap at 3,651 ft/1,113 m and offers grand vistas of the entire park. From Kia Ora hut, it is a forty-five-minute walk to Du Cane hut, which is located in a small clearing in the forest beneath the aptly named Castle Crag. (This hut is not in good condition and is useful only in emergency situations.) There are excellent campsites in the area.

From the Du Cane hut, the trail winds down through dense myrtle beech forests. Popular side trips include stops at D'Alton Falls and Fergusson Falls on the Mersey River. Several huts situated along this section of the trail allow the hiker to take the journey at any pace. Within the forest is Windy Ridge hut, 4.7 mi/7.5 km from Du

The rain forest's lushness in Cradle Mountain-Lake St. Clair National Park is hardly interrupted by the Overland Trail.

Cane. The track then continues through the outer edge of a eucalypt forest, gradually descending to the Narcissus Plains, about 5.6 mi/9 km from Windy Ridge.

The final 10 mi/16 km from Narcissus hut to the Cynthia Bay camping area on Lake St. Clair is easy going. Echo Point hut, 3.1 mi/5 km from Narcissus and on the shore of the lake, is a popular rest stop. The main track follows the shore through myrtle and eucalypt forests to Cynthia Bay. For those who would prefer an easy ride, a daily ferry runs 8.7 mi/14 km across the lake from Narcissus hut to Cynthia Bay.

Signing in and out is very important for walkers on the Overland Trail. Violent storms often besiege the park with little warning. Your safety and the ranger's ability to help you depend on your diligence in making your whereabouts known.

Cradle Valley to Crater Lake. This 2.2-mi/3.5-km walk begins at Waldheim near the ranger station and takes walkers up steep inclines for magnificent views of Cradle Valley. Visitors can look down on the glacially carved Crater Lake and return through some of the park's finest rain forest. The round trip takes about two hours.

Cradle Valley to Cradle Mountain via Marions Lookout. Many cannot resist the temptation to climb to the top of the park's main feature, Cradle Mountain. It is a long journey, taking about seven hours and covering nearly 8.1 mi/13 km of difficult terrain, but on a clear day the view from the top is superb. This trip also includes fine views of the mountains from Marions Lookout, gained by a steep climb up rocky hillsides. Bushwalkers are advised to check with the rangers for weather predictions before attempting this climb. And even then they should be prepared for a sudden shift to inclement conditions.

Cynthia Bay to Shadow Lake. Starting near the ranger's quarters, this relatively easy 6.2-mi/10-km half-day walk takes you through eucalypt and beech forests and around some picturesque lakes and tarns.

Cynthia Bay to Mount Rufus. This is a much more demanding climb of 11.2 mi/18 km, requiring about eight hours to complete. The trek goes across marshy plains before ascending Mount Rufus for a view of many of the park's northern peaks.

CRADLE MOUNTAIN-LAKE ST. CLAIR NP

Cradle Mountain Rd

Dove R

SOUTHWEST CONSERVATION AREA

● Cradle Valley Ranger Station

Waldheim Chalet
CRADLE VALLEY
Crater L.
MARIONS LOOKOUT
CRADLE PLATEAU
＊

L Dove
▲ Cradle Mt

L Dove

Hansons R

Fury R

▲ Mt Emmett

WATERFALL VALLEY
● Waterfall Valley Hut

Barn Bluff ▲

L Will

R Forth

Overland Trk

L Windermere

Windermere Hut ●

Lake Rowallan

WALLS OF JERUSALEM NP

▲ Mt Oakleigh

Mt Pelion West ▲
Pelion Hut ●

Mt Pelion East ▲

Mersey

Mt Achilles
▲ Mt Thetis

● PELION GAP

▲ Mt Doris
Mt Ossa ▲

CENTRAL PLATEAU CONSERVATION AREA

Kia Ora Hut ●
Du Cane Hut ●

▲ Cathedral Mt

D'ALTON FALLS
FERGUSSON FALLS ●

Mt Massif ▲
CASTLE CRAG

DU CANE

Mt Geryon ▲
The Acropolis ▲
RANGE

● Windy Ridge Hut

Murchison R

TRAVELLER

MOUNTAINS OF JUPITER RANGE

Mt Gould ▲

FRANKLIN–
LOWER GORDON
WILD RIVERS NP

Narcissus Hut ●
Narcissus Bay

Mt Byron ●

Lake St Clair

Mt Olympus ▲
● Echo Point Hut

L Petrarch

CHEYNE RANGE

Cuvier Valley Trk

Shadow L

Cynthia Bay

Mt Rufus ▲

Cynthia Bay Ranger Station
Lake St Clair Rd

R Derwent

● Derwent Bridge

LYELL HWY

Lake King William

Legend

— Highways	● Points of Interest		
— Roads-Streets	＊ Scenic Lookout		
— Tracks-Trails	▲ Peaks		

0 ——— 8 Mi
0 ——— 8 Km

N ↑

FRANKLIN-LOWER GORDON RIVERS NATIONAL PARK

Ranger-in-Charge, Collingwood River, c/o P.O. Box 21, Queenstown, TAS 7467, or call (004) 71 1446.

In the vicinity of Strahan, at the west end of the park, there are camper vehicle parks and campgrounds as well as hotels. The remainder of the park has no such organized facilities, although bush camping is possible almost anywhere. One convenient camping location is at the start of the trail to Frenchmans Cap on the Lyell Highway, where cars may be left at a nearby parking area.

Located adjacent to South West National Park, this vast wilderness area has attracted attention both for its World Heritage listing and for the successful campaign to block the building of hydroelectric plants on the park's two major rivers. Although in the early 1970s the power interests succeeded in drowning nearby Lake Pedder for a hydroelectric plant, they were less successful in a bid to dam both the Franklin and Gordon rivers for the same purpose a decade later. Protesters held their ground until Australia's highest court ruled in

Looming to heights of 40 ft/ 12.2 m, pandanis are the tallest heath plants in the world. Their red-bordered leaves are sharp and discourage animals from feeding on them.

July 1983 that the project was not in the best interests of the people or the state.

The park extends from Macquarie Harbour southeast into the interior and includes the former Gordon River State Reserve and Frenchmans Cap National Park. It contains large areas of cool temperate rain forest, the forest floor an impenetrable network of fallen lichen-covered trees and scrub, shrouded in deep, damp shade even on the brightest days. The rare banners of light that do filter through the canopy spark the forest with an ethereal quality. In permanent openings, undergrowth bursts to life in rich tones of green. The moist atmosphere of the higher rain forests often brings forth an abundance of pandani, heath plants found only in Tasmania that can grow as high as 40 ft/12.2 m. Among the trees are the conifer species endemic to Tasmania—the King William pine, celery top pine, leatherwood, and huon pine. Indeed, the park protects much of Tasmania's reserved resources of riverine huon pine. This tree is much coveted for its extremely hard wood, which remains sound even in trees that have been lying on the ground for several years.

The rivers and western harbor can be very inhospitable, the riverbanks a befuddling tangle of sassafras, myrtle, and dwarfing tree ferns. The western coast of Tasmania remains nearly as isolated and uninhabited as when the first European, Dutch explorer Abel Tasman, sailed along the shoreline in 1643. He apparently realized the great difficulty of maintaining a settlement here; two centuries passed before the English succeeded in establishing a colony on the west coast at the head of Macquarie Harbour. That settlement, Strahan, is still the only one on the coast, a striking indicator of the forbidding nature of the topography.

It is still not easy to raft down the Franklin River, but those who do never forget the towering walls of sheer rock or the fast-paced swirl of the white water. A far easier and perhaps better way to view the park's geological and geographical wonders is by taking a ferryboat ride from Macquarie Harbour to the Lower Gordon River. As the boat crosses the large expanse of the harbor, the seascape slowly changes. The water's color changes to a murky, brownish tint, caused by leaching of the peaty soils. On a calm day, the surface of the water provides an almost perfect reflection of both your vessel and the riverbanks.

SOUTH WEST NATIONAL PARK

National Parks and Wildlife Service Head Office, P.O. Box 210, Sandy Bay, TAS 7005, or call the park at (002) 88 2341.
Access to the park is from the north via the Gordon River Road through Maydena, 109 mi/174 km from Hobart. A side road leads to Scotts Peak Dam. There are picnic facilities at Strathgordon and at the Serpentine, Scotts Peak, and Edgar dams. Boat rentals, fishing guides, and tourist launches are available from Strathgordon, and campgrounds with basic facilities are located at Lake Pedder, Scotts Peak Dam, and Edgar Dam.

Tasmania's largest wilderness area as well as some of its best remote bushwalking trails are found in this immense park, which encompasses most of the island's southwestern corner. In its more than 988,400 acres/400,000 hectares, South West National Park boasts five major mountain ranges, more than fifty lakes, breathtaking coastal scenery, long open grasslands, and several prominent river systems.

GEOLOGY

South West National Park is the most vertical landscape in Australia. Many of its mountains – Mount Picton, Pindars Peak, and Precipitous Bluff – resemble the flat-topped, craggy-edged dolerite columns of Cradle Mountain.

In stark contrast to the dolerite peaks, the park's most spectacular spire, Federation Peak is white-crested quartzite. The tops of other quartzite peaks, such as in the Arthur and Frankland Ranges, are very jagged. Recent glaciation has created pronounced moraines (debris deposited by glaciers) and lakes throughout the area, and cirques (natural amphitheaters) in the central and southern parts of the park.

Federation Peak was named in the same year the country's states became federated, 1901. The mountain lies at the southern end of the eastern Arthurs, which is a small but dramatic series of peaks and ridges.

Tall huon pines are a common sight in South West National Park, which is known for its untouched wilderness. Because of the abundant rainfall and mild temperatures, trees in South West grow taller than trees do elsewhere, sometimes reaching over 325 ft/100 m.

WILDLIFE AND VEGETATION

Within its borders, the park protects some of the world's most beautiful temperate rain forest, with an abundance of myrtle beech and tall, slender huon pines, which are endemic to Tasmania. Here, too, one sees large areas of button-grass moorland. Button grass grows in dense clumps (tussocks) that can measure up to 2 ft/0.6 m in diameter. Found in muddy, marshy areas, the tussocks are often the bushwalker's only means of traversing extremely wet regions. Because of the poor drainage, the organic litter of the moorland vegetation does not break down and oxidize but instead forms peat, an organic soil. Peat soils are common over much of southwest Tasmania and are vulnerable to being burned in wildfires.

The moorlands, or high plains, with their long, open vistas, feature many lower-growing plant types, pineapple grass, and snow grass. Taller trees do not do well here because of the strong winds and snowfalls. Typical trees include yellow and varnish gums.

The major hindrance to exploring South West National Park is the infamous "horizontal scrub," which takes its name from the way its weak vertical limbs tend to bend sideways. A slender tree found only in this region, it makes bushwalking not only difficult but dangerous; when tree stems cover a large area, the bushwalker can easily fall through the resulting network of branches.

The park is home to some uncommon bird species such as the ground parrot, emu wren, and yellow-throated honey eater.

Debate continues about the future use of this park's resources—especially its vast stands of virgin forest. Unfortunately, given the growing demand for timber in a relatively unforested nation and the pressure from Asia for wood products, South West's long-term environmental stability is still in question.

BUSHWALKING

Mt. Anne climb. This is an ambitious one-day outing, a ten- to twelve-hour round trip climaxing with a splendid view of neighboring peaks. Atop one of the few dolerite peaks in South West National Park, climbers often are greeted with a blanket of fresh snow in spring and autumn; even summer visitors can expect such a surprise. Anyone attempting a one-day climb should check weather

Hardy Dicksonia ferns, or manferns, thrive in the rain forest along the Weld River.

forecasts closely before beginning. If in doubt, be prepared for a one- or two-night stay.

Junction Creek trek. This walk begins 1.2 mi/2 km west of Scotts Peak Dam at the end of the road near Red Knoll Quarry. It is a relatively easy four- to five-hour trek through small ranges and creeks near Scotts Peak.

Other day trips include a walk via Schnells Ridge, offering fine views of the western Arthur Range and Mount Anne area, and a steep climb for panoramic views of Lake Pedder from Mt. Eliza. Both walks take about seven hours to complete.

South Coast trail. It takes roughly nine days to finish this walk, which skirts most of the state's south coast from Cockle Creek to Melaleuca at Port Davey. While it is only a moderately difficult walk for this World Heritage area, it still requires that those who attempt it be either very experienced walkers or extremely fit first-timers. Each day on the trail offers a wide variety of scene changes, ranging through precipitous ocean cliffs, vast plains of button grass, windswept beaches, dense forests, lofty mountains, and well-hidden coves and inlets. Many of the great tales of bushwalking in Tasmania have originated from journeys in the southwest. Acres of boggy terrain, week-long blinding rainstorms, and walkers stranded by inclement weather—all have added to the mystique of this legendary trek.

South West Cape trek. Access to this week-long walk is from the South Coast trail and involves tramping around a rough granite peninsula that juts out into the Southern Ocean. Rewarded by breathtaking coastal scenery and the excitement of wilderness adventure, walkers nevertheless find this track (which barely exists) and the rough weather exhausting. Days are spent traversing coastal cliffs that are a challenge even in the best of weather. Evenings bring a respite, however, with campsites made, for the most part, in sheltered coves that often provide good fishing.

Western Arthur trek. Many avid bushwalkers consider this the best subalpine trail in this park. The full mountain trek takes a minimum of seven days and offers grand views of huge valleys gouged out by glaciers. The walk skirts many of the range's glacial lakes and tarns, hanging waterfalls, and jagged snowcapped peaks. Walkers should plan each night's camp carefully, since protected sites along the crest of the range are limited.

MOUNT FIELD NATIONAL PARK

The Ranger, Mount Field National Park, P.O. Box 41, Westerway, TAS 7140, or call (002) 88 1149.

The park is located 45 mi/72 km west of Hobart on the Maydena Road. A camping area and camper vehicle park are located near the park's entrance, about 0.6 mi/1 km from the railroad station. There is a privately run kiosk as well as private lodging just outside the park entrance. Huts near the Lake Dobson parking area provide basic accommodation; a reservation should be made with the ranger. A visitors' center includes the ranger's office, kiosk, and interpretive displays regarding the park's history and its flora and fauna. Firewood is provided for use in fireplaces. Picnic shelters and electric barbecues also are available.

Mount Field is probably the most visited national park in Tasmania, largely because of its proximity to the state capital, Hobart, only an hour's drive away. It is the finest one-day park in the state, with well-maintained trails, alpine huts, wilderness interpretive walks, and picnic areas. In addition, 12.5 mi/20 km of smooth dirt road traverse the park, enabling visitors to see much of the forest and the alpine beauty of Tasmania in a single day.

Mount Field National Park includes many scenic bush treks that pass by alpine lakes and tarns. It also offers several areas where water tumbles over higher terrain into lush tree-fern gullies. Russell Falls, located ten minutes from the information center, is the most picturesque and popular of the waterfalls.

Horseshoe Falls is near Russell Falls, on the eastern border of the Mount Field National Park.

Perhaps the park's most striking feature is Russell Falls, a two-drop waterfall of 50 and 100 ft/15 and 30 m, which cascades into a lush valley of ever-growing tree ferns. In 1885 it became the first site, along with a surrounding area of about 370 acres/150 hectares, to be set aside for a nature reserve. Not far from these falls is Horseshoe Falls, and within easy walking distance is the Lady Barron River with its accompanying waterfall.

GEOLOGY

Mount Field contains rock formations more than 220 million years old. Permian mudstone, the oldest rock in the park, has been bared at Russell Falls, but elsewhere in the park, it is covered by a brownish sandstone from the more recent Triassic age. Dolerite rock columns were formed 165 million years ago, during the Jurassic age.

The small mountain lakes and pools were formed by glacial activity 20,000 or more years ago. This same glacial action created huge amphitheaters, like the one at Lake Seal Valley; its several layers of sculpting were caused by the repeated thawing and freezing of the glacier.

Moraines, or clusters of large boulders and other sediments, were left behind when the glaciers retreated, and some of the moraines dammed up lakes. This is the origin of Lake Fenton, one of the major sources of water for the city of Hobart.

WILDLIFE AND VEGETATION

A drive through Mount Field National Park provides a sampling of most of Tasmania's vegetation and wildlife. At higher altitudes, the larger trees and shrubs give way to the tougher kerosene bush, dwarf mountain pines, lemon-scented boronias, and mountain rockets, so-called because of their clusters of red, leaf-like fruit. Other plants of note are the creeping pine, with its bright red cone, the endemic mountain buzzy, and a small relative of the blackberry that produces red, edible fruit.

Spindly pencil pines grow alongside a small lake in Mount Field National Park. Endemic to Tasmania, the trees are found in alpine areas only.

TASMANIAN NATIVE HEN
Gallinula mortierii

One would not have a hard time noticing a Tasmanian native hen, also called the narkie or water hen. With its loud displays of aggression and its tail constantly jerking up and down, it would be difficult to miss. Seemingly hysterical, it runs quickly across roads or even swims to escape if alarmed. Rarely will it fly.

It lives alone or in small groups in open paddocks or on the edges of lakes, streams, and swamps. It is sometimes regarded as a threat to young crops.

During the breeding season, the Tasmanian native hen builds a nest of trampled-down tussocks piled high or a shallow cup of grass, roots, leaves, and twigs in undergrowth. It usually lays six to nine eggs, which are off-white with chestnut spots.

The alpine-subalpine area is typically a patchwork of low heathy shrubland and herbfields. The tremendous soil erosion caused by glacial action during the Pleistocene age left the soils thin and rocky, more suited to low woody species than grasses and herbs. Scoparia is one such plant, well known to bushwalkers for its propensity to scratch. However, where soils are deeper or snow-lie is prolonged, herbfields of pineapple grass and snow grass dominate in company with many other species.

In very wet, boggy places, areas of long snow-lie, or particularly exposed areas, cushion plants may occur. These compact woody shrubs look like carpets or cushions of green. Their shape and density give them protection against freezing and the abrasive action of the strong, ice-bearing winds.

Tasmanian mountains are generally too low to support true alpine vegetation, and much of the treeless snow country is below the climatic treeline. However, frost and waterlogging act to prevent the growth of trees in much of the Tasmanian highland area. Trees that

---

A small creek flows from Newdegate Lake through the northwestern section of Mount Field National Park.

are able to tolerate these harsh conditions include the snow gum, cabbage gum, varnish gum, deciduous beech, myrtle beech, and endemic conifers such as the pencil pine and King William (or King Billy) pine.

Many of the state's mammals are found in the park, including Bennett's wallabies, red-bellied wallabies, Tasmanian barred bandicoots, potoroos, wombats, the two quoll species, and three of the island's five possum species.

The park is a bird-watcher's paradise. The Tasmanian native hen, yellow wattlebird, dusky robin, green rosella, lyrebird, and Tasmanian thornbill are but a few of the many species that may be sighted.

BUSHWALKING

Mount Field's most popular walk is the ten-minute trail to Russell Falls, which weaves its way under huge eucalypts and tall tree ferns. Other easy walks branch out from the huts at Lakes Fenton and Dobson, and there are self-guided nature trails revealing lyrebird habitats and pandanus groves.

Longer, more strenuous trails lead to Mount Field West, a daylong walk that should be started only in good weather. The walk to Tarn Shelf features glacially gouged tarns and small lakes.

Overnight campers are welcome in the park; many go on to explore some of the park's higher peaks and glacial valleys.

SKIING

In winter Mount Field draws people from all over Tasmania for both cross-country and downhill skiing. The park's Mt. Mawson, a skier's mecca since 1922, is southern Tasmania's premier ski resort.

It takes skiers about a half-hour to hike from the parking area at Lake Dobson to Mt. Mawson, where there are four ski tows, equipment rental and instruction, a kiosk, toilets, and public accommodation. Overnight stays are not available on the slopes except in club lodges generally restricted to members and their guests. Huts scattered along Tarn Ridge, however, are available to those wishing to ski into the back country on extended journeys.

WALLS OF JERUSALEM NATIONAL PARK

The Ranger, Cradle Mountain via Sheffield, TAS 7306, or call (003) 63 5187. Department of Land, Parks and Wildlife, 134 Macquarie St., Hobart, TAS 7001, or call (002) 30 2620. Maps and other information about the park can also be obtained from temporary stations for the park at nearby Cradle Mountain National Park.

The park is extremely remote and has no roads leading into it. It is accessible, however, via several walking tracks; the shortest one reaches Herods Gates in about two hours. Bushwalkers get to the park via Sheffield or Mole Creek, heading south past Lake Rowallan Dam to the Fish River.

Park rangers advise anyone entering the region to carry detailed route guides. Bushwalkers are advised to leave their names with local police or Cradle Mountain rangers before setting out.

The Walls of Jerusalem National Park is unique for its five main peaks and grassy valleys, known as Gates. The park is located to the east of Cradle Mountain atop the Central Plateau, a tableland dotted with lakes and tarns.

The most popular way to approach the park is through the open valley called Herods Gate. Beyond this point one sees plates and columns of dolerite ringing the park's largest body of water, Lake Salome. Overshadowing the lake are the West Wall and crest of Mount Jerusalem and The Temple, a rising rock feature. These peaks are not particularly high—the tallest, West Wall, is only 4,920 ft/1,500 m; visitors find them easy climbing from a base camp within the park.

The first Europeans to visit the region were the surveyors and explorers of the early 1880s. Gradually, farmers, trappers, fishermen, and bushwalkers came into the area and built huts, several of which still stand. The Walls of Jerusalem appeared first on a map surveyed in 1849, when it carried the name "China Walls."

Aborigines lived within the region's walls long before Europeans ever settled there. The area's plentiful wildlife was enough to keep the usually nomadic people supplied from spring to late summer.

Walls of Jerusalem National Park, comprising 57,450 acres/23,250 hectares, gained formal status in June 1981, making it Tasmania's newest national park.

GEOLOGY

Like its mountain neighbors to the west and south, the Walls of Jerusalem were left in the wake of huge ice sheets 20,000 years ago as the ice surged and receded across the Tasmanian landscape. The end result was not only a sculpting of the earth into wrinkled, torn rock faces, but the creation of thousands of scattered lakes and tarns; park rangers estimate that the Central Plateau contains more than 4,000 glacial lakes. Some were formed as receding glaciers reamed out holes in the valleys; others filled after leftover debris dammed up smaller bodies of water.

TASMANIAN TIGER
Thylacinus cynocephalus

It is many an adventurer's dream to encounter a Tasmanian tiger, or thylacine or Tasmanian wolf, while visiting Tasmania. But one is not likely to see a Tasmanian tiger because the last known one died in the Hobart Zoo in 1936. It is still not clear why they died off or if, indeed, the species was completely destroyed. Some blame their extinction on the European settlers who destroyed them because they preyed on sheep. Others believe that they may have died from an epidemic. The tiger had long ago become extinct on mainland Australia because it could not compete with the dingo.

It was 3 to 4 ft/90 to 120 cm long and 1.5 to 2 ft/50 to 60 cm high, with coarse tan fur and twelve to fifteen dark stripes across its lower back that became thicker near the rump. It was also called the Tasmanian wolf because of its dog-like head and long, stiff tail.

The Tasmanian tiger used to be the largest marsupial carnivore in Australia. Its diet consisted of kangaroos and wallabies, which it persistently followed until they tired out. Because it was slow-moving, it relied on its perseverance and its powerful jaws to catch and kill its prey.

It stayed in lairs in rocky outcrops and caves during the day and hunted at night in timbered woodlands and open sclerophyll forests.

TASMANIAN DEVIL
Sarcophilus harrisii

The Tasmanian devil is Tasmania's most famous resident. It is Australia's largest carnivorous marsupial—21 to 30 in/53 to 76 cm long—and is known for its slow, clumsy motion as it runs. It has extremely powerful jaws that enable it to eat the bones of its prey.

You are not likely to encounter a Tasmanian devil during the daytime, since it prefers to spend the days in the cool dark of hollow logs, rock crevices, and caves. It emerges at dusk and is active through the night in search of food. It feeds on almost any small living creature that it can capture, but it prefers to eat carrion. Since it moves so slowly, it must rely on the element of surprise to capture live prey.

Tasmanian devils are found only in Tasmania, but remains discovered in western Victoria show that they inhabited the mainland at least 600 years ago. It is thought that the mainland populations were killed off by dingoes while those in Tasmania survived because the dingo does not dwell there.

The Walls of Jerusalem are formed from intrusions of dolerite through sediments. As at Cradle Mountain, wind and weathering have severely eroded the rock, and today the Walls resemble colossal pillars, many fallen in disarray, like the ruins of classical temples.

WILDLIFE

Wildlife is plentiful in the Central Plateau region. Many earlier settlers made a good living from trapping here about 150 years ago. Wallabies, possums, and Tasmanian devils abound. Less fortunate, however, was the thylacine, or Tasmanian "tiger," once common in the area. The large, striped marsupial was trapped and hunted for its high bounties and is now believed to be extinct.

VEGETATION

The Walls of Jerusalem contains many of the state's distinctive sub-alpine and alpine plant species such as the pencil pine, one of several conifers endemic to the state, and its larger relative, the King William (or King Billy) pine. The pencil pine, shaped like a Christmas tree, prefers soggy soil and grows close to streams and lakes. Both species belong to the same family as the giant redwoods found primarily in California. This area is also home to some of the most spectacular species of cushion plant found in Tasmania; plants 6 ft/ 1.8 m in diameter are relatively common in the valley.

BUSHWALKING

Experienced bushwalkers establish a base camp for the length of their stay in Walls of Jerusalem, then foray over the dozen or so day tracks accessible from this central location. Walkers with alpine experience may like the challenge of a return trip within the daylight hours of a long summer's day. It is better to take a slow pace on an overnight journey–the geologic beauty of this park will amply reward you.

Via Herods Gate. The visitor must go via Sheffield or Mole Creek south toward Lake Rowallan Dam. At the dam you will see a sign for the walking track, which begins after another 2.5 mi/4 km. Herods Gate offers sheltered campsites only about thirty minutes from the Gate itself. The campsite can be a jumping-off point for a very leisurely first day or an excellent evening stop for walkers who depart late in the day.

Central Plateau via Higgs Track. This infrequently used track eventually comes to Lake Nameless. The hike takes two days and covers nearly 19 mi/30 km; it should be attempted only by seasoned bushwalkers. Rough terrain and sudden, violent weather changes play havoc with the most carefully prepared plans. The start of the track is located southwest of Deloraine near the settlement of Western Creek. The walk is very rewarding, offering a gamut of terrains and bush habitats, from densely wooded forests of eucalypts to cool temperate rain forest to open moorland grass valleys.

TASMANIAN CAVES

Tasmania has some of the country's largest and best limestone cave formations, four of which are open to the public under the management of the Tasmanian National Parks and Wildlife Service. The cave-rich areas conceal countless underground pockets and alleyways. Indeed, Tasmania remains one of the few places on earth where the "discovery" of a truly new cave and associated formations is possible. Usually the adventure in finding a new cave lies more in locating the cave's mouth than in actually exploring underground. If discovery is your goal, be ready to spend hours fighting through horizontal scrub, wading icy rivers, and battling leeches.

Newdegate Cave, one of the best known in the Hastings Cave State Reserve, is lit to facilitate a thorough inspection.

The caves occur mostly in Ordovician limestone deposited in the ocean between 450 and 500 million years ago. The caves themselves did not form until more recent geologic times—within the past few million years. Over the ages, these spaces have offered shelter from the harsh weather to many creatures. Typical living residents include cave crickets, Tasmanian cave spiders (with a leg span of nearly 5 in/12.7 cm), glowworms, and even the Tasmanian mountain shrimp.

Marakoopa and King Solomon caves. Both formations are located near the village of Mole Creek 60 mi/96 km west of Launceston. King Solomon Cave, named for its profusion of reflecting calcite crystals, is a dry cave that is still actively changing. Marakoopa (the word is Aboriginal for "handsome") has a fine glowworm display. Park rangers offer guided tours at specific times. Fees are charged, and further information is available from the Ranger-in-Charge, Mole Creek, (003) 63 1245.

Gunns Plains Cave. This reserve is situated in northwest Tasmania, some 19 mi/30 km south of Ulverstone. The cave was formed by an underground river that still flows through parts of the high-vaulted cavern. A fee is charged for the guided tours, which are given from 10 A.M. to 4 P.M. year-round. For further information, contact Gunns Plains Cave Guide, 32 Cluan Crescent, Ulverstone, TAS 7315, or call (004) 25 4496.

Newdegate Cave. Named after Sir Francis Newdegate, the state's governor from 1917 to 1920, Newdegate is the only open cave in Australia that occurs in dolomite rather than limestone. It is a prominent feature of the Hastings Caves State Reserve, which also contains remnant patches of rain forest, a natural hot springs swimming pool, and the historical reminders of turn-of-the-century logging operations. Much time and care are spent in maintaining Newdegate. The lighting effects create a beauty and drama unequaled by any other cave in Tasmania and by only a few on the mainland. The forests around Newdegate Cave are dotted with cave entrances, large and small, many unexplored and several yet to be discovered.

Hastings Caves State Reserve is south of Hobart via the Huon Highway. A fee is charged for the guided tours of Newdegate Cave. Times for each day's tours are posted at the cave entrance or are available by calling the Ranger-in-Charge, Hastings Caves State Reserve, (002) 98 3198 or 98 3118.

ROCKY CAPE NATIONAL PARK

National Parks and Wildlife Service Head Office, P.O. Box 210, Sandy Bay, TAS 7005, or call the park at (003) 41 5312.

This small park, nestled on Tasmania's rugged northwest coast, is known for its wave-shaped caves. Aborigines camped here during the frigid winter months, drawn by the shelter it offered and the availability of shellfish and seals. Many of the caves contain faint rock paintings, traces of early Aboriginal activity. Human remains have been found in some of the sheltered caverns.

Short walks lead to three of the better cave sites in the park. These include North and South caves on the eastern side of Rocky Cape, and Lee Archer Cave in the region's midsection.

The park was set aside to protect its diverse heathland flora, among which the sawleaf banksia (*Banksia serrata*) is of particular note. Unfortunately, since the area became a park a fungal disease known as root rot (*Phytophthora cinnamomi*) has swept through, killing many of the heathland plants. Nevertheless, most species have survived and can still be seen here. In addition, the fertile soil and ample rainfall along this section of the north coast have enabled nearly fifty different types of orchids as well as boronias, fringed myrtle, and Christmas bells to thrive here; the floral blooms are most brilliant during spring and early summer. The coast is also a favorite landing site for various seabirds.

Left: The pea bush's flowers always grow in clusters. Right: The dense branches beneath the tick bush's flowers shelter small, tick-carrying animals.

MARIA ISLAND NATIONAL PARK

Head Ranger, Maria Island National Park, c/o P.O. Triabunna, TAS 7273, or call (002) 57 1420.

The island can be reached either by ferry from the Louisville Resort at Triabunna, just north of Oxford and about a ninety-minute drive from Hobart on the Tasman Highway. You can also get there by chartered aircraft. There are no shops on the island; once you arrive you must be self-sufficient.

Facilities on Maria are minimal. At Darlington, there are wood and gas barbecues, toilets, and wash troughs. Some sheltered units are available at Darlington, and there are many designated campsites at different locations on the island.

A singular feature of Tasmania is the presence of many smaller land masses lying off its tortuous coastline. Perhaps none is more intriguing than Maria Island, a 2,000-acre/810-hectare isle 5 mi/8 km off the eastern shore. Originally used as a penal colony, the island was later set aside as a sanctuary for endangered Tasmanian wildlife.

The first thing that strikes visitors to Maria Island, whether they arrive by boat or by light aircraft, is the island's unusual rock shapes. Scientists believe that the island was created in a series of geologic events that may have begun about 40 million years ago when fault movement in the earth produced a high ridge of rock and limestone; a rise in the sea level after the last ice age caused the ridge to be isolated from the mainland by a shallow passage of water. Many of the rocks seen today on the island—including some limestone that is extremely rich in fossils—had their origin some 200 million years ago. The formations called the Painted Cliffs are named for the rusty bands of iron-stained sandstone that run through the rock formations.

HISTORY

Maria Island was inhabited first by Aborigines. Eventually their nomadic settlements were taken over by European explorers. The first of these to make a significant sighting of the island was the Dutch explorer Abel Tasman in the mid-seventeenth century. He had already named the larger island (later Tasmania) "Van Diemen's Land" after the then governor of Batavia; he named this small island "Maria" in honor of Van Diemen's wife.

The magnificent Painted Cliffs of the eastern section of Maria Island National Park bear witness to the several geological periods they have survived.

When the English moved in 200 years later, they set up a penal colony. Just seven years later, however, in 1832, Tasmania's governor ended the island's use as a prison and shipped the inmates to Port Arthur. A brief reopening of the prison colony occurred ten years later. Buildings and ruins are still visible near Darlington.

From the turn of the century until 1930, the island was a center of industrial activity headed by an Italian entrepreneur named Diego Bernacchi. The colonial government leased the land to him for a mere shilling a year in return for his investment of several thousand pounds to make the island a South Pacific resort.

Bernacchi brought in a wide variety of Mediterranean trees and grape vines. He even built a coffeehouse that still stands, but his dream retreat never succeeded. The island's last profitmaking venture was of a very different sort – the production of cement.

In 1965 the state government took control of the island and began introducing animals whose environments on the mainland were being threatened. The Maria Island reserve was established to protect the dry eucalypt habitat necessary to sustain many of these animals. The island gained national park status in 1972.

Foresters kangaroos romp along the shore of Maria Island National Park.

WILDLIFE AND VEGETATION

Maria Island's appearance has changed dramatically over the years due to the clearing of some regions for crops (especially near Darlington and at Port Lesueur), the grazing of sheep and cattle, and frequent burning on the island's western side.

Thorny thistles and other plant species more typically found in the Northern Hemisphere were introduced during the earlier European occupation. Meanwhile, some of the island's higher elevations produce enough rainfall to support rain-forest species more commonly found in western Tasmania. These include native laurel and celery top pines.

During the late 1960s and early 1970s many wildlife species were introduced. The largest of these is the forester kangaroo, whose island population has increased to about 2,000. In addition, there are large numbers of emus, possums, bandicoots, Bennett's wallabies, echidnas, Cape Barren geese, and flightless native hens. The island also has retained a few animals that are holdovers from the early colonial period, such as feral cats, black rats, and fallow deer.

Maria's extraordinary geography of mountains and sea cliffs attracts myriad birds. Albatrosses, petrels, gannets, and short-tailed shearwaters (muttonbirds) are numerous, while the island's many lagoons and swamps are home to white-faced herons and sea eagles. Other birds commonly seen include green rosellas, yellow wattlebirds, kookaburras, Tasmanian thornbills, and black currawongs.

Most important, the island is the final stronghold for the forty-spotted pardalote—found only in Tasmania.

Maria Island is a cornucopia of marine life. Bright red sea anemones, sea stars (starfish), shrimps, crabs, and numerous species of seaweed may be found in rock pools around the island.

Beyond the low-tide level live sponges, rock lobsters, abalone, and at least 105 species of fish. Together they create a marine life environment rivaling that of the Great Barrier Reef, 2,000 mi/3,218 km to the north. Icy, dim waters hide much of this beauty from all but hardy divers. Sharks are plentiful in the waters between Maria and the mainland.

Along the island's northwestern shoreline there is a large underwater forest of giant kelp, a phenomenon found only in a few cold-water regions of the world. Flat areas of sand or mud provide an ideal home for burrowing sea creatures such as crabs, sea cucumbers, and sand urchins.

Although Tasmanian authorities have yet to recognize the richness and value of the waters surrounding Maria by granting them status as a national marine park, the state has set aside Mercury Passage as an official shark-breeding sanctuary.

An inland lake on Maria Island reflects the surrounding grasses and paperbark trees.

FREYCINET NATIONAL PARK

The Ranger, Freycinet National Park, via Coles Bay, TAS 7215, or call (002) 57 0107.

Access to the park is by a road leading from the Tasman Highway. The turnoff is 21 mi/34 km north of Swansea and 16 mi/10 km south of Bicheno. There are shops at Coles Bay and accommodations at a privately owned "chateau" as well as a small youth hostel in the park. Also available are basic camping areas, including some electrified sites, just near the entrance and also farther inside the park. The true Freycinet experience comes beyond the entrance camp, however.

It would be impossible to name one park as the most spectacular in Tasmania, but if there were a contest for the most underrated park, it would have to be this 24,700-acre/10,000-hectare peninsula located about 45 mi/72 km from the east-coast town of Swansea.

Freycinet National Park captures the breadth of Tasmanian geography in microcosm. Vaulting from the surrounding emerald sea, red granite peaks crest at better than 2,000 ft/610 m. From this height on a clear day the panorama is breathtaking. The most dramatic feature of Freycinet is its verticality. Rare is the stretch of trail that isn't either climbing up or switchbacking down a boulder-strewn slope.

The park centers on Mt. Freycinet, which towers over long seaside stretches. There are many beach and hillside hiking trails within the park as well as a 15.5-mi/25-km path whose course runs through the heart of the park's rocky peninsula, over Mt. Graham, and along white crescent beaches and coastline.

Schouten Island, off the tip of the peninsula, was added to the park in 1967. During the last century a whaling station was set up there and some alluvial tin was mined.

GEOLOGY

Freycinet Peninsula features formidable red granite cliffs, the best known of which are the huge rock masses called The Hazards. The granites formed some 375 million years ago, when the heat beneath

Hazard Beach and nearby rock formations were named after Captain Albert "Black" Hazard, who sought refuge here after his ship, Promise, crashed. The eastern section of Great Oyster Bay is called Promise Bay.
Pages 150 and 151: Across the Freycinet Peninsula from Promise Bay is Wineglass Bay.

the earth's surface was so intense that it liquefied even the hardest rocks. Gradually, the molten material cooled and solidified in massive forms.

A lush fern grove covers the forest floor in a eucalypt forest in Freycinet National Park. Most of Freycinet's forests are composed of eucalypts, she-oaks, wattles, and banksias; Oyster Bay pines can also be found.

Those who scale The Hazards will gain a clear view not only of the neighboring peaks, Mt. Graham and Mt. Freycinet, but also of the narrow band of sand, or tombolo, that links the two mountainous parts of the peninsula.

VEGETATION

In sharp contrast to the raw granite, the less hilly areas of the park come to life each spring with wildflowers. Freycinet blooms year-round with dozens of bizarrely shaped orchid species. Even the swamps feature colorful specimens, including bottlebrushes, coral ferns, and sundews.

Dry eucalypt forests occur throughout the park. The forests on the mountain slopes are dominated by a wide range of species, the dominant tree being determined by factors such as soil fertility and drainage. In the higher altitudes of the park the dominant species is commonly the Tasmanian snow gum.

BEN LOMOND NATIONAL PARK

Call Ben Lomond National Park at (003) 90 6279, or contact the Department of Land, Parks and Wildlife, 134 Macquarie Street, Hobart, TAS 7001, telephone (002) 30 2620.

Near the watery northeastern edge of Tasmania rises the Ben Lomond plateau, the highest area in the state's northeastern corner.

The 41,002-acre/16,600-hectare park sits on an alpine plateau atop the range. It offers an extensive list of plant species, such as cushion plants, alpine daisies, and carnivorous sundew plants; its animals include the ubiquitous Bennett's wallabies as well as wombats and several species of possums.

Ben Lomond is best known for its winter cross-country skiing. Park rangers are at a loss to explain why so few visitors come to the park in the summer months, since it offers excellent walking tracks and an abundance of wildlife and vegetation. Summer days upon the high plateau of Ben Lomond are sunny and clear, gentled by soft easterly sea breezes. Yet if you go at this time, chances are you will have the park almost to yourself.

MOUNT WILLIAM NATIONAL PARK

Ranger-in-Charge, Mount William National Park, P.O. Box 1, Gladstone, TAS 7254, or call (003) 57 2108.

The park is reached by gravel road either from St. Helens or Gladstone. Campsites have been set up at several points along the coast road. Fireplaces and picnic tables are available, but there is no permanent drinking-water supply. Facilities in the park are primitive and will probably remain so, as a way of preserving the unspoiled atmosphere. Several crude campsites are maintained at Boulder Point and Musselroe Point. No camping is allowed in the vicinity of Eddystone lighthouse.

Established in 1923, Mount William National Park's rolling grass paddocks and open eucalypt forest are characteristic of the Tasmanian northeast. The great surprise here is the presence of the finest, most accessible beach on the entire island.

The southern extreme of the park, Eddystone Point, features Tasmania's oldest lighthouse. The flashing beacon from this sentinel has warned passing vessels of nearby shoals and reefs since 1889. Giant orange-lichen-encrusted boulders form buttresses to this headland.

The Aborigines of the northeast understood the rich quality of this area. Traveling to the Tasman coast summer after summer, they harvested a bounty of lobsters, abalones, and other marine animals. Today, along the park's northern dunal shores, you come upon the remains of these fruitful harvests—middens of discarded shells, some mounded as high as 30 ft/9 m. Mixed with the debris are fragments of the scraping tools used by the Aborigines.

WILDLIFE

The park is an important reserve for the forester kangaroo, many of which can be spotted at dusk and dawn as they graze with cattle and sheep in the area's ample pastureland en route to Mount William. Inside the park, the foresters, like all animals, are protected from hunters. Many seabirds inhabit the coastline, and other bird species hide in the dense eucalypt forests. One of the most common is the striated pardalote, a tiny bird often seen feeding in the foliage of the large gum trees. The park is home also to the kookaburra, a member of the kingfisher family whose distinctive laughing howl can be heard in the wooded areas.

FORESTER DRIVE

Mount William's wildlife becomes active at night. An evening drive through the park along Forester Drive illustrates the vast number of creatures that dwell here. Turning south onto the track, 1.8 mi/ 3 km past the park's headquarters, you come to the entrance to the drive, well marked by a large display board. The road enters an area of sparsely scattered eucalyptus trees, patchy undergrowth, wattles, and coastal heath. From this point on be ever alert for creatures hopping, waddling, and slithering across the narrow track. A few hundred yards along, the bush opens into paddocks near the emergency airport. Evenings and mornings, these paddocks are jumping with the activity of wallabies and kangaroos. For the next 3.7 mi/ 6 km the road weaves its way through an area where dunes have been enveloped by heath, a good place for spotting wombats. At the junction, the track to the right leads to walking trails on Mt. William; to the left, Forester Drive continues into the open paddocks running to the sea. Here in the twilight hours you will see Tasmanian devils, wombats, rufous wallabies, echidnas, and brush-tailed possums. Forester kangaroos tend to shy away from the road, preferring to browse cautiously near the forest edge. Bennett's wallabies, in contrast, crisscross the paddock in frenzied activity, pausing only momentarily in occasional curiosity.

The Eddystone Lighthouse marks the southernmost point of Mount William National Park.

SOUTH AUSTRALIA

Kangaroo Island
Flinders Chase National Park
Flinders Ranges National Park
Lake Eyre
Mount Remarkable National Park
Cleland Conservation Park
Coorong National Park
Bool Lagoon Game Reserve
Naracoote Caves
Conservation Park
Gammon Ranges National Park

Young joeys of the yellow-footed rock wallaby are usually left in small caves or under overhangs while their mothers search for food; otherwise they remain in her pouch.

IN SOUTH AUSTRALIA, there is little tameness in the bush or among its creatures. Countless explorers and adventurers have traveled into this austerely beautiful landscape. None have conquered it, few have explored more than a fraction of its mysteries, yet all have returned enchanted by what they have seen.

South Australia is the most arid state on the continent. The majority of its 1.4 million people live clustered around the wet region in the capital city of Adelaide or a half-dozen other cities lining the eastern coast. The east's Murray River is the lifeline in this otherwise moistureless environment—and is the largest water system on the Australian continent. Virtually every living creature in the southeast of South Australia depends on it. Along the eastern coast, the Coorong National Park shelters a profusion of marine mammals, birds, and underwater creatures. Offshore a dense population of protected animals, including sea lions, fur seals, and rare bird species, make Kangaroo Island a rich wildlife sanctuary.

North of Adelaide, the thin red skin of earth bubbles and cracks like heat blisters in the Flinders and Gammon Ranges, the only visual interruptions on a barren landscape of mulga scrub and dry creek beds. To the west of Spencer Gulf is the rugged and pristine Eyre Peninsula, and beyond lies the Nullarbor Plain, a parched and lifeless expanse of rolling sand dunes.

KANGAROO ISLAND

Kangaroo Island, National Parks and Wildlife Service, 55 Grenfell St., Adelaide, SA 5000, or call (08) 216 7777.

Island is reached by a half-hour flight or a seven-hour journey by car ferry, both from Adelaide.

As an alternative, you can drive south from Adelaide to Cape Jervis in two hours. A car ferry at Cape Jervis takes you to Penneshaw in one hour.

The range of accommodations includes hotels, cabins, farmhouse bed-and-breakfasts, campgrounds, and caravan parks.

Many visitors to Australia, and indeed many Australians, neglect to visit one of the most beautiful islands in all of Australia. Although it is the second largest island off the coast of Australia (not including Tasmania) and has the fifth largest national park in South Australia, many people do not even know of the existence of Kangaroo Island.

NORTHERN TERRITORY

QUEENSLAND

SIMPSON DESERT

SIMPSON
DESERT NP

SIMPSON
DESERT CP

• Birdsville

GREAT VICTORIA DESERT

L Eyre North

ELLIOT PRICE CP

STUART RANGE

L Eyre South

Marree •

WOOMERA
PROHIBITED
AREA

Arkaroola
Village

GAMMON RANGES NP

Balcanoona

L Frome

L Gairdner

L Torrens

NULLARBOR PLAIN

FLINDERS RANGES

St Mary Peak

FLINDERS RANGES NP

NULLARBOR NP

YUMBARRA CP

WILPENA POUND

Oraparinna

Hawker

Hawker Rd 47

EYRE HWY

Port Augusta

Quorn

LAKE GILLES CP

Wilmington

▲ Mt Remarkable

FLINDERS HWY

Whyalla

MOUNT REMARKABLE NP

Port Germein

Port Pirie

Great Australian Bight

EYRE
PEN

LINCOLN HWY

LINCOLN HWY

Spencer Gulf

YORKE PEN

PRINCES HWY

DANGGALI CP

MT LOFTY RA

Murray R

COFFIN BAY NP

CLELAND
CP

BILLIATT CP

Port Lincoln

Cape Catastrophe

LINCOLN
NP

Thistle I

Gulf St Vincent

Adelaide ★

Murray
Bridge

INNES NP

FLEURIEU
PEN

PEEBINGA CP

KARTE CP

Cape Jervis

Meningie

SOUTHERN

FLINDERS CHASE NP

Kingscote

Encounter
Bay

KANGAROO
ISLAND

COORONG NP

HWY

Naracoorte

BOOL LAGOON RESERVE

NARACOORTE CAVES

SOUTH AUSTRALIA

CANUNDA NP

Mt Gambier

OCEAN

Highways

Roads-Streets

★ State Capital

• Points of Interest

▲ Peaks

⌒ Caves

🌲 Small Parks

0   200 Mi

0   200 Km

N

The Cape du Couedic lighthouse looks out over the Southern Ocean. The Cape's unique limestone formations attract many visitors.

Located off the coast of South Australia, Kangaroo is a wooded island with steep coasts and white beaches. Separated from the mainland by the treacherous "Backstairs Passage," a strait 7 mi/ 11.2 km wide, the island is thought to have parted from the Fleurieu Peninsula at about the same time Tasmania separated from the mainland, during the last ice age.

The sea-tortured coastline of Kangaroo Island has become a graveyard of ships. Though lighthouses dot its precipitous bluffs, warning beams are no guarantee of safety. Even in these days of modern navigational instruments, the waters off Kangaroo continue to claim new victims.

One especially beautiful lighthouse sits atop Cape du Couedic, a promontory created from the skeletons of marine animals together with sand and shell fragments blown up by offshore winds approximately 1.6 million years ago. Over time the limestone of the cape has been sculpted into many strange and beautiful structures.

HISTORY

Kangaroo Island was discovered by Europeans in 1802, when Matthew Flinders landed there from his ship *Investigator*. With rations

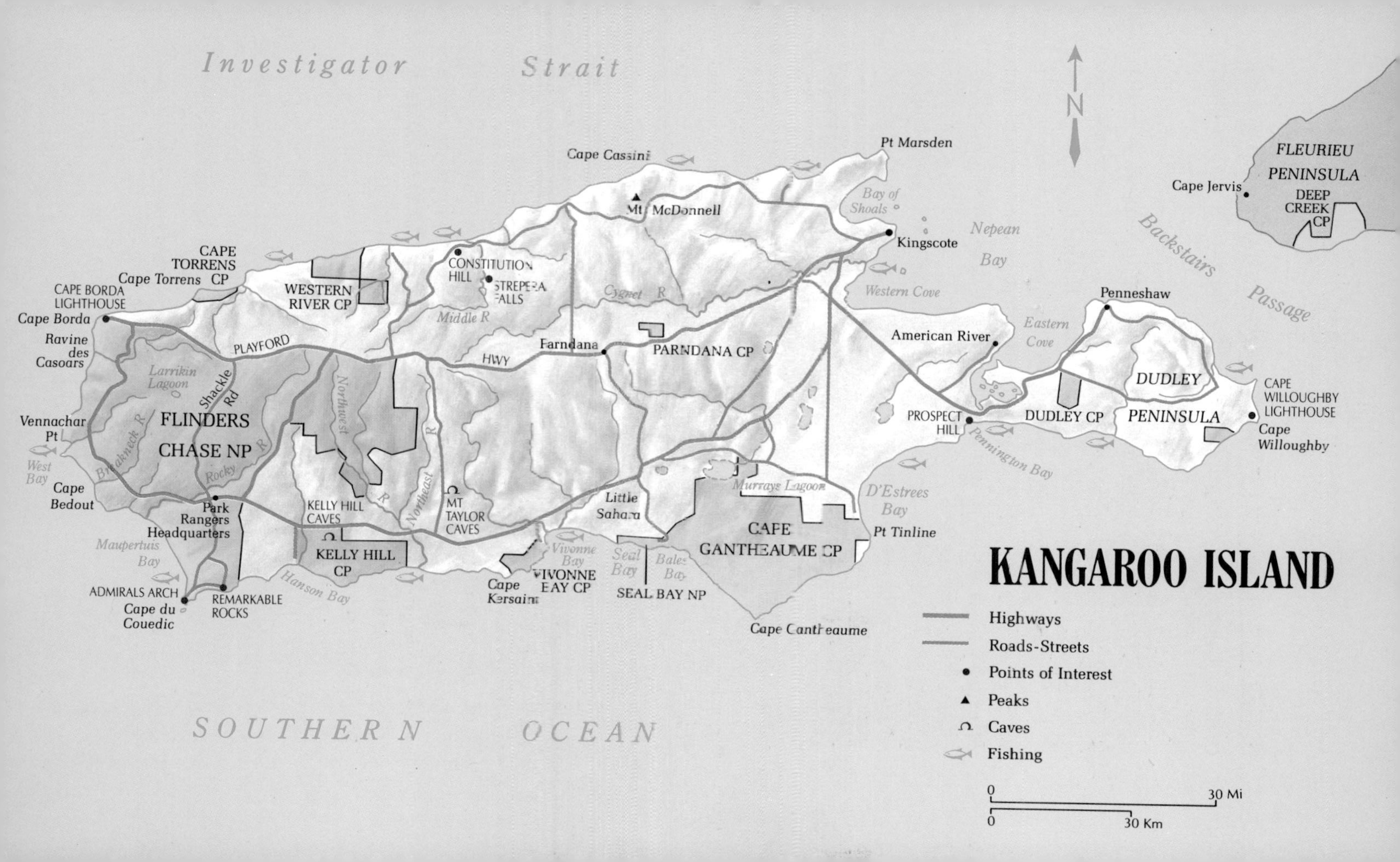

KANGAROO ISLAND

Highways
Roads–Streets
• Points of Interest
▲ Peaks
∩ Caves
Fishing

30 Mi
30 Km

N

FLEURIEU PENINSULA
DEEP CREEK CP
Cape Jervis

Backstairs Passage

CAPE WILLOUGHBY LIGHTHOUSE
Cape Willoughby

DUDLEY PENINSULA

Penneshaw

DUDLEY CP

Eastern Cove

Pennington Bay

Nepean Bay

Pt Marsden

Bay of Shoals

Kingscote

Western Cove

American River

PROSPECT HILL

D'Estrees Bay

Pt Tinline

Cape Cassini

Mt McDonnell

Cygnet R.

PARNDANA CP

Murrays Lagoon

CAPE GANTHEAUME CP

Cape Gantheaume

INVESTIGATOR STRAIT

CONSTITUTION HILL

TREPERA FALLS

Middle R.

Farndana

Hwy

Little Sahara

Bales Bay

Seal Bay

SEAL BAY NP

Vivonne Bay

VIVONNE BAY CP

Cape Kersaint

MT TAYLOR CAVES

Northwest

R

Northwest

KELLY HILL CP

KELLY HILL CAVES

Hanson Bay

WESTERN RIVER CP

PLAYFORD

Shackle Rd

Rocky R.

FLINDERS CHASE NP

Park Rangers Headquarters

REMARKABLE ROCKS

CAPE TORRENS CP

CAPE BORDA LIGHTHOUSE

Cape Borda

Ravine des Casoars

Vennachar Pt

Cape Bedout

Larrikin Lagoon

Breakneck R.

Maupertius Bay

West Bay

ADMIRALS ARCH
Cape du Couedic

SOUTHERN OCEAN

running low, Flinders and his crew were glad to discover the island's abundant population of easily caught gray kangaroos. In gratitude Flinders named the place Kangaroo Island.

At first inspection, it appeared to Flinders that this was one of the few islands never visited by mainland Aborigines. In view of the difficulty sailors had in reaching the island and in navigating its treacherous coast, Flinders' assumption was taken as fact for a century. The theory was negated in 1903, however, when stone tools were found near Murrays Lagoon. Since then, more than 120 tool sites have been discovered. It is believed that the island's last tribes died out 4,500 years ago.

Kangaroo Island saw a variety of inhabitants come and go after Flinders' landing. It was settled first by convicts from Tasmania who found work in a whaling operation on the island. Other industries sprang up, including sealing, trapping, and salt mining from evaporation lakes, carried on largely by rogues and convicts.

In 1836, the island's population went through a major change when H.M.S. *Duke of York* brought over what became Australia's first "free" colony of English gentlemen farmers and their wives. Financed by the South Australia Colonial Company, the settlers were offered tracts of land, the use of a cottage, minimal livestock, and the chance to be successful farmers in a new land. What the farmers did not realize, however, was that the infertile soil and the scant supply of fresh water would make this dream virtually impossible to realize. Most of these settlers became disenchanted and moved to the mainland.

Of the approximately 4,000 people living on Kangaroo Island today, a third of them live near this original settlement in Kingscote. Through the introduction of modern agricultural techniques, they have managed to farm some of the land. American River and Penneshaw are the two other major settlement areas.

GEOLOGY

The geology of Kangaroo Island, in concert with the sea, has created a paradise of raw, wild beauty, a place where one can stand on a southern bluff and gaze on a world unchanged for a hundred cen-

Scotts Cove is one of many peaceful coves on Kangaroo Island's north coast that provides fishing boats refuge from the turbulent seas off the south coast.

Sculpted by wind and sea, the granite monoliths called the Remarkable Rocks over-look the Southern Ocean from Kangaroo Island. Lichen growth and leached iron color the rocks.

Admirals Arch at Cape du Couedic was once a limestone cave but now has two open ings and is more like a tunnel.

turies. Between here and Antarctica, the Southern Ocean washes without interruption for 1,000 mi/1,600 km.

In ancient times the limestone cliffs of Kangaroo Island were part of the seabed. As the sea level began to drop and expose the island, wind and water cut away into the soft landmass, forming the steep bluffs of the island's dramatic coastline. This process of erosion and sculpture is still very evident along the magnificent cliffs and headlands of the island's southern coast, especially in areas such as Cape Gantheaume near Seal Bay.

At Cape du Couedic, one of the island's most spectacular caves has been exposed by erosion from the east and west. Admirals Arch, with its arching ceiling and skeleton-like remains of stalactites, is an especially beautiful sight at sunset.

Several underground chambers of stalactites and stalagmites remain intact in the subterranean world of Kangaroo Island. Of these, only the caves at Kelly Hill are open to the public. Discovered by a man named Kelsey when his horse Kelly fell into a sinkhole, the Kelly Hill Caves are magnificent limestone formations with chambers 120,000 to 140,000 years old. The splendid red, brown, orange, and beige calcite structures draw many visitors during daily tours.

WESTERN GRAY KANGAROO
Macropus fuliginosus

The western gray kangaroo, one of the largest living marsupials, was once believed to inhabit only Kangaroo Island, but subsequent findings discovered an abundance of them on the mainland. Found throughout the southern regions of Australia, the western gray is so prolific that it has become an agricultural nuisance. State fauna authorities have issued licenses permitting residents of South Australia and New South Wales to export their skins and meat.

The western gray's biological make-up is extremely close to that of the eastern gray kangaroo, although it has a different reproductive cycle and a browner coloration. The western and eastern gray kangaroos do not interbreed in the wild, although western males have been mated successfully with eastern females in captivity.

WILDLIFE AND VEGETATION

The island's most famous animal inhabitant is the gray Kangaroo Island kangaroo. Being isolated from the mainland, with plenty of food available and virtually no predators, it has developed into a stockier animal than its mainland cousin, with darker fur, shorter limbs, and slower movement. It is unwary of humans, and in some places on Kangaroo Island barriers have had to be built to keep the friendly creatures away.

Equally famous on Kangaroo Island are the sea lions that dwell on the coast at Seal Bay, representatives of a species that has dwindled to about 5,000 worldwide. The Kangaroo Island population is protected by the National Parks Service, and Seal Bay has been declared a conservation park. For a small fee visitors are granted guided access to walk among the sea lions, except near the nurseries. Though friendly and seemingly tolerant of humans, sea lions

AUSTRALIAN SEA LION
Neophoca cinerea

Found on the offshore islands of western and southern Australia, the Australian sea lion is the only member of the seal family specifically found in Australia. The sea lions were long hunted for their meat and skins, and their populations had dwindled dangerously low when the species finally became legally protected in Australia.

The aggressive sea lions can be very fearsome. Males will staunchly protect the females and their young from intruders, but they are also known to attack sleeping pups and knock them about. Females will protect not only their own pups, but will attend to the pups of other females while the mothers are feeding.

Male and female sea lions look similar during the first two years of life. Starting at age two, the males grow large and bulky, and their body fur becomes dark brown. Adult females are lighter brown in color.

Despite efforts to protect them, there are only 4,000 to 5,000 sea lions living in Australia today, which makes *Neophoca* one of the rarest seals in the world. Their greatest concentrations are in Seal Bay, on Kangaroo Island, and on Dangerous Reef, off Port Lincoln in South Australia.

can be vicious if alarmed, and visitors are urged to be cautious around them.

At Cape du Couedic, in the area of Admiral's Arch, lives a colony of New Zealand fur seals. Made all but extinct by sealers, fur seals are wary of humans and prefer the seclusion of this isolated habitat.

Other native wildlife includes tammar wallabies, echidnas, brush-tailed possums, and bandicoots. Kangaroo Island is one of the few places where it is possible to glimpse the rare glossy black cockatoo. Cape Barren geese are numerous.

It was thought that Kangaroo Island's isolation from the mainland and the relative absence of predators there would give wildlife a better than average chance of surviving. With this in mind, the Flora and Fauna Board introduced several mainland species. These include emus (to replace the now-extinct smaller variety of emu that once thrived there), koalas, ring-tailed possums, and platypuses. Most of these have survived very well on Kangaroo Island, and one of the best places to see wildlife on the island is Flinders Chase National Park.

When Europeans first settled Kangaroo Island they cleared away much of its dense mallee scrub and small eucalyptus growth. Despite this, a considerable portion of the island is still covered by eucalypt woodland. A few of its plant species, like the Tepper's trigger plant, are found nowhere else in Australia.

FLINDERS CHASE NATIONAL PARK

Flinders Chase National Park, Private Bag 246, Rocky River, Kangaroo Island, 5223 SA, or call (08) 483 7235.

Camping is easy here, but permits must be obtained for the Rocky River campground, which has toilet and shower facilities, and to camp in other areas within the park. Strict regulations must be followed about the lighting of fires.

Situated on the western end of Kangaroo Island, Flinders Chase is the fifth largest national park in South Australia. Declared a national park in 1919 while a large-scale clearing of land was being made on the rest of the island, Flinders Chase has retained much of its original beauty. Visitors are able to experience the "rough, untamed" Australia without having to endure unnecessary hardships. Its dense eucalypt forest looks forbidding but is relatively easy to explore by roads that wind their way through the park. For the adventurous, bushwalking is especially rewarding here, where the land seems untouched by human intervention.

Among the most impressive sights in the park are the huge granite boulders called Remarkable Rocks, which sit balanced on the promontory of Kirkpatrick Point. The rocks have been finely sculpted by nature into remarkable shapes.

There is an abundance of friendly and bold wildlife in the park. Many of the animals are so used to humans that they come out in

The long sharp nails of the koala help it climb eucalyptus trees in search of choice leaves to eat.

hordes to greet visitors or to pan a meal. Kangaroos, emus, Cape Barren geese, and parrots form the usual welcoming party. Visitors can usually spot koalas in the nearby eucalyptus trees.

More than fifty species of orchids grow in the park, along with several types of eucalyptus trees, including the sugar, pink, and swamp gums. These are joined by acacias, colorful banksias, and tea trees.

FLINDERS RANGES NATIONAL PARK

Flinders Ranges National Park, National Parks and Wildlife Service, 55 Grenfell St., Adelaide, SA 5000, or call (08) 216 7777.

The park is located about 287 mi/ 460 km north of Adelaide. To get there, take the Princes Highway to Port Augusta and then turn off toward Quorn. The next town to look for is Hawker, 32 mi/51 km from the entrance to the park.

The park is served by two ranger stations, one at Wilpena Pound and the other at Oraparinna; the latter serves as the official park headquarters.

The Flinders and Gammon ranges swell on the horizon of South Australia like a pale, brick-colored mirage in the heat of the outback sun. Just past Hawker, sloping domes of red sandstone begin to lift on the eastern horizon. From here the ranges continue to increase in height, forming a convoluted maze of canyons and gorges. The ranges actually extend beyond the boundaries of Flinders Ranges National Park, wandering for several hundred miles through much of the northeastern part of the state.

Aborigines believe the ranges to be the work of the serpent Arkaroola, who slithered among the drying water holes in search of one final drink. The arid northeast has always been plagued by droughts. Rains are few, and there are often desperately long intervals between downpours.

GEOLOGY

The Flinders Ranges are a briefly interrupted continuation of the Mount Lofty Ranges, which surround the otherwise flat terrain of

Alpenglow—a reddish luminance on mountains after sunset—lights up the Flinders Ranges and a lone grass tree.

Adelaide. While the two ranges were created from the same geologic upheavals, they look different, due primarily to the greater annual rainfall in the Adelaide area.

Both the Flinders and the Gammon ranges were part of an ancient inland sea that covered the majority of central and southern Australia. As the sea receded, large layers of sediment, composed primarily of mud and sand, were left behind. These deposits, lying undisturbed for eons, eventually were uplifted, folded, and then fractured into mountain ranges by earthquakes and volcanic activity deep within the earth's crust. The prominent ridges of the Flinders Ranges are composed of harder, resistant rock types such as quartzite; erosion of much softer materials, such as mudstone, shale, and siltstone, formed the valleys.

An outstanding example of these geologic wonders is at Wilpena Pound, a natural amphitheater some 10.6 mi/17 km by 4.4 mi/7 km, measured from the enclosing ridges. *Wilpena*, an Aboriginal word meaning "bent fingers," appropriately describes these rolling hills and valleys ringed by cliffs in the form of a cupped hand.

VEGETATION

Many of the park's water holes and riverbeds contain water for only a few weeks each year. They are rimmed by the characteristic river red gums and dotted by native pines. Vegetation is less sparse in the western region of the ranges, where rainfall is greater. Typical bloomers in this region are desert wattles, Sturt's desert pea (the South Australia state flower), Sturt's desert rose, and several varieties of herb plants. A good number of these plants have evolved elaborate systems for protecting their seeds against the desiccating effects of the outback sun.

WILDLIFE

Wildlife abounds in the park. Common inhabitants include the big red kangaroos and euros, as well as a far rarer member of the clan, the yellow-footed rock wallaby. The yellowfoot, distinguished by a

The deep canyons and gorges of Flinders Ranges National Park are richly vegetated with native pines and eucalyptus trees.

blunt, striped tail, once was hunted for its fur. Today, since gaining legislative protection and status on the World Wildlife Fund's list of endangered species, the yellowfoot has nothing to fear but the cunning of the red fox and the power of the wedge-tailed eagle. In this dry environment, both the euro and the yellow-footed rock wallaby manage to obtain what moisture they need for survival from the scant vegetation that grows on the rocky slopes of the ranges.

The park's cool canyons and few water holes also attract many bird species, ranging from wrens, honey eaters, parrots, and galahs to larger species such as brown falcons and numerous kites and eagles.

BUSHWALKING

Flinders Ranges National Park offers a number of splendid walks—both short and long—through rocky gorges and steep, sawtooth ridges as well as over wide, rolling plains.

Wilpena Pound. The pound is most remarkable for its sense of seclusion. The only way visitors can enter or leave is through the narrow gorge along Wilpena Creek. To all, it is a source of wonderment that the creek—during most of the year a meandering trickle of cool water—could be responsible for carving out this impressive gorge.

The track into the pound begins in the shady confines of the Wilpena Pound camping area. From the visitors' information center, follow the track along Wilpena Creek. Towering river red gums grace the route through the ocher and beige gorge walls. As you exit the Pound Gap, you will see the ruins of a stone house nestled among the gums, all that remains of an effort to farm the pound basin in the early 1900s.

A side track climbs to a lookout that offers a fine panorama of the pound's tree-dotted flatland and steep, wooded inner slopes. In the spring this view is a blaze of color as wildflowers burst to life.

The walk across the pound is an open, rolling grade through stands of callitris and sugar gums. For the ambitious, a walk to the far foothills and back can be an invigorating challenge to accomplish in one day. For a more leisurely pace, obtain a permit at the ranger station and camp overnight at Cooinda. From here you can watch the lengthening desert rays cast a golden light on the pound's east-

YELLOW-FOOTED ROCK WALLABY
Petrogale xanthopus

Rocky outcrops, boulders, caves, and large crevices are the habitat of the rock wallaby. There is much speculation about how many species of rock wallaby exist, but most authorities agree that there are no fewer than seven.

The rock wallaby is well adapted to life in stony places. The soles of its feet are granulated rather than smooth, for example. It can move nimbly among the rocks with no hindrance from its tail, which it holds arched over its back. It can even ascend trees with sloping trunks to gather food.

Rock wallabies eat grass, herbs, leaves, and fruit. In drought conditions they will eat the bark or roots of trees to obtain water. Unlike most other wallabies and kangaroos, whose babies always accompany the mother, the rock wallaby mother leaves her young behind while she searches for food in her precarious rocky habitat.

The yellow-footed rock wallaby, once hunted for its beautiful skin, is now an endangered species. Found primarily in the Flinders Ranges of South Australia, the wallabies are now well protected from humans but still must compete with feral goats, rabbits, and foxes.

---

ern rim. Nights in the pound are breathtaking, as billions of stars above form the blue-white swash of the Milky Way.

A challenging day circuit of 14 mi/22.4 km leads the hiker through some of the best scenery and vistas in all the Flinders. With an early start, the far border of the pound can be reached by midday. Near Cooinda Camp the track splits left to Malloga Falls (a pleasant side trip if you are camping in the pound). Follow the narrowing track toward Tanderra Saddle for the short climb to St. Mary's Peak, 3,854 ft/1,175 m high. The final ascent to St. Mary's pinnacle is a strenuous climb. The southwest-bound trail from the junction at Tanderra Saddle leads back to Wilpena campground along the pound rim.

Wilpena Pound has become a mecca for vacationers from Adelaide; during holidays thousands of visitors come to explore and backpack in an enclave vastly different from the countryside surrounding it.

Wilkawillana Gorge. This trail, tucked away in the far northeastern edge of the park, follows Mount Billy Creek past low, undulating hills and the steep, craggy face of Wilkawillana Gorge. Embedded in the gorge walls are small, cone-shaped fossils that show the aquatic origin of this rock. The hike takes about four hours.

Bunyeroo Gorge. This two-hour hike starts from the parking area at the Wilcolo Creek Track junction, located in the extreme southwestern section of the park. The trail follows the creekbed and meanders over a relatively untouched area where there is abundant wildlife.

Old Homestead and Wangarra Lookout. This easy walk provides panoramic vistas of Wilpena Pound and an insight into its geologic and cultural history. It takes between one and two hours to complete.

Arkaroo Rock. About 8 mi/13 km from Wilpena on the Hawker Road is a route to Arkaroo Rock. From the parking area, a walking trail of steep grade leads to this important site. A floor of flintstones and charcoal is evidence that the area was once home to Aborigines. Many red ocher images of emus, bird tracks, and snake lines can be seen on rock walls.

If time is limited, or if you are seeking a more ethereal perspective on the incredible landscape, there are sightseeing flights available from the airfield near Wilpena campground.

LAKE EYRE

Lake Eyre, National Parks and Wildlife Service, 55 Grenfell St., Adelaide, SA 5000, or call (08) 216 7777.

This vast dry salt lake lies far beyond the Flinders Ranges in the great outback region of South Australia. While rarely wet—indeed, two times every hundred years is considered better than average—

An open eucalypt forest can support an array of wildlife, including koalas, possums, and parrots.

this area was once part of a vast freshwater lake called "Dieri." Geologists believe a tilting of the landscape prevented nearby rivers from following their natural courses, leading to the creation of the large lake. Thirty thousand years ago the area's climate became drier, the fresh water evaporated, and large deposits of salt were left behind.

When the area does receive rain, as it did in the mid-1970s, the region becomes overrun with wildflowers, grasses, and a host of creatures that flock to the water in a life cycle that lasts only as long as the basin is wet—a few short weeks at best.

This wilderness region can be reached only by a four-wheel-drive vehicle, and if you should be lucky—or unlucky—enough to be there during a rare wet spell be warned that the roads can be washed out and the surface turned into a glue-like substance. When this occurs vehicles may be stuck on the road for days.

MOUNT REMARKABLE NATIONAL PARK

Mt. Remarkable National Park, Private Bag 7, Port Germein, SA 5495, or call (086) 334 7068 for the Mambray Creek section or (086) 67 5181 for the Alligator Creek section.

The park is about 162 mi/260 km north of Adelaide and about 31 mi/ 50 km north of Port Pirie. Access by car to Alligator Gorge is off the Main North Road at Wilmington. Mambray Creek is reached via the Princes Highway, turning off about 28 mi/45 km north of Port Pirie.

Bush camping is available only during certain times of the year. Open bush fires are controlled under strict codes, and in summer all forms of fire, including portable burners and fuels, may be banned for weeks. Heavy fines and jail sentences may be levied for breaking the rules, so check with the ranger for current fire regulations.

Mount Remarkable National Park, located near Port Augusta in the southern end of the Flinders Ranges, is a scenic and varied region of about 20,000 acres/8,100 hectares characterized by hilly terrain and unusually high (at least for South Australia) rainfall of 18 in/ 450 mm a year. Two creeks, Alligator and Mambray, share an oval basin that is surrounded by hilly ridges, recalling the much larger natural amphitheater at Wilpena Pound.

The park now includes two smaller state reserves—Alligator Gorge and Mambray Creek—which were combined with Mt. Remarkable National Park in 1972.

WILDLIFE AND VEGETATION

Marsupials abound in the park. These include kangaroos, euros, and the rare yellow-footed rock wallaby. There are more than a hundred bird species, including little corellas (a smaller member of the cockatoo clan), laughing kookaburras, and the Adelaide and crimson rosellas. Several different types of skinks and small lizards add to the park's interesting wildlife.

Due to the area's relatively high rainfall, many of the park's gorges are covered with river red gums and white cypress pines. Higher elevations host other trees like blue gums and sugar gums, characterized by gray and salmon-colored trunks, respectively.

Many of the park's wildflowers enjoy an unusually long blossoming season. The most conspicuous flowers are the scores of orchid varieties.

Growing in sandy areas in inland South Australia, the Sturt's desert pea shows its brilliant flowers only after heavy rains.

The nocturnal common brush-tailed possum is usually considered a pest as it damages buildings, flowers, and fruit, eucalypt, and pine trees.

BUSHWALKING

Many trails of varying difficulty branch out from the park's two main entrances at Alligator Gorge and Mambray Creek. There are ranger stations at both places, and it is possible to hike overland from one end of the park to the other in about two days. Park rangers should be consulted for information before you set out.

Alligator Gorge Trail. This short trail, which covers about 1.25 mi/ 2 km, descends into a gorge lined by sheer cliffs of red quartzite. The trail almost becomes a tunnel due to the height and overhang of the gorge walls. The walk begins from the parking area above Alligator Creek and takes about two hours to complete.

Sugar Gum Trail. A 2.5-mi/4-km trail, it begins at the Mambray Creek picnic area and winds along the deep valley through river red gums before ascending by a short climb to the lookout. The trip takes about three hours to complete.

Mount Cavern Trail. This six-hour hike commences from the Mambray Creek picnic grounds and crosses the high ridges of the Black Range to the top of Mount Cavern before going down into the gorge of Mambray Creek. Although the view is restricted by tall trees at Mount Cavern, several good clearings open out along the track. The trail covers nearly 7 mi/11 km and, like the other longer hikes in the park, is recommended only for very fit bushwalkers.

CLELAND CONSERVATION PARK

Cleland Conservation Park, P.O. Box 245, Stirling, SA 5152, or call (08) 339 2581.

An easy half-hour drive from Adelaide in the Mount Lofty Ranges, the park is reached via the Glen Osmond and Mt. Barker roads.

Open every day except Christmas and days of declared high-fire danger. There are a limited number of picnic areas, with a kiosk located in the fauna center. Camping is not allowed; accommodation is offered in nearby Adelaide.

Not far from the center of Adelaide, within the cooler confines of the Mount Lofty Ranges, lies this 3.8-sq-mi/9.9-sq-km conservation park. The park's outstanding feature is its fauna center, developed in the 1960s, which attracts large numbers of visitors eager to view the free-roaming wildlife. The network of trails throughout the remainder of the park takes walkers through flowering gullies, deep wooded slopes, and outlooks offering magnificent vistas. In addition to fine walking tracks, the park also features man-made lakes and swamps where several waterfowl species flock.

WILDLIFE

Many wildlife varieties have been established in different parts of the preserve, depending on the type of geographic environment they prefer. In the western section are western gray kangaroos, emus, and euros, which prefer not only the taller tree cover but the rocky ridges as well. Another section of Cleland has been set aside for Kangaroo Island kangaroos and tammar wallabies.

The tammar wallaby is found in few places in Australia, one of which is Kangaroo Island, where it lives an undisturbed existence. Mainland numbers were severely reduced by the clearing of land for crops (thereby mowing down the tammar's favorite scrub and heath vegetation). Predators like feral cats also played an important role in the mainland demise of tammar wallabies.

Cleland is known also for its koala and wombat enclosures. Each day, one of the furry koalas is brought out for feeding and viewing. The park also features two walk-through aviaries and a large lake where many waterfowl species such as black swans, pelicans, cormorants, spoonbills, ibises, and Cape Barren geese congregate each day.

COORONG NATIONAL PARK

Coorong National Park, Park Ranger, Private Bag 43, Meningle, SA 5264, or call (085) 75 7014.

The park is reached via the Princes Highway, and there are two crossings that join the Coorong to the beaches: 42-Mile Crossing and Tea-Tree Crossing, both accessible by four-wheel-drive vehicles only.

Camping is by permit only. Apply at park headquarters, Salt Creek, located near the southern end of the Coorong.

Some 130 mi/208 km southeast of Adelaide, the coastline forms an almost perfect arc for a considerable distance. This stretch, known as Younghusband Peninsula, is but a thin wafer of built-up sand fronting a network of lagoons and sand islands—the Coorong. This beautiful setting is a haven for migratory and resident waterfowl.

Six thousand years ago, one of the country's largest populations of Aborigines lived in the Coorong, feasting not only on various birds but on mussels, freshwater crayfish, and other aquatic creatures. Aboriginal shell middens—large mounds of discarded shells—dot the park's landscape.

The 33,000-acre/13,500-hectare park, which was created in 1966, also includes a game reserve where licensed hunting of certain waterfowl species is allowed during a limited season.

The word *Coorong* is derived from an Aboriginal root *karangh*, meaning "narrow neck." It is an apt name for this area, which, from its northern border at the mouth of the mighty Murray River to the southern coast, looks like a long, narrow neck when viewed from the air. The Coorong extends southward for more than 80 mi/128 km.

Farther inland from both the Younghusband Peninsula and the lagoon lie older dunes and flats that represent coastlines from previous periods of higher sea levels. The deepest lagoons are at the northern end of the park near the Murray River. The pools become much shallower farther south, with salinity levels three times that of sea water.

WILDLIFE

The park contains several small lagoonal islands that attract flocks of sea birds such as pelicans and terns, which come here to breed. The islands are off limits to visitors.

Coorong claims the largest Australian pelican rookery in the state. Sea birds such as the crested and fairy terns also have established large permanent breeding colonies on the limestone-based isles that seem to float in the lagoons. Other bird species, including pied oyster-catchers, ibises, black swans, cormorants, and countless ducks, use the shallow protected waters of the lagoons for breeding and nesting. Among the rarities that inhabit the Coorong is the orange-bellied parrot. Nearly extinct, the few remaining parrots winter in the area and return in spring to southwestern Tasmania.

The most common ibis in Australia, the straw-necked ibis has been known to gather in breeding colonies of more than 200,000. During courtship, a red patch of skin is displayed behind the eyes and on each side of the breast; after mating, the patches fade.

BOOL LAGOON GAME RESERVE

Bool Lagoon Game Reserve, National Parks and Wildlife Service, 55 Grenfell St., Adelaide, SA 5000, or call (08) 216 7777.

Bool Lagoon Game Reserve is located just 15 mi/24 km south of the township of Naracoorte. The park headquarters is located at the lagoon. Limited bush camping is permitted at the reserve, and hotel/motel accommodations are available in Naracoorte.

A considerable portion of the southeast of South Australia, from the Coorong to Mt. Gambier near the Victorian border, is comprised of small lakes and swampland extending several miles inland. While many of these wetlands have been drained for grazing and agriculture, some 7,000 acres/2,833 hectares near Naracoorte have been set aside as a breeding area for waterfowl.

Over the past 600,000 years, the sea—which covered much of southeast South Australia—has receded from the Naracoorte Range, leaving behind a series of twenty parallel sand ridges or dunes. Annual floodwater from the heavy winter rainfall pools between the dunes, and in the lowest basins, which have heavy clay bases, the water remains over the summer, providing a home for many types of waterbirds.

Bool Lagoon offers spectacular observation of more than 120 bird species; the reserve is especially famous for its large ibis, egret, and cormorant rookeries. Spring and summer evenings here are a cacophony of beating wings and squawking voices as countless thousands of adult birds return to their nests.

Any disturbance in the breeding areas can cause a high death rate among the young birds, thus visitor access to these areas is heavily restricted. In late summer, when the surrounding countryside dries out, Bool Lagoon becomes a very important drought refuge for waterbirds. From the perimeter road visitors can observe a wide variety of ducks, geese, herons, egrets, spoonbills, ibis, and many other types of waterfowl and wading birds.

Clockwise from top: red-necked avocets; fairy tern; fairy penguin; head of a curious emu.
Pages 184 and 185: Crested terns gather in huge colonies to breed but build their nests an orderly 3 ft/1 m apart.

AUSTRALIAN PELICAN
Pelecanus conspicillatus

The Australian pelican is one of the most conspicuous sea birds in Australia. It can be found in large bodies of shallow water, both on the coast and inland. It is an impressive sight, with its large bill and neck, its body up to 5 ft/1.5 m long, and its wingspan of up to 7 ft/2 m.

The bird uses its huge bill and bill pouch to fish, preferring waters no deeper than the length of its bill and neck. Pelicans are cooperative fishers and will often be seen fishing in groups, each bird with its bill in the water. This tactic confuses fish, which dart away from one bill only to be trapped by another.

Pelicans usually are seen on calmer waterways because their massive

bodies need a smooth surface for take-off. Although they appear large and top-heavy, their flight is quite graceful and they can attain heights of up to 10,000 ft/3,000 m with little effort.

NARACOORTE CAVES CONSERVATION PARK

Naracoorte Caves Conservation Park, P.O. Box 134, Naracoorte, SA 5271, or call (087) 62 2340; or c/o

National Parks and Wildlife Service, 55 Grenfell St., Adelaide, SA 5000, (08) 216 7777.

Located 7 mi/11 km from the township of Naracoorte in the southeast of South Australia, Naracoorte Caves Conservation Park includes twenty-six known limestone caves. Three of these have been developed for visitor inspection on guided tours. In addition, exploration tours – accompanied by an experienced guide – can be arranged to many of the undeveloped caves.

A major fossil deposit, discovered in 1969, is still being excavated by paleontologists from the Flinders University of South Australia. Here, in the famous Victoria-Fossil Cave, scientists are likely to be seen digging as visitors pass through on one of the many tours conducted daily. From the safety of a viewing platform, observers may share in the discovery of some unique fragment of Australia's curious faunal past.

In breeding season each year hundreds of thousands of bent-wing bats migrate from their winter roosts to the Maternity Chamber of Bat Cave. From late spring through summer nightly tours are conducted to allow visitors to see the spectacular exodus of many thousands of bats as they leave the cave to feed on night-flying insects.

For tour schedules, check with the ranger at the visitor center; here, too, you will find an excellent museum on cave science and exploration, including the history and status of the fossil deposit.

Park facilities include campgrounds, caravan sites, a kiosk, picnic areas, and walking trails.

GAMMON RANGES NATIONAL PARK

South Australia National Parks and
Wildlife Service, District Office,

Balcanoona via Copley, SA 5732, or
call (086) 42 3800.

North of Flinders Ranges National Park, much of the traditional mountain region of the Adnjamathanha Aboriginal tribe was made into a national park in 1970. Now the plains extending to Lake Frome have been incorporated as well, to constitute the Gammon Ranges National Park. An arid, isolated wilderness of extreme rugged beauty, Gammon Ranges offers the visitor an opportunity to bushwalk through 500 million years of Australian natural history.

The park is unique in its close and active relationship with the Adnjamathanha people. Gorges and valleys of the park have numerous grave sites, etchings, paintings, and other evidences of the Dreamtime. Local Aboriginal rangers work within the park and at Balcanoona Homestead, the park headquarters. Rangers are available to teach visitors about the natural history of the park and the related stories and legends of the Adnjamathanha.

The park is accessible only to experienced bushwalkers. With few established tracks and campsites, the Gammons remain largely in pristine condition.

Camping is available at Italowie Gorge and Weetootla Gorge. Both sites are near Balcanoona headquarters, where a camping permit should be obtained. Water is available at the headquarters. While water holes and creeks are designated on most maps of the area, they should not be depended upon to provide an adequate or safe permanent water supply.

North of Balcanoona is Arkaroola, a large tract of land contiguous with the national park. Just outside the park boundary, Arkaroola Station has been privately developed as a bush resort. The station

provides most visitors to the Gammons an enjoyable base from which to explore the region.

Within the Arkaroola area are some of the best wildlife-viewing water holes in the entire region. Most exciting among the possible sightings in the Gammons is the elusive yellow-footed rock wallaby.

The many yellow-footed rock wallabies here are difficult to spot among the boulders and rocks in which they live. Even in the Flinders Ranges, it is unusual to see such a number of these rare animals together.

WESTERN AUSTRALIA

The Kimberley
Geikie Gorge National Park
Windjana Gorge National Park
Bungle Bungles
Hamersley Range National Park
Cape Range National Park
Nambung National Park
Rottnest Island
Leeuwin-Naturaliste National Park
Walpole-Nornalup National Park
Stirling Range National Park
Cape Le Grand National Park

The pinnacles of Nambung National Park are spectacular examples of the varied geology of Western Australia.

Western Australian Tourist Centre, 772 Hay St., Perth, WA 6000, or call (09) 322 2999. Department of Conservation and Land Management, 50 Hayman Rd., Como, WA 6152, or call (09) 367 0333.

WESTERN AUSTRALIA IS A STATE of immense size and natural diversity. While one season's monsoonal rains and cyclones batter the isolated coastlines of the extreme north, 1,500 mi/2,400 km to the south, another season's snows may be dusting the crest of the Stirling Range. In between, the climate of the coastal region near the capital city of Perth is ideal.

The state comprises the entire western third of the continent. Its million square miles encompass an amazing array of creatures that have many similarities to the plants and animals of eastern Australia and strange affinities with those of other continents as well. In the remote Kimberley region of the north, a species of baobab tree suggests an ancient tie to Africa, as do numerous flowering shrubs. Palm trees in Western Australia are reminders of an ancient Australian continent where a lush tropical environment thrived in what is now arid landscape. A multiplicity of marine creatures, many unique to these waters, swim in the Indian Ocean, which laps the state's shores.

The great wildernesses and national parks of Western Australia are clustered in roughly equal proportions in the mild temperate forests and coastlines of the southwest and in the dramatically sculptured sandstone country of the Pilbara and Kimberley regions.

The state is largely a parched wasteland of prickly spinifex scrub and powdery red sand. A few Aboriginal tribes have managed to survive in this unforgiving land, while attempts at settlement by Europeans have ended in misery and failure. From south to north, the Nullarbor Plain, Great Victoria Desert, Gibson Desert, and Great Sandy Desert merge imperceptibly into a vast environment of climatic hostility. The desert acts as a natural barrier to the migratory ebb and flow of wildlife. The consequence of this separation is the development of a fragile world of specialized plants and animals scattered along 7,500 mi/12,070 km of Western Australian coastline.

A journey from the southwest to a destination in northern Western Australia can take days. Careful seasonal planning is extremely important in order to avoid impassible roads resulting from monsoons and cyclones in the north.

The Great Northern Highway runs along the coast and the western edge of the Pilbara district, skirting the coast of the Indian Ocean and avoiding the immense void of sand, dust, and spinifex called the Great Sandy Desert. At Broome, it turns east and eventually north toward Darwin. It serves as the main avenue of exploration in the north and links many of the national parks.

September rains invite a brief and extraordinary explosion of blossoms in the countryside near Geraldton.

WESTERN AUSTRALIA

TIMOR SEA

Highways   ▲ Peaks
★ State Capital   🌲 Small Parks
● Points of Interest   🐟 Fishing

0   300 Mi
0   300 Km

Cape Talbot
Cape Bougainville
Joseph Bonaparte Gulf
Bonaparte Archipelago
DRYSDALE RIVER NP

THE   Wyndham
GARDNER PLATEAU   Kununurra
Buccaneer Archipelago
Cape Leveque
KIMBERLEY
L Argyle
BUNGLE BUNGLES

INDIAN
King Sound
NAPIER RA
KING LEOPOLD RANGES

N

OCEAN
Derby
Broome
WINDJANA GORGE NP
GEIKIE GORGE NP
TUNNEL CREEK NP
Fitzroy Crossing
Fitzroy R
GREAT NORTHERN HWY
Ord R

GREAT

SANDY DESERT

Port Hedland
Dampier Archipelago
Barrow I
Karratha
CHICHESTER RANGE NP
PILBARA
RUDALL RIVER NP
Fortescue R
CHICHESTER RANGE
North West Cape
HAMERSLEY
Wittenoom
Exmouth
RA
YAMPIRE GORGE
CAPE RANGE NP
DALES GORGE
Mt Bruce
Mt Meharry
NINGALOO REEF
Ashburton R
HAMERSLEY RANGE NP
TROPIC OF CAPRICORN
L Disappointment

Exmouth Gulf
NORTH WEST COASTAL HWY
GIBSON DESERT

Shark Bay
Carnarvon
COLLIER RANGE NP
Gascoyne R
L Carnegie

Dirk Hartog I
Faure I
Murchison R
GREAT NORTHERN HWY
GREAT VICTORIA

ZUYTDORP NP
KALBARRI NP
DESERT

MOORE RIVER NP
Geraldton
Houtman Abrolhos
L Moore
L Barlee
L Yindarlgooda

NULLARBOR PLAIN

ALEXANDER MORRISON NP
WATHEROO NP
Kalgoorlie
L Cowan
Cervantes
NAMBUNG NP
HAMPTON TABLELAND
AVON VALLEY NP
WALYUNGA NP
BOORABBIN NP
ROTTNEST ISLAND RESERVE
Perth
GREAT EASTERN HWY
EYRE HWY
DARLING RANGE
BRAND HWY
Great Australian Bight
Fremantle
FRANK HANN NP
CAPE ARID NP
SOUTH WESTERN HWY
Bunbury
Cape Naturaliste
Jerramungup
Ravensthorpe
Esperance
Yallingup
Ongerup
Gnowangerup
Hopetoun
CAPE LE GRANDE NP
LEEUWIN-NATURALISTE NP
Cranbrook
FITZGERALD
Recherche Archipelago
Cape Leeuwin
Mt
BREMER RIVER NP
SIR JAMES MITCHELL NP
Barker
Bluff Knoll Bay
STIRLING RANGE NP
WALPOLE-NORNALUP NP
Walpole Albany

SOUTHERN OCEAN

THE KIMBERLEY

On the northern edge of the Great Sandy Desert flow the waters of the Fitzroy River. The Fitzroy plays a role of tremendous importance, belying its subtle first impression. North of the river, the topography departs from the monotonous, rolling red-brown sand of the desert and becomes a spectacular sculptural landscape of carved gorges and uplifted domes. No major roads penetrate this wilderness. Aborigines have trekked it for thousands of years, but such are the difficulties and hazards of traversing this land that it remains virtually unknown to outside explorers. Similarly, the northwest's rugged coastline has thwarted countless attempts to discover the Kimberley from the north. Its defenses here are submerged coral reefs, enormous tidal fluctuations, mangrove labyrinths, and towering sandstone cliffs.

"The Kimberley" is a largely subjective term, although there are generally recognized boundaries. The Indian Ocean and the Timor Sea define the northern edge of the Kimberley, and the Fitzroy River limits the region across the south. Roughly 104,000 sq mi/ 270,000 sq km of wilderness—including the King Leopold Range, the Kimberley Plateau, and the northern Gardner Plateau—make up the region commonly called the Kimberley.

GEOLOGY

The most striking geological feature of the Kimberley was created by the plants and animals of a huge marine coral reef system. This extraordinary geology is wonderfully displayed in the eastern Napier Range at Geike Gorge National Park and Windjana Gorge National Park. The Lennard River in Windjana Gorge has sliced into the limestone as deep as 300 ft/90 m, revealing stunning samples of ancient marine life.

WILDLIFE AND VEGETATION

There is a surprising diversity of plant and animal types within the Kimberley. Generally, this large, isolated tract of land is considered to be a single, homogeneous environment. Abutting the Timor Sea, however, are isolated patches of monsoonal rain forest, reminiscent of Arnhem Land in the Northern Territory. More widespread are large parcels of land composed entirely of eroded sandstone, with open woolly butt eucalypt forest. There are also broad flood plains, the habitat of paperbark trees and estuarine crocodiles.

In the Kimberley, as in Arnhem Land and Cape York Peninsula, the constant high temperatures and the seasonal occurrence of rain dominate the ebb and flow of life. Caught in the flux between the climatic extremes of wet and dry seasons, plants and animals of the Kimberley are forced to adjust their lifestyles constantly in order to survive.

The northern region is always hot. Along the coast, wildlife must deal with minimum temperatures of 94° F (34° C) in summer (December), while in July, the coolest month, the temperature may only drop a few degrees. Inland, in the absence of sea breezes, solar radiation pushes the mercury in excess of 100° F (38° C).

The dry season brings with it the constant threat of natural bush fires. Water from shallow wetlands quickly evaporates under the

Steeply eroded walls of Manning Gorge in the Kimberley shade and protect a water hole and its surrounding vegetation, creating a good habitat for wildlife.

intense northern sun. Soon the mud deposited by wet-season floods begins to crack and peel. Giant weeping paperbarks, or melaleucas, like stranded botanical islands, collect a thick mat of sickle-shaped leaves and fragments of bark around their roots. Even creatures normally active in the daytime drift toward a seminocturnal existence, feeding and hunting at dusk and dawn to avoid the searing heat of day.

Cyclones in the heart of the wet season cause periodic violence. Thunderstorms and powerful winds tear at the earth, uprooting swamp mahogany trees and stripping foliage from baobabs, giggy-giggy bushes, and cycads. Lightning discharges split trees and shatter rock outcrops. Torrential downpours soon follow these apocalyptic displays. In the aftermath, water deluges the previously parched earth. Dry creekbeds fill up and spill over their banks. In the narrow gorges, torrents of muddy water move boulders and scour the sandstone walls, carving deeper into the ranges and revealing yet more of the geological past of the Kimberley.

Known for their graceful, seemingly effortless flights, fork-tailed kites live on a diet of carrion as well as live rodents, insects, and small lizards.
Pages 200 and 201: The naked branches of the baobab, or boab, grace the winter landscape of the Kimberley. Large white blossoms will liven the tree's appearance by mid-December.

Soon a green world awakens. Life explodes with a violence nearly as intense as that of the past storms. Snakes, such as the olive python and the common tree snake, slither in search of higher ground. The usually nocturnal narbarlek, a rare diminutive wallaby, ventures from the shelter of sandstone crevices to take advantage of rich new grasses. Double-barred and zebra finches fluff, preen, and dry their soaked plumage, their muted voices a sharp contrast to the nasal cries of the red-tailed black cockatoo.

GEIKIE GORGE NATIONAL PARK

Geikie Gorge National Park, c/o Post Office, Fitzroy Crossing, WA 6765, or call (091) 91-5030.

The campsite at Geikie Gorge National Park is flooded during the wet season, November to April. Dry-season sites are available for a nominal fee. The Parks Service operates tours by flat-bottom boats, departing twice daily from the campground, at 9 A.M. and 2:30 P.M.

About 12.5 mi/20 km north of Fitzroy Crossing a muddy river enters a spectacular narrow passage cut through the eastern Napier Range. For millions of years the Fitzroy has funneled its energies through the limestone landscape to form Geikie Gorge, one of Australia's unforgettable geological sights.

In the midst of the dry season, June through September, the river meanders through the pools and passageways of the gorge, masquerading as a gentle force of nature. Less than 18 in/450 mm of rain falls annually in the Kimberley Plateau and Napier Range region. It comes in flash floods, however, and the land can sponge up only a fraction of the valuable moisture. The remainder spills into the passages of the Fitzroy and its tributaries. The water comes instantly, in a volume of unimaginable proportions from a catchment the size of Tasmania. With no other exit but Geikie Gorge, a juggernaut of water, mud, and debris as much as 53 ft/16 m high tears violently at the gorge's narrow limestone cliffs. Months later, river red gums and mangroves display muddy watermarks and festoons of debris in branches as high as 33 ft/10 m.

The nankeen kestrel, smallest of all the Australian falcons, lacks typical falcon speed. It hunts small reptiles, mammals, and insects from a perch or while hovering over an open field.

Drifting through the gorge by boat, one sees walls of cream and reddish brown vaulting above the mangrove-lined river. Over eons, erosion by wind and water has created caves and overhangs and opened narrow fissures in the walls. The scouring effects of the annual wet seasons keep the geologic and biologic history of this breathtaking wilderness exposed to view.

The true nature of this landscape was not understood until 1924, when it was discovered that the Napier Range and adjacent Oscar Range are the remains of a marine coral reef second in size only to the Great Barrier Reef.

Between 350 and 400 million years ago, during the time known geologically as the Devonian period, a tropical extension of the Indian Ocean engulfed much of northern Western Australia. Surf pounding the rugged coastline—at the time 220 mi/350 km east of the present coastline—tossed warm waters into the flanks of the Kimberley Plateau and King Leopold Range. Off these shores ancient corals, stromatoporoids, formed an extensive barrier reef, including fringing reefs, barrier reefs, coral reef islands, and atolls. Today, the ranges between the Fitzroy River and the Indian Ocean are all that remains of a reef complex that may have encompassed a swath of sea floor more than 620 mi/1,000 km long and 185 mi/ 300 km wide, built to a depth of 330 ft/100 m. In the centuries following the sea's recession, erosion from mountain ranges deposited layers of silt atop the dead reef. The current reddish-brown color of the gorge is the result of iron and other minerals leaching from deposits and staining the chalky white limestone. In places, the limestone shows its natural color, thanks to the constant scouring action of the floodwaters. The clear difference between the two areas on the cliff face dramatically records the high level of the floodwaters.

WILDLIFE AND VEGETATION

In areas of weathered limestone, fossilized marine creatures—sponges, seashells, and a variety of coral types—can be discerned, their outlines protruding from the worn surface of the walls. Yet it

The usually tranquil Fitzroy River in Geikie Gorge changes, in the wet season, into scouring floodwaters.

is not the dead but the living creatures of Geikie Gorge that are its greatest attraction. Here one sees plants and animals with affinities to Devonian times and to later periods when tropical vegetation assumed dominance over territory vacated by the receding sea. Innocuous mangroves line the dry-season banks of the river. Because mangroves commonly grow throughout the tropical north, they might inspire little interest—until one realizes that this is anything but typical mangrove habitat: the usual tidal estuaries, salt marshes, and muddy coasts are several hundred miles removed from present-day Geikie Gorge.

Even more astonishing are the fish species that dwell in the opaque waters of the Fitzroy River. Recently, new species of sawfish and stingray were discovered living and breeding in these fresh waters. Both are known to inhabit rivers in South America, but in each case there is some connection with salt water. In the Geikie Gorge, they are isolated by natural barriers and cannot reach salt water.

The archer fish is another exotic inhabitant. Generally, these fish, up to 10 in/25 cm in length, are common in brackish waters along northern coasts of Australia; occasionally they venture upstream to breed. The archer fish of Geikie Gorge spend their entire life in its water holes. They have the remarkable ability to spit water at insects near the water's edge and can even shoot down flying insects.

EXPLORING THE GORGE

The banks of the Fitzroy are restricted as a flora-and-fauna sanctuary. Only researchers and park rangers are allowed within 660 ft/ 200 m of the river from either side, excluding the campground on the western bank. Much of the wildlife can be seen from this area and from a short walking trail that begins near the boat launch and circles up onto the gorge wall and plateau. Numerous birds, including kingfishers, sulphur-crested cockatoos, parrots, and greater bower-birds, frequent the area around the campground.

Since the banks of the Fitzroy are restricted areas, the only way to explore the gorge is by boat. A two-hour guided excursion offers views not only of spectacular geology and galleries of sculptured limestone but of the park's wildlife as well, including Johnstone's freshwater crocodiles, herons, darters, cormorants, and fruit-eating bats. The bats, which line the branches of mangroves and gum trees, are estimated to number nearly three quarters of a million in the park.

FRESH-WATER CROCODILE
Crocodylus johnstoni

The fresh-water crocodile – or Johnstone's crocodile – lives in lagoons, water holes, and in fresh-water rivers along the northern coast of Australia. It is readily distinguished from the saltwater crocodile by its narrow, smooth snout. Also, the mature Johnstone's crocodile measures 8 to 9 ft/ 2.4 to 2.7 m in length, a far less fearsome size than the sometimes 20-ft/ 6-m length of its saltwater relative.

Though active during the day, it is nocturnal in its feeding habits, gobbling birds, frogs, fish, shellfish, and other small creatures. It does not normally attack humans.

The Johnstone's crocodile reproduces near the end of the dry season, when the female lays an average of 20 eggs in a sandbank.

WEDGE-TAILED EAGLE
Aquila audax

With a wingspan of up to 8.2 ft/ 2.5 m, the wedge-tailed eagle is the largest bird of prey in Australia. From a perch on a dead limb or telephone pole, the ever-alert eagle scrutinizes the plains below in search of rabbits, its favorite food. Despite its majestic soaring ability, it is relatively inept at capturing live prey, however. Carrion therefore constitutes an important part of its diet, although it will also feed on small lizards, birds, and mammals.

At one time it was believed that wedge-tailed eagles were responsi-

ble for the deaths of many sheep and other livestock and bounties were paid for their destruction. It is now known that the eagles prey only on sick or disabled sheep; it is now illegal to kill them.

EMU
Dromaius novaehollandiae

Australia's largest and most popular bird is nomadic, constantly wandering about most of Australia. The emu will eat pebbles or charcoal to

help its gizzard grind food. It has also been known to eat such improbable things as discarded batteries and so has earned the false reputation of being a bird that will eat anything. Its preferred foods are seeds, fruits, leaves, flowers, and insects.

Among emus, unlike most birds, it is solely the male's responsibility to hatch the eggs and raise the five to eleven offspring. During incubation, the male forgoes eating, drinking, and defecating and loses a large percentage of its body fat. The female often will spend this time mating with another male and only occasionally stays to watch her chicks hatch.

WINDJANA GORGE NATIONAL PARK

Windjana Gorge National Park,
c/o Department of Conservation and Land Management, Post

Office Box 242, Kununurra,
WA 6743, or call the park at
(091) 68 0200.

The mineral-stained cliffs of the Windjana Gorge are weathered
remains of a 350-million-year-old coral reef that now forms the backbone of the Napier Range. Unlike the Fitzroy River, 72 mi/116 km
southeast, which cuts through these same formations, the Lennard
River of Windjana flows only for brief periods, during and briefly
after the wet season. The rest of the time, its waters stand in quiet,
serene ponds. Only an occasional breeze disturbs the surface of the
water, which reflects the brick-red, black, and cream of the gorge
walls like a huge natural mirror. Small caves and overhangs in the
walls hide traces of Aboriginal rock art. At each end of the 2.5-mi/
4-km main gorge, the vertical landscape dissolves into a semiarid
plateau laced with dry riverbeds.

Windjana Gorge National Park is accessible only during the dry
season. Despite the presence of Johnstone's freshwater crocodile,
the pools are safe for adults to swim in and invite exploration of the
back reaches of the gorge. There are no permanent trails, since
floodwaters each wet season deposit fresh silt and debris along the
narrow banks. Visitors should prepare for wilderness bush camping if considering a stay near the gorge. Be sure to carry all supplies, especially water.

WILDLIFE AND VEGETATION

Low-growing trees and shrubs crowd the sandy strip between the
Lennard River and the base of the gorge walls. These include river
red gums and assorted eucalypt species; numerous tropical fig varieties predominate. On the plateaus above, and trailing off at each
end of the gorge, is an open patchwork of dark green eucalypt scrub
and beige grass tussocks. The barren riverbed of the Lennard River
is lined with a green corridor of eucalypts, though this vegetation

is stunted in comparison with that nearer the heart of the gorge, where there is a permanent water supply.

The gorge's precipitous walls, as high as 300 ft/90 m in places, keep the deep pools cool and refreshing for the countless species that seek refuge there. Jabiru wading the shallows in search of fishes, frogs, and small reptiles find the motionless water an ideal hunting ground. Herons and darters vie with them for aquatic edibles. The waters attract several species of the cockatoo, cockatiel, sulphur-crested cockatoo, galah, and little corella. Occasionally, flocks of lorikeets alight in the gorge to drink and feed, their screeches ricocheting between the limestone faces.

The shingle-back lizard, a skink found in dry regions of the southern coast of Australia, has also been called a double-headed, stumpy-tail, or bobtail lizard because of its bizarre shape.
Pages 212 and 213: The famous beehive domes of the Bungle Bungles were eroded from ancient seabed sediments.

Several reptiles sun on the sandy exposed banks between the eucalypt stands, the most impressive being the reclusive Johnstone's freshwater crocodile, a shy lizard less than 9 ft/2.4 m in length. To visitors they are living reminders of Windjana's prehistoric origins.

BUNGLE BUNGLES

Bungle Bungles, c/o Department of Conservation and Land Management, P.O. Box 242, Kununurra, WA 6743 or call (091) 68 0200.

For safety reasons, one should contact a park ranger before visiting this park; access is by four-wheel-drive vehicle only. Self-contained camping is permitted, and drinking water is available at Bellburn Creek crossing.

Under the late-afternoon sun, the weathered earthen domes near the crossing of the Ord River and the Great Northern Highway on the eastern Kimberley glow a brilliant brick red. These formations, called the Bungle Bungles, comprise 3,000 sq mi/7,770 sq km of eroded sandstone.

A mixture of siliceous sandstone and a type of algae that binds the sandstone grains creates the unique sculptural forms of the Bungle Bungles. Alternating bands of silica and algae create the orange and black stripes seen from ground level. The domes of the Bungle Bungles can resist considerable weathering, but if the algae bonding is disturbed, the sandstone layer below is quickly destroyed by erosion.

The park is filled with huge gorges and cliffs over 328 ft/100 m high. Growing profusely in the gorges and clinging to the cliff faces is the Bungle Bungle fan palm, a variety of the Kimberley fan palm. Well suited to tropical regions with drier climates, the palm adapts both to the heavy rains of the wet season (December through March) and to the dry season that the rest of the year constitutes. It is a slender tree that grows a sparse crown of leaves.

The local Kidja Aboriginal people had known the Bungle Bungles for centuries, and evidence of their habitation is common throughout the park. They called this labyrinth of bubble shapes Purnululu. It was only in 1983 that the existence of the Bungle Bungles was publicized. It is amazing that this geologic masterpiece could be so close to the main highway (only 19 mi/30 km away) and yet go undiscovered for so long.

HAMERSLEY RANGE NATIONAL PARK

Ranger-in-Charge, Hamersley
Range National Park, Post Office
Box 73, Wittenoom, WA 6752,

or call (091) 86 8291.
   Full accommodations and supplies
are available at Wittenoom.

South of the Great Sandy Desert, the landscape of Western Australia rises in layers of shale and conglomerate sandstone to create the Hamersley Range. The earth here is considerably older than the limestone of the Kimberley and Cape Range regions. Steady weathering in this parched country has exposed bands of mineral-rich earth in striations of yellow, red, brown, and black.

These mineral layers began their upward journey nearly 2 billion years ago with the deposit of silts on an ancient sea floor. The Hamersley formations are equal in age to the oldest land found anywhere on earth. Over the millennia, the retreat of shorelines and the slow but violent sequences of uplifting and tilting left this part of the country high and dry.

The buckled earth of Hamersley Range extends 200 mi/320 km east–west across the Pilbara district. From the air, sections of the range appear as a flat, monotonous plateau of gray-green mulga scrub with dots of spikey spinifex grass. Occasionally the land splits open in plunging fissures hundreds of feet deep. Here and there erosion has widened the iron-rich red sandstone into gorges of formidable size. This is especially true at the headwaters of the Fortescue River, the only major river cutting through the Hamersley Range.

GORGES

The ruggedly beautiful gorges are the enticement for most visitors to make the long, 930-mi/1,500-km journey from Perth. After two days of driving across largely featureless landscape, the Hamersley Range appears like a visual Eden on the eastern horizon.

Dozens of gorges splinter the range, most cutting nearly north-south on the northern slope. The majority of the larger gorges that contain water are accessible by dirt roads and conventional vehicles. Their cool, shady confines, lined with the soft greens and stark

The parched and weathered landscape of the Pilbara district belies its origins below ancient seas over 200 million years ago.

white trunks of river red gums, are both a visual and physical oasis from the searing sun on the plateau.

Dales Gorge. Considered the premier gorge of the Hamersley Range, Dales Gorge offers unexpected beauty and spectacular sights. A dark green permanent water hole fills the gorge floor, which in most places is 120 to 200 ft/36 to 60 m wide. Dales' jaggedly eroded walls vary greatly in height but are mostly under 260 ft/80 m. The gorge's two most prominent features are Circular Pool, a large, deep water hole a short walk from the campground, and Fortescue Falls, not far from Circular Pool and reached via a trail cut in the gorge wall. En route, the trail passes through shady tree-and-fern grottoes. Nearer the falls, more ferns and epiphytic mosses thrive in the fine, refreshing mist from the tumbling cascades.

The white-cheeked honey eater is one of sixty-eight species of honey eater, a group credited with spreading many Australian plant species.

Wittenoom Gorge. Much of Wittenoom Gorge lies outside the park boundary and is the site of a large asbestos mine. Asbestos in the rocky layers of Wittenoom is the source of the gorge's characteristic blue color. Visitors can approach the gorge from the south. Once Wittenoom Gorge enters the park, it travels scarcely 1.2 mi/2 km before forking into Hancock Gorge, the incredibly narrow Red Gorge, and Weano Gorge, the shortest of the three. Before reaching Joffre Falls, at the head of Wittenoom Gorge, the creekbed squeezes through chasms so narrow that light strikes the floor only during the few moments daily when the sun is directly overhead.

Yampire Gorge. A rough-cut road runs the entire length of Yampire Gorge, offering access to the interior of the park from Wittenoom township. There is an information site at the entrance to the gorge road.

Hamersley Gorge and Rio Tinto. Much smaller than the main gorges to the east, Hamersley and Rio Tinto are reached easily on the main road between Tom Price and Wittenoom. Hamersley

Gorge enjoys protected status as a separate piece of national park a short distance from the main park. The road bisects Rio Tinto, giving travelers en route a convenient introduction to the area's geologic sculptures.

Other Gorges. For visitors with arid-country bushwalking experience, there are several other gorges—including Bee, Range, Munjina, and Dignam—that offer rugged scenery and wilderness isolation. Use preparedness and caution when venturing into gorges.

Mt. Bruce. As a diversion from hiking down into gorges, energetic bushwalkers can attempt the two-hour trail ascending Mt. Bruce. At 4,051 ft/1,235 m, this shale-and-conglomerate sandstone mountain is the second highest in Western Australia. Start early and carry ample water.

CAPE RANGE NATIONAL PARK

Ranger-in-Charge, Cape Range National Park, P.O. Box 55, Exmouth 6707, or call (099) 49 1676.

Visitors to the park should plan to carry water, since there is only one assured water site, near Mangrove Creek about 3 mi/5 km inside the northern boundary. Yardie Creek often contains ample water, but its potability is not reliable. Camping is allowed along the beach via an access track behind the dunes; a fee is charged. Four-wheel-drive vehicles are necessary beyond Yardie Creek.

When you first arrive at Cape Range National Park from the dusty, arid inland and gorge country, you might take the incredibly gorgeous landscape for a mirage. This isolated coastline, the most westerly projection of the Australian continent, has known the voices and footsteps of white Europeans longer than any other place in Australia. On a course from southern Africa, captains of European sailing vessels would head east across the southern Indian Ocean to the west coast of this little-known wasteland, then navigate north for the rich spice islands of the East Indies. Many ships' captains laid regrettable courses too near the shore and ended their voyages on the countless reefs and shoals near Cape Range.

The vastness of the Indian Ocean on the west of the cape and of Exmouth Gulf on the east hints little at the profusion of marine life beneath the surface. White sharks top the food chain of these warm tropical waters. Avoiding attacks from these giants became the first obstacle in the sailors' gauntlet of difficulties after marooning. Adjacent Ningaloo coral reef hosts a great variety of marine fishes and invertebrates. As Ningaloo Reef Marine Park, it is one of the few reef areas in Western Australia to enjoy protected status, a testament to its value and beauty. Ningaloo, however, is a mere vestige of a reef structure that took shape 15 million years ago when a vast proportion of the northwest corner of Australia was flooded by a warm, shallow sea. Marine life was abundant, and corals especially flourished, constructing gigantic sections of reef. Spasmodic actions in the earth's crust caused crumpling, creating the huge anticline that now underlies the Cape Range area. A limestone island was formed, and along its western shore corals once again began establishing reefs. In the ensuing eons, ice-age sea levels fluctuated. Today sea levels are low enough to expose a land bridge between the mainland and this one-time island. The resultant land mass constitutes a 50-mi/80-km peninsula jutting into the Indian Ocean.

Away from its shores, the cape resembles the chasm-crazed limestone of the Kimberley's Napier Range. After the uplift of the anticline, Cape Range was severed by deep ravines leading down from the central plateau. Wet-season waters flooding across the eastern and western escarpments cut jagged gorges. Yardie Creek, which flows inland from the beach at the southern end of the park, is a vivid example of the tremendous weathering forces at work here. As in many of the western ravines, cool, deep water holes dot the creek's course to the sea. In contrast, ravines on the eastern shore facing Exmouth Gulf experience water only during the heaviest rains.

WILDLIFE AND VEGETATION

There are few areas of Western Australia where the profusion and diversity of wildlife are as great as in Cape Range National Park and Ningaloo Reef Marine Park. Dusk and dawn bring a flood of hopping, crawling, and flying creatures into view. Euros, the large gray-rust kangaroo of such climes, are well established on the cape, where they can be seen in large numbers browsing on coastal heath.

Kangaroo paw flowers are known for their thick layer of soft fur-like hairs. There are at least eight varieties of kangaroo paws found in Western Australia.

Birds are the cape's most numerous residents. The mixture of marine and arid-country species creates a haven for bird watchers. Gorges, especially those with permanent water, attract scores of galahs and little corellas, which find nesting crevices in the pitted limestone. Red-capped robins are a flash of scarlet as they flit through the scrub in search of insects.

Several kites, including the most elegant raptor in Australia, the black-shouldered kite, cruise the stiff breezes along the cape. Ospreys, too, are frequently spotted drifting over the lagoonal waters between the beach and Ningaloo Reef.

In springtime the banksias' honey-orange blossoms attract a variety of honey eaters—the brown, singing, and gray-headed especially.

During periods when Cape Range was bridged to the mainland, an exchange of plant and animal species occurred. But alternating periods of island isolation have allowed many species to develop characteristics unique to the cape. Species like the soft knob-tailed gecko have flourished there while becoming less common elsewhere. Others, such as the native land snail, are solely endemic and have adapted to the near-desert conditions of the cape's plateaus.

Famed for its acrobatic aerial displays while catching flying insects, rainbow bee-eaters feed principally on stinging insects.
Pages 222 and 223: Fossilized roots and fused sand grains carved by wind and time create the bizarre and beautiful pinnacles of Nambung National Park.

The most fascinating examples of isolated development in Cape Range National Park are the marine creatures that inhabit the lightless caves of the cape's limestone underworld. At an earlier time in the geologic history of Cape Range, a variety of marine creatures became entrapped in submerged caves pocketing the limestone structure of the cape. Many of them adapted to a life of total blackness. Today, the blind gudgeon fish, an eel species, and at least two shrimp-like animals have become colorless and completely sightless. Little is known about the biology of these mysterious creatures of darkness.

NAMBUNG NATIONAL PARK

Nambung National Park, P.O. Box
62, Cervantes, WA 0511, or call
(096) 52 7043.

Western Australia is a kaleidoscope of strange geological shapes, but the pinnacle formations of Nambung National Park, 155 mi/ 250 km north of Perth on the Indian Coast, must be among the most curious in Australia. The pillars, knobs, and strange characters of limestone seem to rise up from the surrounding iron-beige-colored sand like uncompleted sculptures. They are no less various in size than in shape: some are pencil-thin—only inches tall—while others form massive mounds larger than a car.

The pinnacles offer few clues to their origins. The vegetation of the surrounding countryside is a dense mixture of wattles, banksias, and coastal heath with an understory of gaily hued flowering annuals. It is here, however, that geologists believe lies the secret of the thousands of tombstone-like formations.

Nambung's pinnacles reflect the root structures of ancient vegetation that stabilized this area of dunes in much the same manner that the adjacent heath scrub now functions. Similar types of heath scrub blanketed the coastal dunes 25,000 to 30,000 years ago. The theory suggests that shifting, unstable dunes eventually engulfed the trees and shrubs, killing them; in time buried rainwater minerals and lime leaching from topsoils trickled down channels left by decaying roots. These spaces were plugged as the minerals hard-

ened, forming calcite. Like buried stalagmites, the forms grew slowly with the deposition of additional minerals. The pinnacles we see today are these fossilized root systems, which have become exposed as another unstable dune system passes through.

ROTTNEST ISLAND

Rottnest Island Board, Rottnest Island, WA 6161, or call (09) 292 5044.

The island is about 10 mi/16 km west of Fremantle; it can be reached daily by either ferry or plane. The only private transportation on the island is by bicycle, available for hire at the local bike shop. Although there are nearly a thousand bicycles for hire, midday arrivals may find all the bikes taken during busy summer weekends and holidays.

Camping is permitted on the island, and there is a wide range of other accommodations, including cottages, cabins, villas, and a hotel.

On a clear day, from Fremantle Harbor, the distant limestone cliffs on Rottnest Island can be seen across the Indian Ocean. This tranquil island lies only 10 mi/16 km from the coast of Western Australia, yet its beautiful white beaches and tropical blue waters seem much more removed in time. For decades, visitors have come to Rottnest Island to lose themselves in its quiet seclusion.

Famed locally for turquoise waters and clean white beaches, Rottnest is one of the little-known islands of Australia.

OSPREY
Pandion haliaetus

Since fish are their primary diet, ospreys are usually found hovering near coasts and large rivers. Swooping from great heights, the osprey lands feet first in the water and sometimes submerges completely in pursuit of its prey. These birds have a 90 percent success rate in catching food, the highest rate of any raptor.

The body of the osprey is well adapted to fishing; its feathers are extremely compact and give little air resistance as the bird plummets to the water. Rough padding on the bottom of its feet enables it to grip its prey securely.

Ospreys are known for their spectacular aerial displays during court-

ship and for the huge nests they build and maintain for many years. Although there is only one species of osprey, it is one of the most widely distributed species in the world.

Rottnest was one of the first points of Australian land to be discovered by white Europeans. During the late 1600s, Dutch sailing captains crossing the Indian Ocean in search of faster and safer routes to the East Indies found themselves skirting the Western Australian coastline. In 1696 Holland's Willem de Vlamingh first sighted the small island.

While exploring the island, the early Dutch navigator discovered short-tailed wallabies, miniature marsupial creatures. Mistaking the animals for large rats, he named the island Rottnest, which means rat's nest in Dutch. Today, the island's quokkas, so named by the Aborigines, are one of its main attractions.

Rottnest was the site of the state's first settlement in 1830. The island also served as an Aboriginal prison and was still in use until the turn of this century. Many penal buildings from this time, as well as other examples of colonial-style architecture (dating back to

QUOKKA
Setonix brachyurus

Resembling a furry rat, the quokka, also called short-tailed wallaby and short-tailed pademelon, is a marsupial found in coastal southwestern Australia. Their heaviest concentration is on Rottnest Island, even though the arid conditions and low vegetation there are not the ideal quokka habitat. Their existence on Rottnest is a continual struggle for access to the scant water supply and adequate shelter, especially on hot days in the dry season. Many members of this endangered species do not survive the summer.

Like many other marsupials, the female quokka may mate while her first offspring is developing in her pouch, right after its birth. Only if the firstborn dies within its first six months, however, will the second develop and be born. This adaptive strategy increases the female quokka's chances of bearing at least one young in a season.

1840), still remain. After years of neglect, most of these structures have been refurbished for nonbusiness use. During its varied past Rottnest has been a military fortification protecting Fremantle Harbor during World War II and a holiday resort for the affluent. Its popularity as an escape from the faster pace of life in nearby Perth has helped to preserve its natural getaway atmosphere.

WILDLIFE

Rottnest seldom is singled out for its wildlife, yet this small island attracts dozens of migratory shorebirds and wetland species. Among the birds drawn to the shallow salt lakes dotting the interior of the island are the Australian shelduck, the wood duck, the red-necked avocet, the banded stilt, and a collection of dotterels and plovers. Rock parrots and rainbow bee eaters are two of the more interesting land birds that come to Rottnest to breed each November. Above the island, one of the most beautiful birds of prey in the world–the osprey–sails on the warm ocean breezes. Nesting and breeding on several of the less accessible limestone cliffs, ospreys have become a symbol of Rottnest's protected wild heritage.

Rottnest is positioned at the confluence of ocean currents–currents sweeping south and cool temperate currents reaching the island from the Southern Ocean. This creates a marine environment unlike any other in Australia. Colorful coral reef fishes swim near giant disks of plate coral. In dark grottoes and submerged archways live a diverse assortment of brightly colored marine invertebrates, such as sponges, crabs, and shrimp, unusual in these warmer waters. The huge crayfish found here–the largest in Western Australia–are the target of dozens of private craypots dropped each weekend by boaters arriving from nearby Perth.

Chestnut-breasted shelducks, also called mountain ducks, are usually strong fliers but become temporarily flightless when they molt.

LEEUWIN-NATURALISTE NATIONAL PARK

Western Australia National Parks Administration, 63 Serpentine Road, Albany, WA 6300, or call (097) 55 2144. Located about 165 mi/265 km southwest of Perth. Camping, by permit, is allowed in the park. Accommodations are available at nearby August and Busselton.

This 38,300-acre/15,500-hectare park, a combination of the former Cape Leeuwin and Cape Naturaliste parks, has magnificent vistas of the Indian Ocean coastline, as well as an inland system of limestone caves deep below the ground. It lies along 75 mi/120 km of the coast, and is traversed by the Caves Road.

Leeuwin-Naturaliste's long stretches of limestone-strewn beaches and rocky shorelines are affected daily by the pounding of the seas. Tall, windswept cliffs and coasts, buffeted by strong westerly and southwesterly winds, have witnessed many shipwrecks. A few isolated coves and bays interrupt the harsh seashore and provide tranquil resting places for wildlife and visitors alike.

VEGETATION AND WILDLIFE

The stunted heaths and mallee scrubs near the coast are filled with colorful plants and flowers, including white clematis and purple pea. Common hovea, a purple shrub that grows to 20 in/50 cm high, is also common on the heath.

The most popular vegetation at Leeuwin-Naturaliste, however, is found in the Boranup Karri Forest. The karris here, growing to heights of 200 ft/60 m or more, thrive in limestone-based soils, a habitat very different from the red clay beds in which they usually are found. The entire forest is only a century old, being composed entirely of trees that were planted to replace forest cut down for timber or destroyed by fire. Other areas of Leeuwin-Naturaliste contain slender peppermint and towering jarrah eucalyptus trees. The more swampy areas of the park support melaleuca (paperbark) trees.

The flowering heath and eucalypt forests attract many different wildlife creatures, including western gray kangaroos, several spe-

Built in 1896, the Cape Leeuwin lighthouse sits at the confluence of two oceans—the Southern and the Indian. The lighthouse still operates to warn approaching ships of the cape's rocky presence. Daily tours are available for visitors.

cies of possums, and a variety of birds. Among the unusual birds frequenting the area are the red-tailed tropic bird, a white bird with long red tail-streamers, which feeds almost exclusively on fish, and the red-eared firetail finch, a solitary bird found foraging among the heath, notable for its bright red bill and the large red patch behind its eyes.

CAVE VIEWING

A large network of caves exists in the Yallingup area in the park. The caves, nearly 130 ft/40 m deep, were formed by a combination of rainwater, carbonic acid from the air, and decomposed plant matter that seeped through the ground and dissolved the limestone.
  Besides several species of bats, a variety of primitive species, including crustaceans and insects, inhabits the caves. These creatures, adapted to life in the darkness, are blind and colorless.
  Four caves–Yallingup, Mammoth, Lakes, and Jewel–may be seen on daily guided tours. Three other caves–Brides, Giants, and Calgardup–are open to the more adventurous. They are unlit, contain no handrails, and should be attempted only by experienced spelunkers.

Stalagmites and stalactites have formed in Jewel Cave from acidic rainwater dripping through the limestone ceiling.

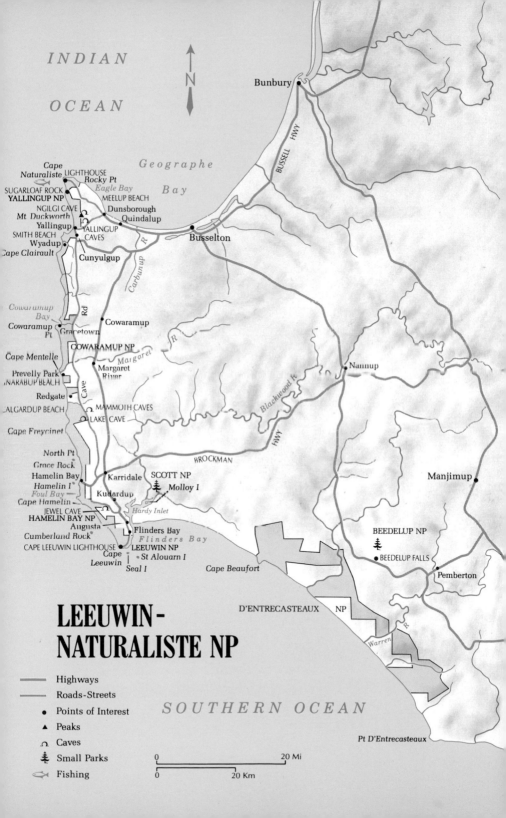

INDIAN

OCEAN

Bunbury

Geographe

Bay

Cape
Naturaliste LIGHTHOUSE
Rocky Pt
Eagle Bay
SUGARLOAF ROCK
YALLINGUP NP
MEELUP BEACH
NGILGI CAVE
Dunsborough
Mt Duckworth
Quindalup
Yallingup
YALLINGUP
CAVES
SMITH BEACH
Wyadup
Cape Clairault
Cunyulgup
Busselton

BUSSELL HWY

Carbunup R

Cowaramup
Bay
Cowaramup
Pt
Gracetown
Cowaramup
Rd
COWARAMUP NP
Margaret
Cape Mentelle
Margaret
River
Prevelly Park
INARABUP BEACH
Cave
Redgate
MAMMOTH CAVES
ALGARDUP BEACH
LAKE CAVE

Nannup

Blackwood R

Cape Freycinet

North Pt
Grace Rock
Hamelin Bay
Hamelin I
Foul Bay
Cape Hamelin
JEWEL CAVE
HAMELIN BAY NP
Augusta
Cumberland Rock
CAPE LEEUWIN LIGHTHOUSE
Cape
Leeuwin
Seal I

Karridale
SCOTT NP
Molloy I
Kudardup
Hardy Inlet

Flinders Bay
LEEUWIN NP
St Alouarn I
Flinders Bay

Cape Beaufort

BROCKMAN

HWY

Manjimup

BEEDELUP NP

BEEDELUP FALLS

Pemberton

D'ENTRECASTEAUX NP

Warren R

LEEUWIN-
NATURALISTE NP

— Highways
— Roads-Streets
• Points of Interest
▲ Peaks
∩ Caves
🌲 Small Parks
🐟 Fishing

SOUTHERN OCEAN

Pt D'Entrecasteaux

0   20 Mi
0   20 Km

WALPOLE-NORNALUP NATIONAL PARK

Walpole-Nornalup National Park, P.O. Box 17, Walpole, WA 6398, or call (098) 40 1026 or 40 1066. There is camping at Coalmine Beach and in several other areas around the park. Some of these areas also have hotel and motel accommodations.

Situated on the Southern Ocean and the Nornalup Inlet, 74 mi/ 120 km west of Albany, Walpole-Nornalup National Park combines a sandy coastal environment with a rugged wilderness area. Visitors who prefer long stretches of beach, quiet inlets, and peaceful bays and coves will enjoy spending hours exploring the heath-covered dunes and sandy shores of this part of the park. The tranquil waters of the inlet are ideal for swimming, boating, and fishing. Cool breezes blow off the Southern Ocean on the southwestern section of the park, bringing refreshment even in the hottest months of the year.

Farther inland you will find Walpole-Nornalup's most famous feature—its awesome karri trees. A eucalypt that grows to heights over 300 ft/90 m, the karri is one of the world's tallest hardwood species. The trees grow best on sandy loam and thus thrive in the Walpole-Nornalup environment. Before the park was declared a reserve in 1910, many karri trees were felled by lumber companies. Today these giants, clad in smooth blue-gray bark, stand protected. Indeed, karri trees dominate sections of Walpole-Nornalup. Their trunks, which turn yellow after they shed their bark each year, seem to gleam in the forest, leading the eye upward to the deep blue skies above.

Even though there is sufficient rainfall, the area is susceptible to frequent bush fires. Unlike tropical rain forests, karri forests do not form closed canopies against the effects of lightning, wind, and sun. They depend on bush fires to regenerate. Only after a fire ravages the dense undergrowth can the karris' seedlings get their share of nutrients from the soil. With the coming of winter rains, the seedlings sprout high in their ashbeds.

Walpole-Nornalup is home to the tingle tree, the only eucalyptus tree with a widened, buttressed base. It is a hardy tree and usually survives the bush fires.

Karri trees, the towering eucalypts of southwest Australia, shade a springtime display of flowering wattles and other forest shrubs.

Extinct or endangered throughout much of the world, peregrine falcons flourish in the remote wilds of Australia.

Many parts of the park have been left as wilderness areas and are accessible only on foot. Nuyt's Wilderness is the most popular location for rugged bushwalkers. There are no campgrounds, picnic areas, or any other signs of civilization, and visitors can be assured of a true wilderness experience.

Two major rivers cross the park's boundaries – the Frankland and the Deep. The Frankland is strewn with large granite boulders, and the Deep often floods its banks. Both are easily maneuverable by boat, however, and many visitors enjoy exploring the park this way.

BUSHWALKING

Valley of the Giants. This short track features some of the park's towering tingle trees as well as many of the area's bright-blooming wildflowers, such as the white crowea. Only 1,312 ft/400 m long, the walk is located between the South Coast Highway and the Valley of the Giant Road.

Rockwood Trail. This 1-mi/1.6-km track is located near Mt. Frankland in the park's northern section. It takes hikers around the base of the mountain in an area of lush ferns and mosses. Rangers suggest that you combine this hike with the short climb up Mt. Frank-

The rocky shores and jutting granite headlands near Albany are treacherous to navigate and have been the cause of many shipwrecks.

land that starts from the picnic area and winds its way to the summit. The climb is strenuous, but it is less than a mile/1.6 km to the top, and the panorama of the surrounding landscape is superb.

Nuyt's Wilderness Walk. For more experienced bushwalkers, this 9-mi/14.4-km hike wends its way through the Nuyt's Wilderness area in the southwestern part of the park. Along the way walkers meet fine examples of the king karri tree and beautiful splashes of colorful wildflowers. The trail traverses many quiet beaches and hidden bays along the shores of the Southern Ocean.

STIRLING RANGE NATIONAL PARK

Stirling Range National Park, Amelup via Borden, WA 6338, or call (098) 27 9230 or 27 9218. Camping is permitted in the park.

Accommodations of every sort are also available at nearby communities, including Mt. Barker, Albany, Cranbrook, Gnowangerup, and Ongerup.

The Stirling Range dominates the otherwise flat farmland of the southwest. Its lofty peaks often are covered by mist-laden clouds that bathe a profusion of wildflowers and other vegetation. The peaks are composed of hard, metasedimentary rock that was under water 2,500 million years ago. The upper layers are made of quartzite and sandstone, while the plains are granitic. The range has the highest peaks in the southern half of the state—although Bluff Knoll, the highest in the range, is only 3,582 ft/1,092 m high. It still manages to support a wide range of vegetation usually found in much higher altitudes because of its cool and humid conditions, which are optimal for growth.

Some 273 mi/440 km from Perth, Stirling Range National Park is one of the best places on earth for viewing wildflowers. The area was declared a national reserve in the early 1900s and so escaped the farming and settlement that destroyed many of the other natural landscapes in the area. Vegetation has thrived here, and more than 500 species of plants have been discovered thus far.

There are no permanent water holes in the Stirling Range, but after the winter rains, many creeks flow and the park bursts forth in a blanket of brilliant hues. Visitors come from all over the world to experience the visual and aromatic grandeur of this natural garden.

Clockwise from top: wild daisies; pink orchids; spider orchid.

WILDLIFE

Visitors who come to the Stirling Range for the wildflowers are always pleasantly surprised by the area's wildlife. Birds are the most obvious and colorful of the inhabitants, and they enliven every patch of wildflowers. There are honey eaters busily drinking nectar and parrots and purple-crowned lorikeets flitting about in search of delicious seeds. Golden whistlers ring out their pleasure, and wrens delightedly flick their tails as they perch. Wedge-tailed eagles soar high above in search of prey.

Some of the range's larger species include gray kangaroos, brush wallabies, and emus. Numerous smaller inhabitants include honey and pygmy possums.

With so much vegetation, insects also proliferate. The thousands of industrious bees, spiders, and brilliantly colored butterflies seem to keep the flowers in constant quivering motion.

VEGETATION

In the arid period from December through May, the Stirling Range's rolling hills are sedate in browns, greens, and golds. After the winter rains of July and August, however, they become riotous in oranges, reds, blues, yellows, and spring greens. The floors of the eucalypt forests are strewn with low shrubs, and the mountainsides are largely covered with dense scrub. Heaths and woodlands fill the surrounding plains.

It would be difficult to describe every flower species represented here, but a few extraordinary plants deserve mention. Pink mountain bells, also called darwinias, are found in the Stirling Range and nowhere else in the world. Growing over 3 ft/1 m tall on the steep, rocky higher slopes of the eastern peaks, the plants have small clusters of six or seven flowers that hang like delicate churchbells. Red and green kangaroo paws grow in clumps on the flats. The prolific Drummond's wattle, 6.5 ft/2 m tall with yellow brush-like flowers, is a standout among the many wattle species in the range.

Other species endemic to the area are the Stirling Range smoke-bush with its fleshy blue fruit, the Stirling Range coneflower with

BANKSIAS
Banksia spp.

These colorful plants are found primarily in Western Australia, growing mainly in sandy soils. Of the seventy-one species, fifty-seven are found only in Western Australia. Hundreds of flowers are clustered together in impressive spikes, or "cones," up to 12 in/30 cm long. Banksia flowers are colored predominantly in shades of yellow, from a creamy color to a brownish gold. The darkest blooms are an orange- or red-brown.

Named after the famous botanist Sir Joseph Banks (1743–1820), banksias are trees or woody shrubs. They may reach heights of 66 ft/20 m or spread horizontally on the ground. Most species, however, are medium-sized erect shrubs, 33 to 45 ft/10 to 15 m tall.

---

its pink feathery leaves, the deep orange Stirling Range banksia, and the green-and-red Stirling Range bottlebrush.

Because of the altitude and the constant motion of the wind, many of the eucalypts, such as jarrahs, marris, and wandoos, are smaller here than they are in lower environments. Most of the vegetation consists of low-lying shrubs and small trees.

BUSHWALKING

A road traverses the entire park, with several parking areas along the way. There are a few trails leading from parking lots to several of the peaks.

The park's most popular hike is the ascent of its tallest peak, Bluff Knoll. This trip takes about three hours to complete and requires some rock climbing, especially near the mountaintop. The view from the summit is well worth the effort, taking in some of the area's richest farmland and other high points of the range.

CAPE LE GRAND NATIONAL PARK

Ranger-in-Charge, Cape Le Grand National Park, P.O. Box 706, Esperance, WA 6450, or call (090) 75 9022.

The park is 20 mi/32 km east of Esperance. Camping is permitted; fireplaces are provided.

Nestled on the south coast of Western Australia and bordering the Southern Ocean, Cape Le Grand is a relatively small park that is known primarily for its tranquility. It is the perfect park for those who want the serenity of small, isolated coves with sandy beaches and calm waters, ideal for fishing, swimming, and boating. Small granite hills dot the landscape of the park.

WILDLIFE AND VEGETATION

The park's flowers and vegetation are attractive to honey possums and honey eaters, which enjoy eating nectar from the banksias, and to native bees, which inhabit rock caves and overhands. Small families of rock wallabies find Cape Le Grand's granite hills an ideal habitat.

The tranquil waters of Thistle Cove, sheltered from the turbulent Southern Ocean, provide a calm space for swimming, sailing, or fishing.

The most prominent form of vegetation on the Cape Le Grand coast is mallee scrub, a combination of several eucalypt species that grow in relationship to one another. (Originally an Aboriginal word, *mallee* has been accepted into scientific usage.) The park is one of the few places in Australia where mallee can still be seen. Most of the park's vegetation is low-lying due to the constant winds from the Southern Ocean.

From September to February there are beautiful wildflower displays on the sandy heath. The ground-growing purple enamel orchids stretch themselves daintily. Large clusters of leschenaultia, a bushy prickly plant with bright red flowers, are a stunning accent in the hard white earth where they manage to thrive. The aromatic curry flower, with its red, white, and green leaves, and the white spider orchid, with its sharp-pointed leaves, also bloom here.

BUSHWALKING

Exploring any part of this park is rewarding, and several trails are marked throughout. Visitors particularly enjoy taking short walks through the sand plain heaths and hilly mallee scrublands, which offer beautiful views of the coast and the nearby Recherche Archipelago. Thistle Cove is one of the largest and most scenic coves.

For bushwalkers the best way to experience the park is a 9.3-mi/ 15-km trail that links Le Grand Beach to Rossiter Bay. The trail takes a full day to complete, and the western half is especially challenging.

A highlight of the park is the climb to Frenchman's Peak. Only 860 ft/262 m high, the nearly bare basaltic rock is easy to climb from the eastern side; the west presents more rugged going. From the top there are fine views of the Southern Ocean coastline and the bays and coves of the park.

NORTHERN TERRITORY

Uluru National Park

Rainbow Valley

*Ormiston Gorge
and Pound National Park*

Finke Gorge National Park

Kakadu National Park

Katherine Gorge National Park

Only after heavy rains can Rainbow Valley, 60 mi/98 km south of Alice Springs, burst with floral color.

The sandstone domes at Kings Canyon National Park, 200 mi/323 km southwest of Alice Springs, are constantly being reshaped by the wind. Vegetation is scattered throughout the moist crevices in the sandstone and along the mesa above.

THE NORTHERN TERRITORY contains some of the driest and the wettest landscapes Australia has to offer. Within its boundaries are two vastly different worlds that compete for the visitor's attention. At the heart of these worlds are Australia's two most famous national parks—Kakadu and Uluru—whose attractions include a rich Aboriginal history, magnificent landscapes, unusual geologic formations, and fascinating wildlife.

In many respects, the Northern Territory epitomizes the preconceived images of "outback." To some, the outback means miles of uncharted land: open, red-sand country inhabited only by wildlife. To others, the outback means swamps and lagoons, the domain of man-eating crocodiles. The Northern Territory fulfills both these images, with dry outback in the south and "swampy" outback in the north.

Australians refer to the area south of Katherine Gorge as the Red Centre and the area north as the Top End. Visitors to the Top End enter a subtropical landscape that is breathtakingly wild. Among its spectacular sights are Fogg Damm and Butterfly Gorge, both south of Darwin. Butterfly Gorge is famous for its huge array of butterfly species. At Fogg Damm in late winter, the air is thick and orange with the smoke of nearby bush fires; at sunrise, scattered flocks of ducks and geese lift into the sky. Within moments there bursts forth a chorus of avian voices as perhaps 80,000 birds fill the sky: magpie geese, plumed whistling ducks, pygmy geese, plovers, and an odd assortment of jabirus and brolgas.

The Red Centre, in sharp contrast, is sun-baked and dry for most of the year. Its wildlife and vegetation are well adapted to enduring prolonged periods of drought, as is evident in Kings Canyon National Park. Between Alice Springs and the border with South Australia, red sand, dry mulga scrub, and spinifex grass offer the only visual relief in an otherwise featureless landscape. Near Alice, the vermilion and cream cliffs of sandstone form a network of gorges and valleys in the uplifted countryside of the MacDonnell Ranges. The intimate gorges of Simpson and Ormiston offer refreshing relief from the desert sun and bushwalks of exceptional beauty.

ABORIGINAL HISTORY

To many, the Northern Territory immediately brings to mind Aborigines, the Dreamtime, and the droning baritone voice of the didjeridoo. The breadth of Aboriginal culture, both past and present, is represented here. From the far southern border come the Pitjantjatjara people, one of the few surviving desert-dwelling groups; Ayers Rock, near Uluru, is the ancient pilgrimage destination of the Loritdjas; and in the Top End live the famous Arnhem Landers and the Tiwi artisans of Bathurst and Melville islands.

The first people to wander this land of paperbarks, gum trees, crocodiles, and kangaroos arrived more than 30,000 years ago. All indications suggest that groups or clans of migrants made their way initially into the northern regions of Australia near Darwin, the Cobourg Peninsula, Bathurst Island, and Melville Island, and farther east into Arnhem Land, along the Gulf of Carpentaria. The ancestors of these people were most likely inhabitants of Indonesia, Timor, and Papua New Guinea. The exact migration routes taken by these early Australian nomads is unclear. It is thought that they first wandered throughout northern Australia and then radiated across the virgin Australian continent.

In the wake of their travels, the Aborigines left their legacy in stone. Engravings on cave walls have been dated to nearly 20,000 years ago, placing them among the oldest such marks known. Also common are rock paintings crafted by Aboriginal artists over the past 20,000 years. The impression of walking into a gallery of rock paintings for the first time is unforgettable. Walls of dusty-red sandstone arch from the fine powder of the earth at your feet to perhaps 20 or 30 ft/6 or 9 m above your head. Covered in layer after layer of ocher and charcoal and rich brick red, the walls seem covered with a chaotic mixture of lines, shapes, and textures. Then the picture resolves and one can see the paintings: stick-like figures of human form, the faded outline of a child's hand, and dozens of animals – kangaroos, turtles, fishes – become clear.

Little is known of the history, origins, and purpose of rock painting. Much of the art was done in response to the images of dreaming, of being in touch with the Dreamtime – the creation of the world. The paintings provide a wealth of information about seasons, hunting methods, weapons, and the chronology of historical events. Illustrations on the walls at Obiri Rock, called Ubirr by the Aborigines, detail a square-rigged sailing vessel, a European man smoking a pipe, and rifles.

Rock paintings contain some curious and fascinating bits of information about the past wildlife of the area. For the most part, kangaroos, wallabies, and some odd aquatic creatures decorate the walls but there are also occasional drawings of extinct animals. Archaeologists have been able to identify Tasmanian tigers (thylacines), numbats, and long-beaked echidnas (extinct in Australia for at least 18,000 years) in many paintings.

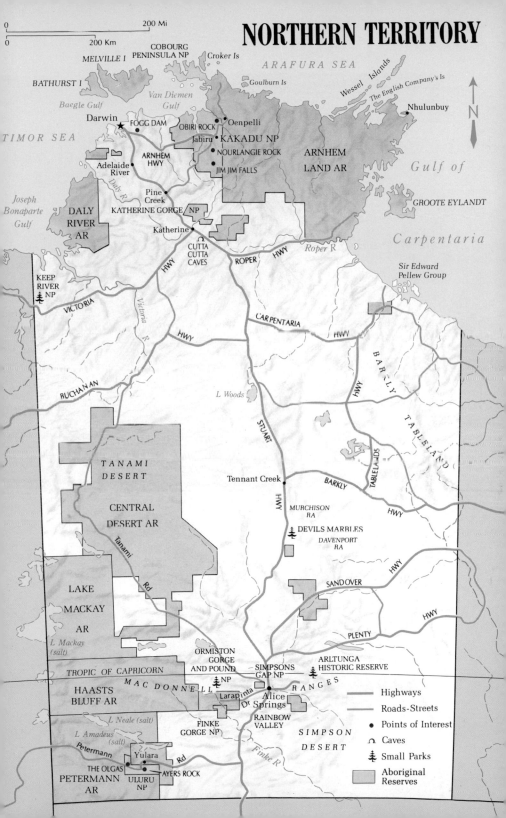

NORTHERN TERRITORY

0   200 Mi
0   200 Km

ARAFURA SEA

COBOURG
PENINSULA NP
Croker Is
MELVILLE I
BATHURST I
Goulburn Is
Wessel Islands
The English Company's Is
Nhulunbuy

Van Diemen
Gulf
Baegle Gulf

Darwin
FOGG DAM
OBIRI ROCK
Oenpelli
Jabiru
KAKADU NP
ARNHEM
LAND AR
Gulf of

TIMOR SEA
ARNHEM
HWY
NOURLANGIE ROCK
JIM JIM FALLS
Adelaide
River
Daly R.

GROOTE EYLANDT

Joseph
Bonaparte
Gulf
DALY
RIVER
AR
Pine
Creek
KATHERINE GORGE NP
Katherine
Roper R.
Carpentaria

KEEP
RIVER
NP
CUTTA
CUTTA
CAVES
ROPER
HWY
Sir Edward
Pellew Group

VICTORIA
Victoria R.
HWY
CARPENTARIA
HWY

BARKLY
TABLELAND
BUCHANAN
L Woods
STUART
TABLELANDS

TANAMI
DESERT
Tennant Creek
BARKLY
HWY
HWY

CENTRAL
DESERT AR
MURCHISON
RA
DEVILS MARBLES
DAVENPORT
RA
Tanami
Rd
HWY
LAKE
MACKAY
AR
SANDOVER
L Mackay
(salt)
HWY
PLENTY
TROPIC OF CAPRICORN
ORMISTON
GORGE
AND POUND
NP
ARLTUNGA
HISTORIC RESERVE
MAC DONNELL RANGES
HAASTS
BLUFF AR
Larapinta
Dr
SIMPSONS
GAP NP
Alice
Springs
L Neale (salt)
FINKE
GORGE NP
RAINBOW
VALLEY
SIMPSON
DESERT
L Amadeus
(salt)
Petermann
Finke R.
Yulara
Rd
THE OLGAS
PETERMANN
AR
ULURU
NP
AYERS ROCK

Highways
Roads-Streets
● Points of Interest
∩ Caves
🌲 Small Parks
Aboriginal
Reserves

ULURU NATIONAL PARK

Uluru National Park, c/o Northern Territory Conservation Commission. Gap Road, Alice Springs, NT 5750, or call (089) 50 8211.

Ayers Rock is a five-hour drive from Alice Springs. The park is reached by leaving the Stuart Highway, which connects Alice Springs and Adelaide, to travel west along the Petermann road. There also are daily bus services and flights both to and from Alice Springs, and an airstrip operates near the park in conjunction with the village of Yulara.

There are all forms of accommodation at Alice Springs, as well as deluxe hotels, a budget motel, and a campground at Yulara, just 20 mi/ 32 km from the Rock.

Although climbing Ayers Rock is the main attraction, park rangers also offer guided tours that point out the historical significance of the region and introduce visitors to Aboriginal rock art.

Feldspar, a mineral present in Ayers Rock, is responsible for the rock's reddish glow at sunset.

Like the arching back of a great sleeping giant, Ayers Rock rises from the surrounding red-sand desert, mulga scrub, and golden spinifex. To the west, the squat domes of the Olgas keep the dozing leviathan company. Together with the surrounding desert, Ayers Rock and the Olgas make up Uluru National Park.

Ayers Rock is the largest isolated rock in the world: it swells 2,845 ft/867 m above the adjacent plains, is 6 mi/8 km in circumference, and occupies nearly 1,000 acres/400 hectares of Uluru National Park. The Rock, as the giant sandstone mound is most commonly called, has become the most famous physical terrestrial feature in

Top: Dingoes are the most dangerous predators in Australia. Bottom: The sand goanna's markings vary greatly, depending on the region it inhabits.

Australia. Travel brochures, souvenirs, and shop windows from Sydney to Perth encourage foreign tourists and "Aussies" alike to visit the Rock. From its discovery by Ernest Giles and William Christie Gosse in 1872 until the present, the Rock has cast a spell on all who see it.

After Giles and Gosse discovered what the Aboriginal people of the desert had revered for centuries, their journal entries could barely contain their excitement: "more ancient and sublime," "marvelous in extreme." What seems curious to present-day visitors is that these accolades were not prompted for the most part by what Gosse described as the "immense pebble"–Ayers Rock–but by the thirty-six domes of the nearby Olgas.

The Olgas bubble up 14 mi/32 km to the west of Ayers Rock. Most visitors are content to view them from the vantage point of the Rock. Those who venture to investigate the Olgas close up should be sure to wander through the Valley of the Winds and explore the secluded ravines. The experience will leave an indelible impression.

Ayers Rock and the Olgas remained virtually unknown to outsiders for many years after their discovery by Giles and Gosse. But now, more people climb the sloping face of Ayers Rock each morning than trekked cross country to visit the entire area during the seventy-five years following Giles and Gosse's exploration.

In 1958, the beauty of these stone monoliths inspired the creation of Ayers Rock and Mount Olga National Park. More than pure geologic aesthetics were at issue in establishing the park. For many centuries, the Loritdja people of the desert had journeyed here to seek food and water in the surrounding area and to find shelter in the rock's caves; the caves were spiritually important to the Loritdja as well. Recognizing that the area played a "supremely important role in the lives of Aborigines," the Parks Service changed the name to Uluru National Park in order to acknowledge its Aboriginal background. Uluru is now cooperatively managed by the national government and the Aborigines.

The shambles of tiny huts and sheds that was the old "village" has been removed from near the base of Ayers Rock. The government of the Northern Territory has built the hotel-resort and camping facilities of the modern village of Yulara outside the park boundary, restoring the isolated beauty of these domes to much the same condition in which the Aborigines were wont to leave them.

Rock Paintings

It is virtually impossible to leave Uluru National Park without some sense of the Aborigines' reverence for these rocks. The Aboriginal association dates back several centuries, but it is difficult to determine exactly when it began.

Of the numerous Aboriginal groups said to have ties to the area, the Loritdja people enjoy the closest bond. From the Loritdja comes one of the best interpretations for the origin of the word *Uluru*. Their word for "fluted" or "forehead" is *Luru*. Loritdja refer to the *Luru* when describing the parallel gutters on the west wall of Ayers Rock. Another possible explanation is that the word *Uluru* was derived from a term meaning "place of shade," probably referring to the numerous caves and sun shelters that Ayers Rock offers near its base. Uluru would have had great importance because it provides the only shade for several dozen miles in any direction.

In Aboriginal mythology, every tree, rock outcrop, and water hole in the area is evidence of the conflict that took place during the *Tjukurpa*, or time of creation. Mythology illustrated at the painting sites usually centers on the titanic struggle among the three ancestors: Kunia, the carpet snake; Liru, the poisonous snake; and Wanambi, the serpent. It is believed, for example, that the pitted spot where most people begin the climb of Ayers Rock shows the markings made by Liru's spears during a struggle.

The rounded minarets of the Olgas were also sacred to the local Aborigines, who called them the Katatjuta, meaning "many heads." One legend tells about the creation of the domes encircling the Valley of the Winds. In it, the Mingarri, virgin mice-women, had come to the area to camp. Unfortunately, they were discovered by Pungulung, a woman-chasing giant, and his companion, Mudjura, the red lizard of the sand hills. Pungulung and Mudjura attacked the Mingarri, who turned into dingoes and counterattacked. Pungulung put Mudjura on his back and used him as a shield until Mudjura tired, got off Pungulung's back, and turned to stone. Pungulung then defended himself with his boomerang and managed to knock out the dingoes' teeth. When Pungulung tired, he turned to stone; the Mingarri eventually turned to stone as well. The shiny pieces of quartz found in the Olgas are said to be the dingoes' teeth.

Aboriginal art in the park appears in three distinct forms: sacred objects (spears, clubs, and other weapons), rock engravings, and paintings or cave art. Relatively little of this rich artistic history remains. Sacred objects have all been removed to the ownership of the original Aboriginal tribes of the area or have been acquired by private collectors. Years of weathering have taken their toll on rock engravings; the few remaining sites are now off limits to the general public. At Ayers Rock, as throughout much of the desert, art is scattered and is not as apparent as the art of western Arnhem Land. For the visitor, rock paintings are the best preserved and most easily accessible of the three art forms.

The most prominent painting at the Rock is at Maggie Springs. It depicts the story of Wanambi, the serpent, who lives in the springs. Related to all forms of water, Wanambi can, if necessary, be summoned to bring rains to fill the drying water holes. After the rainfall, Wanambi rises skyward as a rainbow before returning to his home in the water.

"The Blue Paintings" at Little Nourlangie in Kakadu, which may be more than 30,000 years old, exemplify the x-ray style of Aboriginal art.

The thirty-six domes of the Olgas are only 20 mi/32 km away from Ayers Rock.

GEOLOGY

Ayers Rock is like a terrestrial iceberg, showing only a fraction of its buried sandstone mass. Some geologists estimate that the Rock may extend more than 10,000 ft/3,000 m below the earth's surface. They believe that the monolith was originally part of a huge bed of sediment laid down on the floor of an inland sea more than 500 million years ago. As the eons passed, the harder portions of the sediment fused, and then, during the northward movement of the Indo-Australian plate, the fused sediments were tipped on end, exposing this giant rock mass. The Olgas were shaped in a similar fashion, although Mount Olga, at 1,700 ft/510 m, is nearly 600 ft/180 m higher than Ayers Rock.

The exterior of Ayers Rock is pockmarked with caves, ridges, crevices, and ravines. The top is flat but contains deep gouges created by the action of wind and rain over thousands of years as well

"The Brain" is one of many geologic sites at Ayers Rock that are sacred to the local Piljantjatjara people.

as by temperature changes between the intense heat of day and the cold of night. Fluctuations in temperature also play a major role in the cracking and splitting of the giant domes.

Ayers Rock and the Olgas are geologically very different from each other, not only in shape, but also in composition and texture. The Olgas are an amalgam of small stones, large boulders, and a cemented filling of fine sand grains. In contrast, Ayers Rock appears smooth. Its sandstone is worn down at an imperceptibly slow rate, wind and rainwater being the master sculptors.

Some believe that the setting sun makes Ayers Rock shine red, but the color of the Rock is a result of the geology of the monolith. It is composed primarily of arkose sandstone, which is rich in feldspar, a grayish mineral in its pure state. When feldspar is exposed to the air, it oxidizes and turns reddish brown. As the sun sets over Ayers Rock, this rust color becomes more apparent.

THORNY DEVIL
Moloch horridus

The thorny devil's frightening name and forbidding appearance are in sharp contrast to the generally timid nature of this slow-moving lizard, which is dangerous only to the black ants it eats. Reaching an average length of 6 in/152 mm, it is covered with spines growing from conical mounds on its body, which effectively discourage predators. It earned its "devilish" name from the horn-like spines that grow over its eyes.

Found in the deserts of central Australia and the drier regions of Western and South Australia, it is most active in the daytime (except in the extreme heat) and spends its evenings in burrows or hiding under shrubs.

Its patterned body is an excellent camouflage that can change color as the temperature varies, becoming darker in cooler weather and brighter in warmer weather. Its skin has the ability to channel moisture by capillary action to its mouth, enabling it to utilize even droplets of dew for survival.

VEGETATION

Plants living anywhere in the Red Centre face a desperate struggle for survival. Very little rain falls in this region. The plants that grow in Uluru National Park have features, such as airtight leathery shells, that help them survive long periods of drought. Every seven to ten years, usually during the early winter, the desert is soaked by heavy rains that last for several days. Only after these shells become thoroughly waterlogged by the standing rainwaters do the seeds begin to germinate. Flowers breach the soil and stretch skyward from every square inch of earth. Rock crevices, notches on dead stumps of river gums, gutters, and dirt ruts are ablaze with the whites, yellows, and reds of desert daisies and cassias and the golden yellow of the usually pale mulga. This floral spectacle is rivaled in few other places on earth.

The casuarina, or desert oak, and the desert poplar are two of the few tall plants that decorate the landscape in times of little rain.

At the heart of Kings Canyon National Park are massive sandstone cliffs that have been deeply etched by the periodic flooding of the Kings Creek.

They tend to spring up close to shade or permanent moisture, finding water even if it lies deep within the earth. The long root systems of both these species are the key to their survival. Using a similar strategy for obtaining water in times of prolonged drought are the Sturt's desert rose and the native hibiscus, the state flower of the Northern Territory.

RAINBOW VALLEY

Rainbow Valley, c/o Northern Territory Conservation Commission, Gap Road, Alice Springs, 5750 NT, or call (089) 50 8211.
The valley is about 40 mi/65 km south of Alice Springs between the Stuart Highway and Tarcoola Railway, near the James Ranges. Access to the area is by four-wheel-drive vehicle only.

The main attraction of Rainbow Valley is the Hermannsburg sandstone formation. The towering rock wall is a dramatic backdrop for a usually parched red claypan that rarely–perhaps once every seven years–fills with water. Spinifex grass and spreading desert oaks grow in the surrounding sandy plain which, after the rains of August and September, becomes a sea of yellow, then purple, wildflowers.

The valley is a natural showplace of rock ferrugination, a phenomenon common in Central Australia. Millions of years ago, rainwater and underground water movement leached iron oxide from deep in the rock, coloring the upper areas red and hardening them. Meanwhile, the same water action bleached the lower rock. The result is the contrast between brick-red and cream, which can be seen most clearly in late afternoon when the sun's rays shine directly on the rocks. Because the lower parts of the stone are not ferruginated, they erode more quickly than the upper rock and good examples of honeycomb weathering can be found here. Rare ripple-marked sandstone exists in the rock as well.

Petroglyphs and rock paintings are in gullies surrounding the valley, and much of the area is important in the active traditions of the local Southern Aranda (Arrente) people. One of the rocks, called Ewerre, in the southern area is a registered sacred site. A scattering of large black rocks below the northern cliff is also significant.

Pages 258 and 259: Rainbow Valley's main attraction is its two-tone sandstone cliff formation.

ORMISTON GORGE AND
POUND NATIONAL PARK

Ormiston Gorge National Park, Northern Territory Conservation Commission, Gap Road, Alice Springs, NT 5750, or call (089) 50 8211.

There is a designated camping area inside the park entrance. There are no fees, but visitors are required to camp in pre-existing sites only. Showers, lavatories, and firewood are provided. About 2.5 mi/4 km beyond the Ormiston turnoff along the main road from Alice Springs is a lodge where cabin accommodation is available.

Rising east and west of Alice Springs are the MacDonnell Ranges, one of the largest mountain systems in Australia. Surrounded by desert—a sandy expanse studded with spinifex tussocks and the hardy mulga bush—the eroded escarpments, gorges, and tilted mountains of the MacDonnell Ranges offer a spectrum of inviting wilderness areas.

Where creeks and rivers have carved a passage through the uplifted earth, a number of steep-walled gorges and gaps have been formed. Of these, Ormiston Gorge, the heart of Ormiston Gorge and Pound National Park, is the most striking example of nature's sculptural ability.

Seen from above, the Ormiston landscape looks inhospitable to all but the most perfectly adapted desert creatures. Earth rifts, rich in mineral-saturated quartzite, run in parallel ridges far toward the distant horizon. In the center of the 10,120-acre/4,600-hectare park, the dry bed of Ormiston Creek snakes its way between the ridges.

Ormiston Creek maintains water in only a few scattered pools. About halfway through the gorge there is a water hole measuring 300 ft/90 m long and up to 40 ft/12 m deep. Even during the hottest summers, this pool remains cool and refreshing.

There is an Aboriginal legend about this deep, permanent source of fresh water—indeed, most major water holes in the dry northern regions of Australia have a legendary past. In this case, the local Aranda (or Arrente) Aborigines told of a gigantic serpent, or watersnake, that inhabited the water hole. The practical effect of this legend was to prevent swimmers from polluting this precious source of fresh water.

Ormiston Gorge and Pound National Park is an easy one-day trip from Alice Springs. The road to the park, paved for 82 mi/132 km, passes several lesser gorges, including Simpson Gap, Ellery Creek, and Serpentine Gorge.

Where the road enters the park, red river gums line the dry bed of Ormiston Creek. During the late evening and early morning dozens of birds, including the beautiful spinifex pigeon, can be spotted. The abundance of vegetation and wildlife in the gorge creates an oasis-like atmosphere, but away from the creek and gorge, the landscape quickly resumes the parched appearance typical of central Australia.

Deep inside the heart of Ormiston Gorge, as you travel north up the creekbed, a deep overhang prevents the western wall from receiving direct sunlight for most of the day. An assortment of shade-preferring ferns and mosses flourishes there, fed by water seeping out of the rock. Among these plants are some rare varieties that have survived for thousands of years, descendants of plants that thrived here when the region was green and tropical.

Beyond the gorge the dry Ormiston Creek opens into Ormiston Pound, the creekbed winding across the pound floor for nearly 6 mi/ 10 km. The pound walls encircle the area, culminating on the eastern wall in the summit of Mt. Giles (1,283 ft/4,210 m). Walking through the pound when the angular light of evening or morning is reflected in the scattered water holes is a prized experience for visitors to the MacDonnell Ranges.

WILDLIFE

Ormiston Gorge offers a rare opportunity to observe dozens of creatures who make their home in the arid landscape of central Australia. Because of their long association with humans, especially in the park setting, many of the animals have become accustomed to the activity of people and tolerate their approach, in some cases to within a few feet.

Butterfly Gorge National Park, 133 mi/214 km south of Darwin, is a small 257 acre/ 104 hectare park, which was named for the hordes of butterflies that sometimes gather here. It also has fine swimming areas.

SPINIFEX GRASS
Triodia and *Plectrachne*

Hummocks of spinifex grasses comprise the majority of the vegetation of arid inland Australia. These are among the hardiest grasses in the world, and in the hot, dry Australian desertlands, the needle-like spinifex leaves provide home, shade, and nourishment to many creatures. Aborigines used to grind spinifex seeds into flour.

Spinifex grows in circular clumps up to 20 ft/6 m in diameter. The well-known rings form through the death of the older, central part of the plant, and regeneration from the stems takes place on the periphery, leading to successive annual enlargements of the ring.

During times of extreme drought, growth is extremely slow. After summer or fall rains, growth speeds up and the spinifex produces flowers.

The spinifex pigeon, a small ground bird, is among the most beautiful of the many birds in the gorge. During August and September, the male and female pigeons strut about the campground, displaying their fine red-clay-colored plumage.

The walks along the small water holes in Ormiston Creek are excellent places for observing the common as well as the rarer birds of the park. Early morning draws flocks of exquisitely marked painted firetail finches and lime-green budgerigars. Also called parakeets, the budgerigars are the wild stock from which the well known household pets were derived.

The Ormiston Gorge area supports an interesting array of non-native wildlife. Feral animals—cats, dogs, horses, donkeys, and even camels—roam much of the area. While these animals, the wild descendants of domesticated and agricultural types, are curiosities for the visitor, they are a serious problem for the park management, causing widespread destruction of native plants and animals. Feral cats, in particular, destroy large numbers of reptiles and small birds.

SPINIFEX PIGEON
Petrophassa plumifera

Superbly adapted to life in the dry desert, the spinifex pigeon is usually spotted darting in and out of spinifex grass and nearby rocks in the desert. Existing on the seeds of available plants and on the flowers of the spinifex, the pigeons must also have access to water or they die.

With a remarkably low metabolic rate, the pigeons need little energy to survive. They roost in close-knit groups to preserve heat on cold desert nights. Most of their time is spent walking on the ground, but they have the ability to fly great distances when in search of water.

When male spinifex pigeons compete, they perform a bowing display, lowering their heads and bodies and attacking each other with their wings. They usually breed during rainy seasons, when food and water are most plentiful.

FINKE GORGE NATIONAL PARK

Northern Territory Conservation Commission, Gap Road, Alice Springs, NT 5750, or call (089) 50 8211.

Traversing the route to Finke Gorge National Park is perhaps as much an adventure as actually discovering the gorge. A four-wheel-drive vehicle is the only possible mode of transport, and even under the most favorable conditions, the going is slow along the dry river-bed. Here the traveler enters a genuine outback wilderness.

The red sandstone gorge was carved over time by the Finke River as torrents of floodwater poured down off the plateaus and through the narrow slots and gorges. Today the scene is much quieter; except during floodtime, the Finke River is a series of water holes with giant river red gums arching out from the dry banks. Where there is water, the birds of the gorge congregate in abundance to drink and bathe.

Travelers who make the journey up the Finke River are justly rewarded, for at the heart of this 101,200-acre/46,000-hectare national park is an oasis called Palm Valley. One of Australia's most unusual environments, the area is named for the tall palms and similar-looking but much shorter cycads that line the narrow water holes.

Palm Valley is an environmental relic. Eons ago, the entire region of the western MacDonnells was submerged beneath a shallow tropical sea. Where the land was exposed, it was much like present-day tropical Queensland—moist and fertile with a warm, stable climate. Seas receded and sediments were uplifted and tilted to form the MacDonnell Ranges. Trapped in the geologic upheaval were several species of cycad, plants even older than the palm family, and a species of cabbage-tree palm called *Livistona mariae*.

Palm Valley now hosts hundreds of cycads and nearly 3,000 of the unique *Livistona*. The trees are botanical survivors of an ancient era, and grow nowhere else in the world. In a sense Palm Valley is a journey back in time. Its magical quality is matched by few other places in the outback of Australia.

The red kangaroo is one of the largest marsupials in the world, reaching 4.5 ft/1.5 m tall. Though called "red," most females and some males are blue-gray; females are sometimes called blue fliers.

KAKADU NATIONAL PARK

Kakadu National Park, Box 71,
Jabiru, NT 5796, or call (089) 79 2101

South of Darwin on the Stuart Highway, the Arnhem Highway turns off abruptly to the left. Screaming lorikeets dart across the sky, and as one travels east, the eucalyptus trees thicken along the narrow stretch of road.

Far to the north, plumes of gray-black smoke spiral above the tree line—another bush fire revitalizing the bush. During the dry season, from April/May to October, a dozen fires may belch forth smoke and cinders as they race through the bush in a torrent of heat and flames. The very survival of the land depends on these fires; if they fail to ignite on their own, either from lightning strikes or from embers blown from nearby fires, rangers must play the starter's role. Without the fires, the dry low-lying grass and scrub would grow too high and dense and thus pose the hazard of all-consuming fire to the forests. Trees that have evolved fairly thick disposable bark survive the small fires unscathed, but they would not be able to tolerate the longer and hotter fire of a major burn.

Only two hours after leaving the Stuart Highway, the road enters Kakadu National Park, which UNESCO called one of the world's last great natural reserves in 1981. It was declared a World Heritage Site, to be preserved for all humankind because of its profusion of wildlife and vegetation and because it has the richest known treasure of Aboriginal artwork.

Kakadu only recently opened its doors to the outside world. For centuries, the secrets hidden here were the private possession of the western Arnhem Landers, the Aboriginal peoples of the low marsh and escarpment country. Under the provisions of the Aboriginal Land Rights Act of 1976, ownership of Kakadu National Park was granted to the traditional occupiers of the area—the Aborigines. The Aboriginal owners then leased the land to the government of Australia for use as a national park.

In the past century, the trail carved out by early outback explorers and anthropologists was widened to allow entry to pastoralists, buffalo shooters, poachers, and missionaries. Recently, the trail has

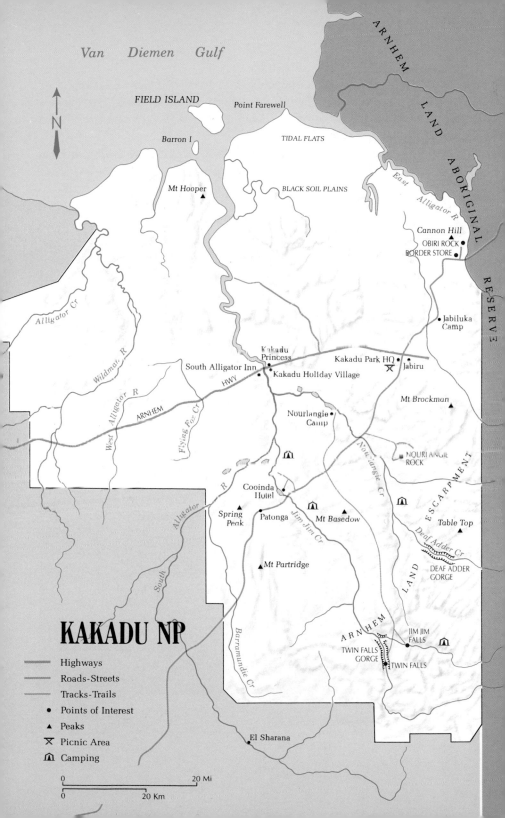

become a bitumened two-lane flow of tourists. With the completion by 1990 of the Kakadu Highway south to Pine Creek, the greater accessibility of Kakadu will bring a flood of the curious to the land of man-eating crocodiles.

The majority of the 12,500 sq mi/20,000 sq km of Kakadu National Park spread out across a maze of marshes and lily-matted backwaters and a series of twisted creeks and waterways that lead into the East and South Alligator rivers. Water, in all seasons, is the lifeblood of this land. By late September and October, it will have been months since the last rainfall. Every creature tries to make its way to the permanent water sites.

Late April through October/November, the dry season, is the best time to witness the spectacle of Kakadu. Ponds and water holes have dried, forcing most of the wildlife of the park to share a few narrow waterways. The visitor is thus offered an excellent opportunity to view many wildlife species at close range. Yellow Waters

Periodic small fires in the area help to keep the understory short, preventing later fires from doing more severe damage.

Campground, at the heart of the park, has become a mecca for naturalists and bird watchers during the dry season because it is one of the few areas that maintain an actively flowing water supply even in the driest conditions.

During the build-up to the wet season, high humidity and temperature stretch the tolerance of every creature in the park. Even the normally composed nankeen night herons feel the pressure, restlessly snapping at buzzing insects. Finally, at year's end, the tension breaks as the overcast sky opens and releases its moisture on the flat plains of western Arnhem Land. Water spills over banks and saturates the thirsty earth.

Despite the weather's torment, this is the time when the park truly opens its soul and bares its treasures. In the backwaters of the South Alligator River, trees are alive with nesting egrets, herons, and cormorants. The falls of Jim Jim Creek swell and thunder as water plummets 120 ft/36 m into the emerald pools below.

Over thirty species of freshwater fish have been found in the creeks and floodplains of Kakadu, including the popular barramundi.

Rock Paintings

The listing of Kakadu National Park as a World Heritage Site was a recognition of the importance of the rock art of western Arnhem Land. Kakadu has some of the most magnificent galleries of this kind in the world. Of these, only a few are accessible to the public: Obiri Rock (Ubirr), Nourlangie Rock, and Cannon Hill area.

Figures and images of the rock art can be grouped into two major styles: Mimi and x-ray. Both styles were executed simultaneously for about 2,000 years, and layers of images sometimes render even the simplest figures indiscernible.

Of the two styles, Mimi is the older. Mimi art generally depicts spirit creatures in the shape of humans. Paintings are often small, thin-lined, and painted in red ocher. Aboriginal tradition has it that the Mimi figures were painted by the Mimi spirits themselves. They were light, delicate creatures who were believed to inhabit the crevices of the western Arnhem Land Escarpment.

Mimi figures most often appear in composed scenes. Groups are

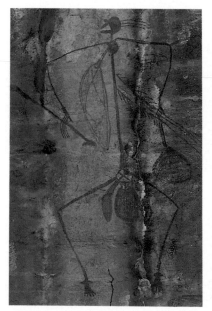

Clockwise from left: Mimi art near Obiri Rock (Ubirr); x-ray art in the main gallery at Nourlangie; turtle depicted in the x-ray style.

depicted acting out rituals, making love, hunting, or battling fiercely. At Obiri Rock (Ubirr), 35 mi/56 km north of Jim Jim on the road to Oenpelli, a spectacular frieze of running Mimi figures armed with spears and goose-wing fans and adorned with assorted body ornaments enlivens the wall opposite the main gallery.

Mimi art was executed during the pre-estuarine period, dated at 7,000 to 20,000 years ago. Freshwater systems had not yet developed throughout the escarpment country of Arnhem Land. The significance of this environmental demarcation point is the sudden disappearance of some animals from the paintings, possibly because of their extinction, and a major shift in rock-painting style.

X-ray art is a generic category that encompasses almost all the rock-art styles rendered in Arnhem Land between about 7,000 to 9,000 years ago and the present. As the name suggests, x-ray art depicts internal features of the subject. The art of rock painting appears to have blossomed under this new style of expression. Nourlangie Rock, halfway between Jim Jim and Yellow Waters on the park's central highway, is the most brilliant display of x-ray art known in Australia. Here the x-ray artists used a wide range of colors to illustrate the wildlife of the area. Because the style paralleled the emergence of freshwater sources, and as a consequence, renderings of giant perch dominate many friezes. Much of the fishes' anatomy is revealed in great detail, including backbone and intestines.

On the wall at Nourlangie are male and female figures in the company of ancestral heroes painted in many colors. The scene represents the birth of the tribe. A white figure in the upper right-hand corner is that of Namarrkon, the lightning man, feared by Aboriginal people of the area for his power and violence.

Many have compared the Arnhem Land galleries with the cave art in France and Spain. But the Australian artwork varies greatly in detail and technique from the European. One major difference is that the rock art of Arnhem Land was kept alive into modern times by the Aborigines. Until only a few decades ago, Aborigines used to repaint the art, helping it to withstand the effects of wind, rain, and time and physically renewing their ancestral ties to the Dreamtime. Although the art is rarely retouched at present, the sites are of continuing significance to the living religion of the Aboriginal people.

WILDLIFE

For many tourists visiting Kakadu National Park, there is only one animal to see—the creature that many believe to be the Lord of Kakadu, the saltwater crocodile. "Scaled death," the "devil's lizard," or the "man-eater," the saltwater crocodile has become at Kakadu what sharks are at the Barrier Reef. Despite the danger, all who visit the park want to see this fearsome creature close up.

Kakadu is perhaps Australia's premier bird sanctuary. Its varied and readily accessible habitats afford the bird watcher an easy opportunity to view over seventy species in a day. Indeed, more than one-third of all the avian species recorded in Australia have been sighted in the park.

The best way to enjoy the wildlife of Kakadu is by boat. Gliding through the maze of paperbark-lined channels in a motorized punt, one enters a world far removed from that of the public campgrounds. Among the tangled lilies and mangroves, lotus birds, with their gypsy-like existence, wander about in search of small aquatic plants and insects. The prehistoric-looking saltwater crocodiles register the boats' passing, but they seem undisturbed, their eyes mere slits viewing the human intruders. Visitors should not be fooled, how-

A blue-winged kookaburra in Kakadu National Park. Kookaburras are known for their raucous calls.

SALTWATER CROCODILE
Crocodylus porosus

There are many stories of saltwater, or estuarine, crocodiles growing as long as 20 ft/6 m, being able to catch birds in flight, and stalking humans Indeed, they are one of the few animals that will deliberately hunt humans. They hide from their prey by floating submerged in the water, with only their nostrils, eyes, and a small strip of body showing.

Saltwater crocodiles live primarily in coastal rivers and swamps, but they are often found in fresh water and even in the open sea. Their main sources of food are crustaceans, fishes, small reptiles, birds, and mammals.

More than 1 million saltwater crocodiles once inhabited Australia, but human predation has greatly reduced this number. Protected since 1979, their population in the Northern Territory is estimated now at between 15,000 and 30,000.

---

ever. Those eyes notice every action and reaction in this watery world and are ever alert for opportunity.

Kakadu is also home to nearly fifty fish species, including the primitive archer fish, the rare Gilberts grunter, the sharp-nosed grunter, the saratoga, and the area's prime gamefish, the barramundi.

Some of Kakadu's wildlife is only found at the park's higher elevations. Among them are black wallaroos, rock wallabies, and the northern quoll, a carnivorous marsupial that looks like an opposum. A recently discovered member of the python family and the more familiar large gecko also live in these areas, as does an array of unusual bats, including the diadem horseshoe bat, the orange horseshoe bat, and the very rare lesser warty-nosed horseshoe bat.

BIRDS OF KAKADU

The behavior of Kakadu's birds is vastly different during the wet and dry seasons due to the varying availability of fresh water.

During the wet season, water holes fill to capacity, allowing the green pygmy geese to spread to the various swamps and ponds throughout the park. Here they find plenty of water lilies, supplying them with ample seeds and buds to live on.

The noisy magpie geese busily prepare their nests on floating platforms in the middle of the swamps. Herons and egrets stand by the shore of waterways with their wings spread, casting shadows on the water. The shadows attract fish seeking to "hide," and these become easy prey for the long-legged birds. Cormorants, which fish submerged, are seen on surrounding naked branches and stumps, drying their

outstretched wings in the warming sun.

By day the nankeen night herons roost high in the trees. At dusk, their loud croaks announce that it is their turn to forage along the shores of the waterways. They fish by vibrating their bills back and forth in the water to draw fish and small crustaceans within striking distance.

During the dry season, as water holes dry up, the birds must adjust their feeding and living habits. The green pygmy geese go in search of more permanent lagoons, where they flock by the hundreds. Plumed whistling ducks, more adept on land than on water, move to be within reach of water, even if it is just a small muddy pool. They must change their diet from the grasses, legumes, and herbs of the wet season to the more available sedges found near the lagoons.

As the swamps dry out, the young magpie goslings molt and their families move together in search of water. If they do not find it quickly, the young will die. The bulbs of spike-rushes, their dry-season diet, may not be enough to sustain life.

Wedge-tailed eagles appear at Kakadu more frequently during the dry season. With the tighter concentration of birds on the permanent water sources and the relative unavailability of kangaroos, wallabies, and rabbits, the eagles resort to preying on birds.

Plumed whistling ducks. Facing page: pied herons like to congregate near fishermen and visitors in anticipation of handouts. The birds are especially common at Yellow Waters.

VEGETATION

The vegetation of the plateau of the Arnhem Land Escarpment consists mainly of wiry grasses, spinifex, and large gum trees. Deep within the escarpment country are remnant patches of tropical rain forest. The low-lying areas to the west of the escarpment extend for several hundred miles. Open eucalypt forest and extensive scrub and grasslands are the principal vegetation south of the Arnhem Highway. North toward the Cobourg Peninsula, in deltas of the East and South Alligator rivers, lowland vegetation meets areas of the estuarine flood plains. There are pockets of coastal rain forest green with palms and broad-leafed species, in many places merging with thick mangrove forest.

Closer to the sea are true flood plains consisting principally of sedges and paperbark trees. The paperbark has long been a tree of prime importance to the Aboriginal tribes of western Arnhem Land; it was used for clothing and medicinal purposes and in rituals.

Near the sea, the flat, mud-choked banks of the East and South Alligator rivers become overgrown with bright-green thickets of estuarine mangroves. *Mangrove* is a generic term embracing a variety of trees and shrubs that have adapted to salt marshes and mud flats along the coast. Mangroves create an environment favorable to diverse and specialized forms of wildlife, from small fishes and crustaceans that lurk on the mud bottom to the animals that shelter in the canopies high above the tides.

Mangroves are a common feature of northern Kakadu. These trees, of the genus *Rhizophora*, are supported by stilt-like roots that arch from the main trunk and end in a cluster of smaller roots. These root systems provide shelter and nutrients to many tidal creatures. By trapping debris, seaweed, and sand, the roots also raise the level of the mud flats and thus contribute to the extension of the tidal lands. In effect, they stabilize the shoreline and provide an increased area for wildlife habitation.

Mangroves, through their ability to shed salt and take in air directly from the surrounding atmosphere, have adapted to an otherwise inhospitable marine environment. This is extremely important in northern Kakadu, where the unusually flat landscape is susceptible to flooding from high seas and coastal storms. Trees with less tolerance for high salt levels would die quickly in such an environment.

KATHERINE GORGE NATIONAL PARK

Katherine Gorge National Park, c/o
Northern Territory Conservation

Commission, Box 344, Katherine,
NT 5780, or call (089) 72 1866.

Katherine Gorge is a spectacular example of the erosive power of the water that sweeps through the Northern Territory during the wet season. During the dry months, the Katherine River runs peacefully through a series of long, deep pools before it reaches the township of Katherine. Surrounding the pools, cliff walls of iron-stained reddish cream sandstone soar 300 ft/90 m into the blue sky. Near the river level the sandstone is worn slick from centuries of scouring. Higher up on the walls, deep scars and gouges tell of the tremendous force exerted by the debris-laden flood waters.

One approaches the Katherine Gorge through a flat, monotonous landscape of mulga scrub and spinifex tussocks. There is no hint of the magnificent geologic formation that lies ahead, and first-time visitors are taken by surprise.

WILDLIFE

With its bountiful permanent water supply, Katherine Gorge is a huge natural oasis for the wildlife of the north-central Northern Territory. Salmon gums and pandanus trees at the campground and visitors' center teem with bird life. September through February, when the vast majority of the species are breeding and nesting, is prime bird-watching time. You may be able to spot as many as forty different species, including red-shouldered parrots, northern rosellas, rainbow bee eaters, and an assortment of wrens and fly-catchers in the dense undergrowth.

Two prominent birds live near the visitors' center. The first is the blue-face honeyeater. One of the largest of the honeyeater family, the blue-face has a brilliant sky-blue patch over each eye. This is the southernmost extent of its range in northern Australia. It can be found here feeding among the paperbark trees and flowering grevilleas, or peeling away loose bark in search of beetles, ants, and weevils.

The other is the emu. The emus of Katherine Gorge can be ardent beggars, soliciting all manner of edibles from picnic tables and campsites. If they are not given food, they will steal it, and these giant birds are capable of gulping down practically anything they can fit into their bills.

The park's mammals include euros, antelopine kangaroos, dingoes, and echidnas, but the most common by far are the agile wallabies. Just after dusk each evening these appealing animals invade the open paddock areas in the campground to feed on grasses. A bonus during October and November is the sight of the young joeys, just out of the pouch, bounding about with their mothers.

A trip up the gorge should provide a glimpse of one of the park's main wildlife attractions–Johnstone's freshwater crocodile. Typically nocturnal, freshies, as these reptiles are called, can often be seen basking in the sun along the mud and sandstone banks of the river.

Black-footed rock wallabies are common in the MacDonnell Ranges where the rocky outcrops are an ideal habitat.

BROLGA
Grus rubicundus

The brolga, or Australian crane, is one of the few Australian birds that have retained their Aboriginal names. Known for its graceful and elaborate dancing rituals, the brolga is the inspiration for the Aboriginal brolga corroboree, a dance where participants dress up and imitate brolga courtship displays.

During courtship, the cranes dance in groups of up to several hundred on grassy plains and swamp areas near lakes and streams. The dance has many movements: jumping, bowing, a steady fluttering and arching of wings, picking up twigs and flinging them into the air. Pairs join together with loud, bellowing calls.

Brolgas are found in northern and eastern Australia. They eat tubers of plants in the dry season as well as

grass seeds, insects, and sometimes maize when available. The nest may be a low. platform of sedges and grasses which the birds build on an island in a swamp; sometimes it is a mound built up above water level.

EXPLORING THE GORGE

Up to four times a day during the dry season, flat-bottomed boats leave the campground on gorge exploration trips. Visitors see striking evidence of the awesome forces at work each wet season when a torrent of water comes rushing through the narrow passages. Up to a height of 33 ft/10 m, the walls appear whitewashed where the flooding Katherine has scraped the sandstone clean. From the high-water mark to the plateau above, the walls are continually being carved and sculpted by the action of wind, rain, and root growth. This area of the cliff has been stained in dark shades of brown, red, and black by iron and other minerals leaching from the earth.

At the end of the first gorge, visitors disembark, walk around the falls, and board a waiting boat for the journey through the second gorge. Before boarding, however, they should try to explore the first level of cliffs above the high-water mark. Wall paintings below the sandstone overhangs here depict creatures that have long inhabited the gorge and the surrounding plateau—wallabies, kangaroos, and echidnas. The paintings are the only evidence of the Djauan Aboriginal people who once spent long periods in the gorge, hunting, fishing, and living along the shores of the Katherine River.

For some reason, many visitors to the park confine themselves to the river and gorge, without venturing into the surrounding countryside. Yet, if they choose, walkers can take any of four primary trails, varying in length from 1.5 to 47 mi/2.5 to 76 km and offering

splendid vistas of plateaus, open sandstone country, and serene wilderness areas. The trails all begin at the campground and end at various points in the gorge. An exciting way to end the hike is to carry along an inflatable mattress and drift on the river back to the campground.

Soon after the wet season, many of the longer walks offer beautiful displays of wildflowers. Notable among the species are the larger shrub-like wattles and grevilleas as well as smaller annuals like orchids, lilies, and sundews.

During the dry season, the Katherine River flows peacefully throughout Katherine Gorge National Park, bordered by pandanus and tea trees.

QUEENSLAND

Many of Palmerston National Park's major hiking trails are adjacent to creeks and rivers so as to avoid the thickest areas of vegetation—which are often impenetrable.

QUEENSLAND IS A MAGICAL PLACE of contrasts and extremes. Within its borders are virtually untouched tropical rain forests, the world's largest sand island, and the sandstone gorges and canyons of the central highlands. Queensland is, in many respects, a microcosm of mainland Australia, with its various habitats condensed into a single state.

More than 60 percent of Queensland extends north of the Tropic of Capricorn. Affectionately called the Sunshine State, Queensland incorporates a variety of tropical environments. In the far north, it presents the classic vision of the tropics, with dense, verdant rain forests that seem to drip from the hillsides. Here the early explorers encountered vines and trees that could sting with the ferocity of a giant insect and kangaroos that climbed among the treetops. Along the coastline, mangrove swamps interrupt long stretches of coral sand beach.

In the southeast corner of Queensland, remnants of the subtropical rain forests that once covered the mountainous areas of this part of the state remain protected in a cluster of national and environmental parks. The forest is cool, its colors muted. The roots of these giant trees first tapped the forest floor years before the earliest Europeans arrived.

Running from the far north to the southeast, the weathered spine of the Great Dividing Range separates the tropical environments of central Queensland. East of the range, dry, open eucalypt forests ring out with the screeching cries of lorikeets and sulphur-crested cockatoos. In this part of tropical Queensland, the dry season can become torturously long as temperatures consistently exceed 100°F/ 38°C. The wildlife of the area tends to cluster near the coast, where the cooling sea breezes bring relief. In a few scattered areas, remnant rain forests punctuate the landscape with a flush of bright green – reminders of the ancient Queensland.

On the western slopes of the Great Divide, the air is parched and thin as the tropical sun assaults the countryside at the beginning of the Australian "outback." River red gums form graceful corridors along silent riverbeds. Narrow gorges house permanent water holes

Pages 288 and 289: The morning fog lifts gently over the Archer River in Cape York.

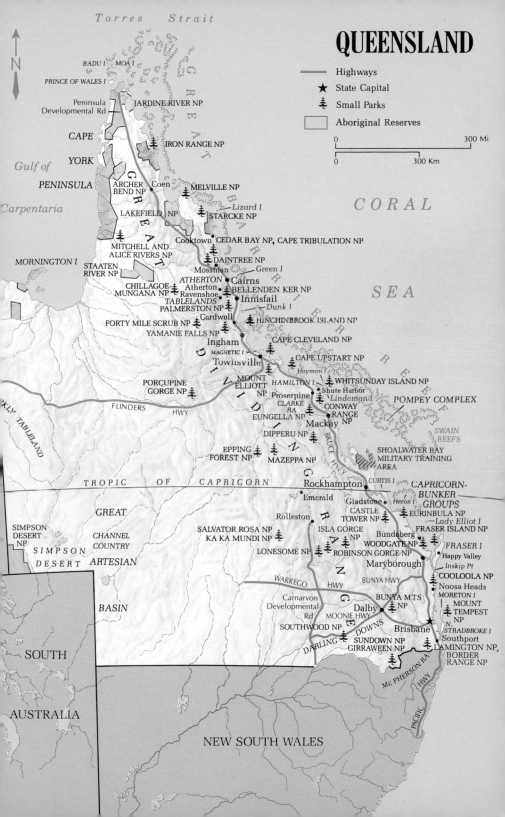

QUEENSLAND

Highways
★ State Capital
🌲 Small Parks
▨ Aboriginal Reserves

0   300 Mi
0   300 Km

Torres Strait

BADU I   MOA I
PRINCE OF WALES I

Peninsula
Developmental Rd   JARDINE RIVER NP

CAPE

YORK

PENINSULA

Gulf of

Carpentaria

ARCHER   Coen
BEND NP

LAKEFIELD NP

MORNINGTON I

STAATEN
RIVER NP

MITCHELL AND
ALICE RIVERS NP

CHILLAGOE
MUNGANA NP
TABLELANDS
PALMERSTON NP

FORTY MILE SCRUB NP
YAMANIE FALLS NP

Ingham

MAGNETIC I

Townsville

PORCUPINE
GORGE NP

MOUNT
ELLIOTT
NP

FLINDERS   HWY

*KLY
TABLELAND*

EPPING
FOREST NP

MAZEPPA NP

IRON RANGE NP

MELVILLE NP

Lizard I
STARCKE NP

Cooktown   CEDAR BAY NP, CAPE TRIBULATION NP

DAINTREE NP
Mossman   *Green I*
ATHERTON   Cairns
Atherton   BELLENDEN KER NP
Ravenshoe   Innisfail
   Dunk I
Cardwell
   HINCHINBROOK ISLAND NP

CAPE CLEVELAND NP

CAPE UPSTART NP
Hayman I
HAMILTON I   WHITSUNDAY ISLAND NP
Proserpine   Shute Harbor
CLARKE   *Lindeman I*   CONWAY
RA   RANGE
EUNGELLA NP   NP
Mackay

DIPPERU NP

CORAL

SEA

POMPEY COMPLEX

*SWAIN
REEFS*

SHOALWATER BAY
MILITARY TRAINING
AREA

TROPIC   OF   CAPRICORN   Rockhampton   *CURTIS I*   CAPRICORN-
   BUNKER
   GROUPS

Emerald

GREAT

SIMPSON
DESERT
NP

CHANNEL
COUNTRY

SIMPSON

DESERT   ARTESIAN

BASIN

SALVATOR ROSA NP
KA KA MUNDI NP

LONESOME NP

Rolleston

Gladstone   *Heron I*
CASTLE
TOWER NP   EURINBULA NP
   —*Lady Elliot I*
ISLA GORGE   FRASER ISLAND NP
  Bundaberg
  WOODGATE NP   FRASER I
ROBINSON GORGE NP   Happy Valley
Maryborough   *Inskip Pt*

COOLOOLA NP
Noosa Heads
MORETON I
MOUNT
TEMPEST
NP

*D
I
V
I
D
I
N
G*

*R
A
N
G
E*

BRUCE   HWY

WARREGO   HWY   BUNYA HWY

Carnarvon
Developmental
Rd   Dalby
MOONIE HWY
SOUTHWOOD NP

BUNYA MTS
NP

Brisbane

N.
STRADBROKE I
Southport
LAMINGTON NP,
BORDER
RANGE NP

SOUTH

AUSTRALIA

DARLING   DOWNS

SUNDOWN NP
GIRRAWEEN NP

McPHERSON RA

PACIFIC   HWY

NEW SOUTH WALES

GREAT

*B
A
R
R
I
E
R*

*R
E
E
F*

GREAT

DIVIDING

that erupt each evening in a celebration of life as creatures from every niche in the arid environment gather to drink.

Though much of the 667,000 sq mi/1,727,530 sq km of Queensland is remote and distant to the visitor, some of the most beautiful and fascinating areas in the state have been preserved in national parks. Generally accessible by conventional vehicle, the majority of the national parks dot the coastal slopes of the Great Dividing Range between Cairns and the New South Wales border.

THE CAPE YORK PENINSULA

Queensland National Parks and Wildlife Service, Far North Region, P.O. Box 2066, Cairns, QLD 4870, or call (070) 51 9811.

For more than a century, the Cape York Peninsula, with its strange plants, wild rivers, and odd creatures, was the destination of a select group of scientists, missionaries, bold adventurers, and treasure seekers. They each came in search of the wealth such legendary places were certain to contain. Today, during the dry season, ever-increasing numbers of tourists and adventurers with four-wheel-drive vehicles venture into the area to explore the virgin forests.

Many of the plants and creatures of the Cape York Peninsula are found nowhere else in Australia. The eclectus parrot, the cuscus, and several butterfly species, all common across the Torres Straits in Papua New Guinea, are uniquely present on the Cape as sub-species. The peninsula contains not only dry, monsoonal, and lowland rain forests, but coastal mangrove swamps as well.

The Cape experiences only two seasons: wet and dry. From December to April the area is beset by cyclones and frequent, heavy monsoonal rains. Many of the roads in Cape York are unpaved and of widely varying grade, and these become impassable during the "wet." During the dry season, the Cape receives less than one-fifth of its total annual rainfall. Toward the final weeks of the dry season in late November, the wildlife of the forests and open woodlands collects around precious, dwindling water holes. Creeks dry up, and natural bush fires become a hazard in many areas.

WILDLIFE OF THE MONSOONAL RAIN FOREST

Compared to tropical or temperate rain forests, the monsoonal rain forests may at first seem deserted and lifeless. A small skink might dart beneath the leaf litter, and the flashing emerald of a Cairn's bird-wing butterfly, largest in Australia, will arrest the eye, but otherwise all is quiet.

Late in the afternoon, however, the rustling of a rainbow pitta in the undergrowth begins a subtle but steady stirring to life. The sun drops quickly in the tropics, and the swoosh of wings starts the evening's activities. Gray-headed flying foxes and other fruit bats begin their siege on fruit trees. By the hundreds, these large bats invade the forest canopy, consuming copious amounts of ripening fruit (and, in the process, distributing the seeds across the rain forest, since most of the seeds pass through them undigested). The canopy of the monsoonal rain forest soon becomes a hive of activity.

Several species of possums and rodents share foraging activities in the treetops with one of the strangest Australian creatures, the cuscus, a possum relative. The two cuscus species found in Australia's monsoonal rain forest are relatives of cuscuses found in Papua New Guinea. They are especially numerous in Iron Range National Park.

An animal unique to tropical rain forests is the striped possum. Distinctive black and white stripes run the length of this active little creature, whose excitable temperament and quick actions are very unpossum-like. In contrast to its larger cousins, most of which are quiet, robustly built, and often sluggish animals, these striking possums behave in a fashion similar to the squirrels of other continents, racing up and down vines and tree trunks.

Rats are common forest mammals. Along with bats, they comprise some 40 percent of all Australian mammals. Little is known about their behavior, and many are found only in northern rain forests. One kind of rat, the melomys, is represented by three species in Cape York; mostly arboreal, these timid little animals feed primarily on fruits. The extreme contrast to the shy, gentle melomys is the giant white-tailed rat. This aggressive rodent prowls the night like an eating juggernaut. Its powerful jaws and sharp teeth are capable of gnawing through the hardest seeds or delivering a deadly bite to formidable adversaries such as snakes and lizards.

Pademelons occasionally appear, bounding through the tangle of vines and fallen trees. Dingoes also are known to frequent monsoonal rain forests, although in these forests, as in all its other habitats, the wary dingo is careful not to show itself.

Birds are not as numerous in the monsoonal rain forest as in other types of rain forests. September through November is their most active period. A number of species utilize the forest only for nesting and rearing young. A spectacular member of the kingfisher family, the white-tailed kingfisher, is just such a seasonal resident, migrating here from New Guinea.

Also crossing the Torres Straits for the forests of Cape York are three of the forty-three species of birds of paradise. Two of these are species of riflebirds, so named for their unusual penetrating call that rings through the rain forest with unmistakable clarity. The third of this group is the trumpet manucode, a glossy black bird with a distinctive vermilion eye; it is endemic to Cape York and does not migrate.

Two of the Cape's unusual birds are primarily ground dwellers, and one is flightless. The Australian cassowary belongs to the most primitive group of living birds, the ratites (which also includes the ostrich, emu, and rhea). The brush turkey also inhabits the rain forests of Cape York. Brush turkeys are one of three Australian megapodes, or mound builders. Males of the species use powerful legs to scratch and toss leaf litter into huge mounds, which they use for incubating eggs. As the material in the compost pile decays, it generates considerable heat. The male is able to check the temperature by digging into the mound; then, by displacing or adding compost, he regulates the heat on the eggs.

Snakes of the rain forest are accomplished tree climbers and dwellers. Pythons are a common group, including the green, carpet, and amethystine pythons. The amethystine is the largest snake in Australia, recorded at a length of 28 ft/8.5 m. The snakes' prowling in the rain-forest canopy often brings screeching calls of alarm from birds such as the double-eyed fig parrot. These parrots are among the smallest in Australia, and the Cape is the sole habitat of one subspecies.

Countless insects live in every conceivable niche in the rain-forest mosaic. By far the most flashy and colorful are the tropical butter-

Clockwise from top: the non-venomous carpet snake; bird-eating spider; gray-headed flying fox.

CASSOWARY
Casuarius casuarius

The elusive cassowary is a solitary bird. Except during breeding season, when it becomes social enough to mate, it lives its life quite alone. It is recognized by its huge size and the distinctive rumbling noise it emits when approaching strange objects. If threatened or alarmed, it will hiss and raise its feathers high; if this tactic fails, the bird scurries quickly away.

The cassowary has many similarities to the emu besides its flightlessness. Females are dominant; the male incubates the eggs and rears the young, while the female is free to mate with other males.

The bird's diet consists mainly of fruit that falls from rain-forest trees,

though it will eat practically anything – including fungi, snails, dead rats, and dead birds.

flies and moths. Two butterflies, the Ulysses and Cairn's bird-wing, should be on everyone's list to see. The iridescent blue of the Ulysses makes it nearly impossible to miss. The Cairn's bird-wing is remarkable for its wingspan – 6 in/15.2 cm in the male to 7 in/20.3 cm in the female.

VEGETATION

The Great Dividing Range originates near the tip of the Cape York Peninsula and runs down the eastern coast of Queensland for nearly 700 mi/1,126 km before it weaves southeast and south. The growth and development of vegetation in northern Queensland is strongly influenced by this mountain range.

West of the range, where there is little rain, open eucalypt forests and woodlands with a grassy understory dominate. In the east, dry, monsoonal rain forests grow over slopes and plateaus down to the sea. In small pockets along the coast, mangrove forest forms the third major vegetative zone.

The dry, monsoonal rain forests of the Cape receive a large percentage of the almost 70 in/178 cm of annual rainfall during the monsoon season of November to late April. Despite the fact that they experience similar rainfall to that of the tropical rain forests in the south, their limited wet season inhibits the diversity of plant species and the ecological relationships that result when there is more even rainfall. The most glaring difference is in the overall height of the forest canopy: 30 ft/9 m on average, compared to the more than 210 ft/65 m farther south.

From late November to early December, the dry time prior to the onset of the wet reaches its peak. Semideciduous trees in the monsoon forest drop their leaves to conserve precious water. Leaves pile up on the forest floor and do not decay. This leaf fall and the marked shortage of ferns, orchids, and mosses give the forests a very different appearance from that of the more southerly tropical rain forests of the Atherton Tableland.

The most unusual natural area on the Cape is the lowland rain forest, which once extended from Townsville to the tip of the Cape, but it has been largely cleared for agriculture and grazing. Only a few dwindling areas, such as Cape Tribulation National Park, still exist. Lowland rain forests are of two major types, depending upon the drainage of the soil. On rich, well-drained basaltic soils, lush forests of lacebarks, Australian teak, hoop pine, and figs form a framework for myriad vines and epiphytes. Swampier lowland forests feature several palm species capable of surviving nine to ten months a year in nutrient-poor soil. Palm swamps, as they are called, usually occur near watercourses along the coast. Walking through one is like venturing through a prehistoric jungle.

The destruction of lowland rain forests has resulted in the decline of many specialized species of reptiles, birds, mammals, frogs, and invertebrates. Because of the disappearance of the termite mounds in which it nests, the spectacular white-tailed kingfisher, with its scarlet bill, metallic blue wings, orange body, and elongated white tail feathers, has been particularly affected.

IRON RANGE NATIONAL PARK

King Park, Lockhart River, QLD 4871.

The park has no telephone and no special facilities, but bush camping is allowed by free permit, issued by Ranger at King Park.

Iron Range National Park is reached by four-wheel-drive vehicle either from Cairns or Cooktown.

Tracks are impassable after heavy rains, and four-wheel drive is necessary at all times. Unless you are quite skilled and comfortable in the tropical bush, you are well advised to contact the Queensland National Parks and Wildlife Service in Cairns for guidance.

Until recently the wilderness of Iron Range National Park was extremely difficult to reach. Even though the park is now more accessible, it still holds the magic of adventure and undiscovered secrets. A forgotten vestige of tropics, the park contains an astonishing variety of plants and animals that do not exist farther south on the Australian continent.

Iron Range is one of the few places that harbor both species of cuscus, the spotted and the gray. Preferring to live in lowland monsoonal rain forests, the slow, musky-odored cuscuses are among the largest members of the possum family in Australia. They are mainly

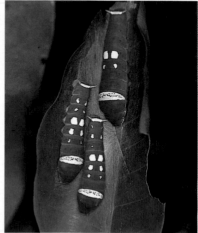

Caterpillars can be just as varied in appearance as butterflies, as evidenced by these from the papilionidae and the nymphalidae families.

nocturnal, sitting out the daylight hours in trees or clumps of foliage. At dusk, these round-faced balls of fur peer out at the world through large, marble-like eyes and begin their search for food. With incredible diligence, they steadily traverse the network of branches and vines in the forest canopy, gathering ripe fruits and leaves. The work is facilitated by the animal's strong hindfeet and its seminaked prehensile tail. Indeed, its round, furry face and curling tail have caused it to be mistaken for a monkey.

Cuscuses share the dimly lit recesses of the Iron Range with an assortment of rain-forest creatures. The striped possum, the most animated resident, races about the treetops, snatching up insects, centipedes, and scorpions with deadly speed and accuracy. This 16-in/40-cm possum is unusually adapted for removing beetle larvae and other foods from difficult locations. A modified fourth finger on each front foot deftly reaches into cracks and crevices of rotting wood in search of insects. If one is found, sharp teeth send wood chips flying, and the prey is devoured.

Twenty-five percent of all the known butterflies in Australia can be found in Iron Range National Park. The parade of colorful flitting wings seems endless in late November as species after species completes its metamorphosis. Unmistakable is the metallic blue of a

Lacewing butterflies are known for the white edging on their wings. There are almost 400 species of butterflies in Australia, many protected by law.

The spotted cuscus, with its soft thick fur and big round eyes, has often been mistaken for a monkey. The arboreal marsupial lives mainly on leaves, fruit, and flowers.

5-in/12.7-cm Ulysses butterfly as it gently swoops through breaks in the canopy. Larger still is the male Cairn's bird-wing, floating on its 6-in/15.2-cm wings of metallic green and velvety blue with yellow spots. You must wait until dark to see the ruler of this winged world, the Atlas moth. One of the largest moths on earth, the Atlas takes to the night air on magnificent teardrop-shaped wings measuring 10 in/25 cm across. The Atlas female is unable to feed and must live off food stored during her months as a caterpillar. After mating, she deposits eighty to a hundred eggs on several rain-forest food plants and then dies.

It is not unusual to hear the raspy screech of the palm cockatoo or the less abrasive voice of the eclectus parrot. Both varieties are found only in the Cape and across the Strait in Papua New Guinea.

CAPE TRIBULATION

Queensland National Parks and Wildlife Service, Far North Region, P.O. Box 2066, Cairns, QLD 4870, or call (070) 51 9811.

Reaching the park in any season except the dry is extremely difficult. The last 25 mi/40 km of the 65-mi/104-km trip north from Cairns are unpaved. The downpours of the wet season and the steep grades throughout the park often combine to make the roads impassable. Even during drier months, roads within the park should be attempted by four-wheel-drive vehicles only. A vehicle ferry carries passengers across the Daintree River from 6 A.M. to 6 P.M. daily except Christmas Day and Good Friday.

The park offers facilities for camping, by advance reservation, at Noah Beach, 5 mi/8 km south of Cape Tribulation; a permit is required. Public camping is available also at Thorntons Beach; there are private camping areas at Myall Creek and Cape Tribulation. All these sites have toilets and water. Fuel, telephone, and limited foodstuffs are available from the kiosk at Thorntons Beach.

The rain forests and beaches of this undeveloped park offer bushwalkers the chance to see an exceptional variety of plants and animals. From Thornton Peak, at 4,511 ft/1,375 m, the vista stretches in waves of green down slopes and across valleys and mangroves, giving way abruptly to broken coastline along the Coral Sea.

Along this thin margin of sand and surf worn boulders, two of the richest environments in the world abut each other. The eastern slope of the McDowall Range, between the Bloomfield River in the north and the Daintree River in the south, comprises Cape Tribulation's 41,920 acres/16,965 hectares. The eastern border runs adjacent to the Great Barrier Reef. Here lives an extraordinarily diverse community of plants and animals—many of them (such as the Bennett's tree kangaroo) endemic to Cape Tribulation and nearby areas.

The north–south length of Cape Tribulation is crossed by dozens of creeks. The creekbeds, especially during the dry season, provide the most accessible routes into the rain forest. The banks of permanent creeks and rivers appear like green corridors between massive tree trunks hung with ferns, orchids, and other epiphytes.

Reptiles are a common sight at Cape Tribulation. Most, such as the amethystine python, prowl the night in search of possums and sleeping birds. During the daytime, lizards such as the banded gecko and Boyd's forest dragon bask in patches of sunlight. Estuarine

(saltwater) crocodiles are diurnal and occur in both the lower Daintree and Bloomfield rivers as well as in many of the larger creeks. Visitors should be aware of their presence and use caution when approaching any area where they may be active. Marine stingers are a danger to ocean swimmers from October to April.

ATHERTON TABLELAND

The Atherton Tableland is northern Queensland's great hidden treasure. A dozen scattered national parks dot the rolling landscape of the Tableland, protecting the remaining vestiges of upland tropical rain forest. Despite its close proximity to Cairns, and the hundreds of thousands of visitors that pass through that tropical city each year, the Tableland's two largest parks, Palmerston and Bellenden Ker, receive relatively few visitors.

Inland from the coast between Cairns and Innisfail is the Tableland's rich, rolling countryside. From coastal fields of sugarcane the terrain rises sharply through the hillsides of broken granite and dense, lush rain forest that form Bellenden Ker National Park. At nearly 3,000 ft/900 m the countryside levels off into a sea of rolling green farms with scattered patches of the tropical rain forest that once dominated the landscape of northern Queensland.

The climate, topography, and geology of the Atherton Tableland have combined to create one of the richest growing regions in Australia. Ample rainfall and rich volcanic soil invited farmers in the late 1800s to test the Tableland for what it could yield agriculturally. Acre after acre of tropical rain forest was cleared in this pursuit. Today parks are all that remain of a once-great tropical rain forest.

Water is the dominant element in the life of any rain-forest environment, and the Atherton Tableland is no exception. Mist, fog, midday downpour, all-night drizzle, and the rumble of water cascading over falls demonstrate the omnipresence of water. Less than 14 mi/ 22 km away, the coastal towns of Cairns and Innisfail may be basking in the hot morning sun, while in the Tableland mist rises from ravines and valleys along the North Johnstone and Barron rivers, leaving behind a thick blanket of soaking dew.

The Tableland is home to an incredible collection of trees, all

Dense tropical rain forest lines the eastern slope of the Atherton Tableland.

dependent upon constant rains and rich basaltic soils. Giant hoop and kauri pines, growing as tall as 160 ft/50 m, dominate the jungle-like atmosphere. The patter of drops plummeting from these heights to the forest floor is a counterpoint to the voices of rain-forest birds.

The Atherton Tableland is fairly dry, receiving about 20 to 40 in/ 50 to 100 cm of rainfall annually. Precipitation is much greater along the eastern edge of the Tableland, however, where 3 to 4 in/7.5 to 10 cm of rain may fall in a single hour.

WILDLIFE

Bird-watching is undoubtedly the most rewarding daytime activity. Near clearings in the forest, and along roadsides and picnic grounds, dozens of species of tropical birds can be observed darting in and out of the forest. Early mornings and late afternoons are especially active times, as insect-catching varieties such as the gray-headed robin, pied flycatcher, Bower's shrike-thrush, and golden whistler take advantage of the abundance of flying morsels. From Cairns, several one-day guided trips feature Lake Eacham and Lake Barrine as major stops for bird watching.

Clearings also provide an opportunity for many flowering varieties of plants to grow. Their blossoms attract several members of the honey-eater family, including the eastern spinebill and the Macleay's and bridled honey eaters.

The dense green canopy of the rain forest is home to a range of parrots, cockatoos, and pigeons whose screeching and cooing sounds filter down to the forest floor. Among the treetop dwellers are the exotic purple-crowned pigeon, the raucous sulphur-crested cockatoo, and the red and green male king parrot. During October and November many of these large fruit- and seed-eating birds raise their young in the forest crown.

A search for birds in the dense rain forests of the Tableland is often more a case of bird listening than of bird watching. High in the canopy, birds with flashing feathers – greens, purples, reds, yellows – produce a symphony of whistles, trills, booms, and strange cat-like meows. The watcher needs persistence and a good pair of binoculars. Often, though, the sight of a golden bowerbird, a Victoria's riflebird, or a spotted catbird will reward the hours of stalking. And even if not a single bird is sighted, the beautiful concert of sounds is itself an unforgettable experience.

Possums are the largest mammals commonly seen in the Tableland. There are four major species in the area. They include the green and lemuroid ringtails and the coppery brushtail. The fourth member, the Herbert River ringtail, is much more reclusive and difficult to discover. (It is also the symbol of the Queensland National Parks and Wildlife Service.)

Possums awaken just after dark and then climb through the forest canopy in search of fruits, insects, and leaves. The three ringtail species make little noise in their progress through the vine-tangled crowns of trees. Their dexterous feet and a semiprehensile tail, naked at its ventral tip, allow them to move with great ease and fluidity.

In contrast, the coppery brushtail crashes noisily about the forest. Brushtails spend a portion of the night combing the leaf litter for beetles and fallen fruits and nuts. The copper-color phase of the brushtail is unique to the Queensland rain forests.

The lemuroid and Herbert River ringtails are found at altitudes over 1,476 ft/450 m. The soils here are principally basaltic, and the forest is draped in cool misty shrouds throughout most of the year. Both species are considerably rarer in the lower elevations

Heavy clouds obscure the peak of Mount Lewis in the Atherton Tableland. The misty peaks here support diverse vegetation that benefits from the abundant moisture.

(above 820 ft/250 m), where green ringtails and copper brushtails are more common.

September through November is an especially rewarding time for possum-watching. The young are increasingly active during these months and travel with their mothers, clinging piggyback. One or two young are common, depending on the species.

Another interesting mammal of the nocturnal rain forest is the black-footed tree rat. About 11.5 in/29 cm long, these rodents feed voraciously on fruits, flowers, and insects.

VEGETATION

The Tableland rain forests are a maze of vines and buttresses. One of the largest trees is the impressive curtain fig. An epiphytic plant, its seeds germinate on the branches of host trees, from which the young figs let down dozens of aerial roots. These vine-like roots form thick curtains and choke out their hosts after only a few years of growth.

An impressive sight in the rain forest is the manner in which giant trees buttress themselves for stability. The buttress is a combination of roots and trunk that looks like a skirt as its large curving wall grows out from the tree 6 to 10 ft/1.8 to 3 m above the ground. Occasionally these walls may curve out and around the axis of the tree and extend several feet into the forest. Besides helping to anchor the tree, which may reach up over 100 ft/30 m into the forest canopy, the buttress serves to collect scarce nutrients.

Rain forests experience an extremely high degree of nutrient turnover as warm temperatures and constant moisture assist fungi and bacteria to break down debris. Nowhere is this more evident than when one of the mighty trees finally relinquishes its hold and topples over. As the tree falls, it clears a wide swath through the forest. This sudden break in the otherwise dense canopy allows sunlight to flood in on the forest floor and awaken dormant seeds and spores. Within days, the clearing teems with bright green leaves, lianas, and ferns. These newcomers consume the space with unbelievable speed, soon dominating and lending a jungle-like aspect to the forest.

The wide-spreading leaves of the bird's nest fern, one of the most abundant epiphytes in the rain forest, catch forest debris and rainfall that become the plant's nourishment.

Fungi grow in surprising shapes and colors in the rain forest. Their digestion of decaying plants helps return vital nutrients to the soil.

One of the most unusual trees in this rain forest is the stinging tree, of which there are two species and a related shrub. With its heart-shaped leaves and hairy stems, the stinging tree physically resembles a half-dozen other rain-forest species, but it has one dangerous difference. It possesses a highly toxic fluid in those stiff hairs, and if stung one should seek medical care at a hospital immediately. In many of the Tableland parks, rangers have placed labels clearly identifying the trees and warning of their harmful potential.

Unlike their monsoonal counterparts in the north of Cape York, the tropical rain forests here host a diverse collection of epiphytes, fungi, and mosses. Spectacular among these are the huge staghorn and bird's-nest ferns. On the higher altitudes of Bellenden Ker National Park these ferns may grow to three times the diameter of the host trees. Clinging to their hosts with vine-like roots, the epiphytic ferns catch falling debris and moisture and convert these elements to usable nutrients.

0   10 Mi
0   10 Km

Barron R

Clohesy R

HWY

BRUCE

HWY

BARRON
FALLS NP

Cairns

YARRABAH

ABORIGINAL

RESERVE

CORAL

SEA

N

KENNEDY

Mareeba

DAVIES CREEK NP

L A M B
R A N G E

MALBON

THOMPSON RANGE

Gordonvale
Walshs
Pyramid

Mt Massie

Mt Sophia

Mt Harold

BELLENDEN

North
Peak

KER NP

Centre
Peak

RUSSELL RIVER NP

GRAHAM RANGE NP

BABINDA FALLS

South
Peak

Babinda

GREAT

DIVIDING

*Tinaroo Falls
Reservoir*

Tolga

Kairi

Gillies

Rd

Mulgrave R

BELLENDEN

KER

RANGE

LAKE
BARRINE NP

L Barrine

Atherton

Yungaburra

CURTAIN FIG

Mt
Quincan

*L
Eacham*

LAKE EACHAM NP

Mulanda

erberton

Mt Bartle
Frere

TOPAZ ROAD NP

EUBENANGEE
SWAMP NP

Pawngilly

THE CRATER NP

North Johnstone R

MT MARIA
NP

Millaa Millaa

PALMERSTON

Innisfail

ETTY
BAY NP

PALMERSTON
NP

NORTH
JOHNSTONE
RIVER
GORGE

HWY

Ravenshoe

HWY

MILLSTREAM FALLS NP

CRAWFORDS LOOKOUT ✳

BRUCE

HWY

KENNEDY

MT MAJOR NP

South Johnstone R

CANNABULLEN FALLS NP

McNAMEE
CREEK NP

D
I
V
I
D
I
N
G

R
A
N
G
E

ELIZABETH GRANT
FALLS NP

TULLY FALLS NP

ATHERTON TABLELAND

⎯⎯ Highways	✳	Scenic Lookout
⎯⎯ Roads-Streets	▲	Peaks
• Points of Interest	⸙	Small Parks

BELLENDEN KER NATIONAL PARK

Ranger at Josephine Falls, Bellenden Ker National Park, P.O. Box 93, Mirriwinni, QLD 4871, or call (070) 67 6304. Access to the park is at Josephine Falls below Mt. Bartle Frere. A paved road veers off the Bruce Highway 27 mi/43 km south of Cairns. From the turnoff it is 5 mi/8 km to the park headquarters. There is a large parking area carved out of the rain forest at the trail head to Josephine Falls. Camping in undeveloped areas of the park is permitted depending upon conditions. A permit is required and can be obtained from the Ranger.

Traveling south from Cairns to Innisfail along the Bruce Highway, you will notice that the hillsides to the west steadily increase in elevation. Throughout much of the year the loftiest heights are covered with clouds. The deep rich green of the jungle-covered slopes contrast with the acres of sugarcane fields at their base. These rugged hillsides, on both the eastern and western slopes of the Bellenden Ker Range, form Bellenden Ker National Park.

The park protects a 40-mi/65-km stretch of undeveloped rain forest, the single largest tract of upland rain forest left in Australia. Bellenden Ker's borders also contain lowland rain forests, now rarely found in Australia.

The park climbs in elevation from approximately 266 ft/81 m near the Bruce Highway to 5,287 ft/1,612 m atop Mt. Bartle Frere, making it the highest park in Queensland. On the slopes between lowland and upland rain forests, the foothills occasionally take on a jungle-like appearance.

A chaotic matting of vines inundates broad openings. These openings are the result of cyclones that hit the tropical Queensland coast during January and February, early in the wet season. Their violent actions leave scars in the rain-forest canopy, and vines and swift-growing trees take immediate advantage of the openings, shooting forth new growth that retards development of preexisting tree species. If cyclones strike the same forest during successive wet seasons, the effect can be severe and long-lasting. In some areas of

A popular destination for bushwalkers, Josephine Falls cascades into Josephine Creek in the only area of Bellenden Ker National Park that is developed.

TREE KANGAROOS
Dendrolagus spp.

Many visitors to Australia are amazed when they encounter a kangaroo climbing a tree. It is believed, however, that most early ancestors of kangaroos were well adapted to tree-climbing and only stopped climbing as ground food became plentiful. There are now seven species of tree kangaroos in the world. Two live in Australia: the Lumholtz and Bennett tree kangaroos. The other five species live in New Guinea.

Tree kangaroos, found in mountainous rain forests of the eastern side of northern Queensland, are well adapted to their arboreal existence, having rough foot pads, long uniform tails, and long curved claws that help them climb and jump among the branches. They are far more clumsy on the ground, where they forage for fallen leaves and fruit.

Bellenden Ker National Park, forest damaged by cyclones several decades ago can be recognized by a patchy, uneven canopy strewn with vines.

The upper slopes of the park change dramatically in vegetation and animal species as the altitude increases. Lower temperatures and stronger winds are active forces in modeling the ridges and slopes above 5,000 ft/1,500 m. These altitudes include not only several unique plant species but also a host of unusual rain-forest creatures such as tree kangaroos, lemuroid and Herbert River ring-tailed possums, and the leaf-tailed gecko. The northern barred frog is found only in these rain-forest conditions.

BUSHWALKING

Josephine Falls trail. It is a short walk (0.5 mi/800 m) to the first tier of the falls. Josephine Falls is a popular swimming spot, and visitors enjoy sliding down the slick rock in the falls. Openings in the forest created by Josephine Creek encourage many species of flowering plants to thrive. The brightly colored flowers lure populations of brilliantly hued butterflies.

Mt. Bartle Frere. The access route to the top of the mountain is not developed, but it is well marked. The terrain is quite steep, with rain-forest vegetation dominant initially, changing to low scrub and open grassland on the ridges. Water is available almost year-round from a spring at the old hut near the summit.

PALMERSTON NATIONAL PARK

Palmerston National Park, P.O. Box 800, Innisfail, QLD 4860, or call (070) 64 5115. Also: Queensland

National Parks and Wildlife Service, P.O. Box 2066, Cairns, QLD 4870, or call (070) 51 9811.

To explore Palmerston National Park is to behold one of the last great fragments of upland tropical rain forest. These botanical wonderlands once blanketed the entire Atherton Tableland. The park is filled with an exotic blend of lush wet greenness and natural mystery, colorful and strange tropical birds flitting among tangled branches in a rain-forest canopy nearly 200 ft/70 m overhead, and curious creatures like the platypus, half bird, half mammal. It is a nocturnal world possessed by animals cryptically designed and almost defying description.

The park owes its name to prospector-adventurer Christie Palmerston, who in the early 1880s carved a path through precipitous terrain and dense forest for 62 mi/100 km between present-day Innisfail and Herberton. The two-hour journey today leads through some of the most beautiful tropical rain forest in Australia.

During the rainy season, the ridges and gorges of Palmerston are often submerged in either a damp gray mist or the deluge of a wet-season storm. The area receives over 138 in/3,500 mm of water annually, clearly establishing it as one of the wettest spots on the continent.

The generous water supply, basaltic soil composition, and mild average temperature in Palmerston National Park have made it one of the richest biological regions in Australia. This upland tropical rain forest hosts an astounding 500 different tree species, including trees with giant buttress roots. Clinging vines and a diversity of epiphytic plants complete the picture of the perfect jungle.

EPIPHYTES

Two major traits of these plants are their lack of woody stalks or supporting structure, and the absence of roots tapping into the rich forest soils.

Epiphytes generally attach themselves to the trunk or a large branch of a woody tree by a network of clinging roots. The attachment point is some distance from the ground but in an opportune position to receive light. The plants feed on water draining down the host tree's bark and on rotting leaves, fruits, and other debris that accumulates in and around their roots.

Some epiphytes, such as the bird's-nest fern, have developed magnificent structures for surviving in the lofty rain forest. Growing in a rosette of broad, light green leaves, the bird's-nest fern encircles the host tree's trunk or begins an upside-down crown of leaves along a large upper-story branch. Water collects within this crown and falling debris also mounds up, forming a miniature compost pile that gives the fern valuable nutrients as it decomposes.

Epiphytes include certain kinds of mosses, lichens, fungi, ferns, vines, and flowering plants such as orchids. Although these plants may all seem quite different, the epiphytes share a number of remarkable characteristics.

WILDLIFE

Platypuses are one of the many wildlife attractions of Palmerston National Park. Near the campground at Henrietta Creek, a short path east through the forest brings you to an elevated viewing platform. During the dim-lit hours of dawn and dusk, patience rewards the visitor with the sight of one or two of these amazingly assembled animals as they dive and forage in the clear pools of the creek.

Birds are definitely a feature at Palmerston, and the campground at Henrietta Creek offers the best opportunity for spotting a number of local specialties such as the red-and-green king parrot; green-winged, bronze, and wompoo pigeons; sulphur-crested cockatoos; yellow robins; and the local specialty, the Atherton scrub wren.

The night world of Palmerston comes to life under the spotlight and guidance of park rangers during evening walks. Since the vast majority of rain-forest dwellers are nocturnal, these walks afford an excellent opportunity to meet the residents of Palmerston. Two of its most extraordinary animals inhabit opposite levels of the rain forest. Among the tree buttresses on the forest floor, look for the leaf-tailed gecko. A master of disguise, this 6-in/16-cm gecko blends well with the lichen-spotted bark of the trees. It is the largest of Australia's sixty-odd gecko species.

Meanwhile, high among the leaves and fruits of the tree crowns, the Lumholtz tree kangaroo, one of the oddest members of the kangaroo family, methodically eats its way through the canopy. Unlike its ground-hopping cousins, the tree kangaroo enjoys relative safety in the upper canopy. It is the largest of the rain-forest mammals and rarely feels threatened. Its only natural enemy is the amethystine python.

Since the majority of the rain-forest creatures are nocturnal, a walk through a patch of rain forest in Palmerston National Park at 11 A.M. is vastly different from that same walk taken twelve hours later. During late morning, an occasional skink scuttles through the forest litter of leaves and twigs, a rainbow pitta scratches helter-skelter through the same litter, and if startled a red-legged pademelon thumps its distress against the forest floor before bounding off. Otherwise only the constant cooing of forest pigeons and other birds is heard.

Pink mushrooms spring out from the forest floor when it is time for this fungus to send its spores to other areas of the forest.

Twelve hours later a flashlight illuminates a mysterious kaleidoscope of large-eyed marsupials and outlandish-looking insects. The birds have disappeared. Their sounds have been replaced by the strange hums, bizarre squeaks, and insistent rustlings of the night creatures.

BUSHWALKING

Crawfords Lookout to K-Tree. Allow two to three hours for this 3-mi/5-km circuit. From Crawfords Lookout the trail winds down into the North Johnstone River Gorge, falling about 1,640 ft/500 m in the 0.9-mi/1.5-km walk. The trail then follows the outline of the hill parallel to Douglas Creek and then Henrietta Creek. At Tchulpala Falls, constant mist has encouraged a prolific growth of mosses and ferns. This beautiful area is environmentally sensitive, and slick, water-covered rocks and logs make straying from the trail potentially dangerous. From the falls several flights of stairs lead to the picnic area on the highway near the K-Tree survey point. The 1.2-mi/2-km return to Crawfords Lookout via the highway takes approximately an hour.

K-Tree to Goolagans picnic area. A trail of 1.8 mi/3 km, taking one to two hours. It leads first to Wallicher Falls, which, though relatively small, are spectacular. Access to the bottom of the falls is possible after crossing Henrietta Creek. The trail then ascends and follows the contours above Henrietta Creek through some very tall and dense-canopied rain forest. The 1-mi/1.7-km return to K-Tree via the highway takes approximately forty-five minutes.

Goolagans picnic area to Henrietta Creek camping area. This excellent 0.5-mi/800-m trail takes thirty minutes. It follows Henrietta Creek, joining the picnic and camping areas. Lucky visitors might see the musky rat kangaroo as well as platypuses and tortoises in the creek. The return via the highway takes about fifteen minutes.

Nandroya Falls circuit. Distance to the falls is 1.5 mi/2.5 km; time, one to two hours. From the camping area the trail ascends the ridge that separates Henrietta and Douglas creeks. It then serpentines slowly down toward Nandroya Falls via Silver Creek Falls. Return either along the main Nandroya Falls trail or via the circuit trail, an additional 2.2 mi/3.5 km, two to three hours. The circuit trail first follows Douglas Creek, passing some excellent swimming holes. It then goes around a steep hillside before rejoining the main trail (0.6 mi/1 km) from the camping area.

CHILLAGOE-MUNGANA CAVES

P.O. Box 38, Chillagoe, QLD 4871, or call (070) 94 7163.

Camping facilities include toilets and running water. There are signposted walking tracks and guided tours are at 9 A.M. and 1:30 P.M. daily to the three developed caves. The tours last about one hour and are extremely informative. Exploration is permitted in other caves.

Visitors to northern Queensland usually expect to see beach or rain forest, and some are surprised to discover the unique system of underground caves near Chillagoe and Mungana. This intricate system of caves was formed from large limestone deposits, skeletons of marine creatures left from the time when this area was submerged in a shallow sea.

Only certain caves are open for public viewing, but their beauty is remarkable, with richly colored red-orange and brown stalagmites and gray stalactites that hang like precious jewels, fragile to the touch. The appearance of the caves is ever changing as water percolates through the ceilings, gradually creating new shapes.

The caves of Chillagoe and Mungana are not as thick-walled and resistant to change as many others in Australia, and it is not uncommon for the roof of a cave to collapse, allowing sunshine to filter in. The Royal Arch in Royal Arch Cave pokes through one of these daylight holes.

Royal Arch is one of the largest cave systems in the Chillagoe-Mungana cave area. It has huge, well-lit caverns up to 167 ft/51 m long and 115 ft/35 m wide. Daylight striking certain sections of the cave casts an eerie light on the formations inside, making the stalactites sparkle like silver and the red stalagmites cast a burning glow.

Only 6 mi/10 km from Chillagoe and Mungana you come upon castle-like formations that are a delight to explore and climb. Fossils of marine creatures are easily found within the limestone. This stone is the same as that in the caves, but it is more finely chiseled because it has been exposed to weathering. The formations look like battlements with broken turrets and crumbling walls. Some sections have been so delicately etched that their sharpness can do damage.

MAGNETIC ISLAND NATIONAL PARK

The Ranger, c/o Post Office, Picnic Bay, Magnetic Island, QLD 4876, or call (077) 78 5378. Queensland National Parks and Wildlife Service, Northern Regional Centre, P.O. Box 5391, Townsville Mail Centre, QLD 4810, or call (077) 74 1411. Magnetic Island is 5 mi/8 km from Townsville and can be reached from Townsville via passenger ferry, chartered helicopter, or vehicle barge.

Isolated pockets of sandy beach are interspersed among the boulder-covered shores of Magnetic Island, a small island off the coast of Townsville. It was named by Captain James Cook, whose compass produced incorrect readings while he was sailing nearby. Cook believed that the granite outcrops of the island were magnetic, but no scientific evidence has ever supported his theory.

The island has, however, proven to be a magnet for tourists in search of a tropical island not too far from the mainland. It has

The giant tree frog can grow to 6 in/140 mm. Its large webbed feet give it the dexterity to climb trees in search of food.

coconut palm trees, tropical fruits such as pineapples, mangoes, and papayas (called pawpaws), secluded beaches, and a consistently warm and pleasant climate. Several fringing coral reefs surround the island, and coral cod, coral trout, king salmon, and barramundi are found in its waters.

The island's coast has many isolated coves and bays, the largest being Horseshoe Bay with its 2 mi/3.2 km of beach. Picnic Bay, at the southern tip of the island, is the main commercial area, including a ranger station and passenger ferry landing site.

The northern half of Magnetic Island has been declared a national park; the rest of the island is urbanized. There is a small environmental park at Horseshoe Bay, created to protect waterfowl habitat. Terns, noddies, pelicans, cormorants, and gannets find refuge here.

The wildlife on the island lives virtually free of predators, but a hardy population of feral goats ravages the vegetation. Koalas often are sighted and, although known for their insistence on eating only eucalyptus leaves, they have been seen eating mangoes here.

EUNGELLA NATIONAL PARK

Eungella National Park, c/o Post Office, Dalrymple Heights, QLD 4740, or call (079) 58 4552. Queensland National Parks and Wildlife Service, P.O. Box 623, Mackay, QLD 4740, or call (079) 57 6292. Queensland National Parks and Wildlife Service, Central Regional Centre, P.O. Box 1395, Rockhampton, QLD 4700, or call (079) 27 6511.

There are two camping areas, which include picnic facilities, toilets, and running water.

On the central Queensland coast, 50 mi/80 km from Mackay, the ruggedly beautiful ridges and peaks of the Clarke Range have been preserved in one of the state's largest undeveloped national parks. The Aborigines called these rain-forested mountains and valleys "land of cloud," or Eungella.

The park runs along 20 mi/32 km of the southern end of the Clarke Range. This great expanse of wilderness is a bushwalker's paradise. There are no roads crossing the park; most of the 9.5 mi/15 km of the main walking trail skirts the Broken River.

WILDLIFE AND VEGETATION

Often laced with thin, misty clouds and drenched by rainstorms rolling in from the nearby Pacific Ocean, Eungella has the feeling of a tropical rain forest more characteristic of northern parks. Large, buttressed hardwoods, palms, vines, and a collection of epiphytes create an unexpected jungle atmosphere in a region of Queensland dominated by dry eucalypt forest, open grassland, and valleys of sugarcane.

Eungella is a refreshing escape from the sapping heat of the lowlands. The park's elevation and forests ensure that most visits will be cool and pleasant. Surprisingly, during June and July some of the highest peaks experience harsh cold and frost. The dramatic variation in altitude creates many different environmental zones and habitats for more than 110 species of birds and dozens of mammals.

Among the birds, the pigeons of Eungella National Park are of special interest, because so many are rare or infrequent visitors this far south. Forest-dwelling pigeons are extremely beautiful: the purple-crowned, red-crowned, green-winged, topknot, and white-headed are frequent visitors to the rain forests along Broken River Trail.

Most mammals in Eungella are nocturnal. Platypuses, however, commonly appear swimming about the clear pools by day. The park proudly lays claim to being one of the few places where this little web-footed animal is certain to be observed.

Two locations are especially promising in the search for the shy platypus. Near the campground at Conical Pool they have become surprisingly nonchalant about quiet activity in and around their pool. This is not the case with the platypuses farther downriver in Platypus Pool. Here, deep in the cool, shadowed confines of the rain forest, they receive far fewer visitors and maintain their shy, secretive ways. Spotting a platypus in this pool requires patience and keen observational skills.

BUSHWALKING

Walking-trail systems exist in two areas of the park: south of Eungella township at Broken River, and at Finch Hatton Gorge.

Broken River tracks (Broken River-Crediton Creek). This trail starts at Broken River picnic ground and follows the river for much of the way. It is 5.2 mi/8.4 km – at least 2½ hours – to the Crediton Creek entrance, which emerges on the Crediton Loop Road.

Australian brush-turkeys are solitary and fairly tame mound-building birds that are social only when they breed.

The initial 0.5 mi/700 m is part of the self-guiding Rainforest Discovery Walk. At the two trail junctions follow the signs to Crediton Creek. At Crystal Cascades you may veer off the main trail via a set of steps and enjoy a closer look at the cascades. The trail continues through the rain forest for most of its length, although in several places it approaches the river's edge. Here the contrast between the riverine and forest habitats is apparent. At Platypus Pool, look for bubbles on the surface that may indicate a platypus feeding on the bottom.

Birds such as the pied cormorant, black duck, and azure kingfisher are frequently seen in the area. At the Wishing Pool, 4.5 mi/7.2 km from Broken River picnic ground, the trail forks. The lower trail follows the river for 984 yd/900 m; the upper trail continues for 800 yd/732 m, at which point these two tracks merge. From here it is 400 yd/366 m to the Crediton Loop road. You can return to the picnic ground either via the trail or by turning right and following the road for 4.2 mi/6.7 km.

Eungella fan palms edge the track and epiphytes such as bird's-nest and elkhorn ferns grow high in the trees. Common birds are the whipbird, white-browed scrub wren, brush turkey, yellow robin, golden whistler, and topknot pigeon.

Palm Walk trail (Broken River-Palm Walk entrance). Beginning at Broken River, the trail is part of the first section of the Rainforest Discovery Walk. Follow the signs to Palm Walk and cross the river. At a number of points along this trail, such as Sunshine Corner and Surprise Lookout, the right-hand side suddenly opens to reveal the Pioneer Valley below.

Some 3.1 mi/5 km from Broken River, the Crooked Cedar Trail branches off to the left and joins the Eungella-Broken River road a short distance away. The main trail continues to take you through a beautiful section of rain forest with tall groves of piccabeen palms. Another 1.1 mi/1.8 km will bring you to Bevans Lookout at the side of the road. To return to Broken River picnic ground, turn left and follow the road for 1.7 mi/2.7 km. The Sky Window picnic ground may be reached by turning right and walking along the road for 547 yd/500 m.

Wheel of Fire Falls trail. The trail branches 0.7 mi/1.1 km from the campground. The trail to the left leads to the Wheel of Fire

PLATYPUS
Ornithorhynchus anatinus

You are not likely to encounter the elusive platypus even if you visit its habitats in freshwater streams, rivers, and lakes. One of the two monotremes (egg-laying mammals) that live in Australia (the other is the echidna), it spends its days in burrows along the banks of streams and ponds and its evenings in the water searching for food.

Its diet consists of crayfish, shrimp, worms, snails, tadpoles, and young insect larvae. It moves in water by propelling with its strong webbed forefeet and steering with its partially webbed back feet; on land it walks on its knuckles.

The female platypus builds an elaborate burrow up to 66 ft/20 m long that includes a breeding chamber where she incubates and raises her one to three young.

Though usually docile, the adult male will use the venomous spur on his hind feet to defend himself when competing with other males. More often, however, he uses the spur as a weapon in capturing frogs.

Falls, about 0.6 mi/1 km. A short side branch from this trail leads to Araluen Falls. Here the water falls into a deep pool in the rock. A common resident at this water hole is the Eungella day frog, a small brown frog found only in the Eungella area. At Larapinta Cascades the fast-flowing water has weathered the more susceptible rock, and the swirling action has formed pools where the flow of water is slowed down. This has created the step-like formation of these cascades. After a short climb through the forest, the trail comes to an end at the Wheel of Fire Falls. These run into a large, deep pool, with sheer rock walls and rain forest lining both sides.

Dooloomai Falls trail. Where the trail branches, 0.7 mi/1.1 km from the campground, the right-hand trail leads to the top of Dooloomai Falls, some 2.2 mi/3.6 km from the campground. Along the way you will notice quite a few flooded gums. Since eucalypt seedlings will not grow in rain forests, their presence here indicates that this location was once an open eucalypt forest. The trail ends at the top of Dooloomai Falls. From here you can see the water cascading down the 182-ft/55-m falls into the gorge below.

CARNARVON NATIONAL PARK

The Ranger, Carnarvon National Park via Rolleston, QLD 4702, or call (079) 84 4505. Queensland National Parks and Wildlife Service, P.O. Box 906, Emerald, QLD 4720, or call (079) 82 2246. Queensland National Parks and Wildlife Service, P.O. Box 1362, Rockhampton, QLD 4700, or call (079) 27 6511.

A camping area is maintained at the park. Advance booking is necessary; apply by phone or in writing (enclose a stamped self-addressed envelope) any time up to twelve weeks in advance of your proposed visit. If planning a visit during a holiday period, preregistration is absolutely essential. Alternative accommodation is available at the tourist lodge near the park entrance.

Facilities at the camping area include a visitors' information center, cold showers, toilets, and a public telephone. Firewood is not available in the area; visitors must provide their own gas cooking equipment. The tourist lodge, open every day, sells general merchandise, gasoline and diesel fuel, and ice.

The bush of the eastern and western parts of central Queensland has undergone the most dramatic change in appearance of any area in Queensland. Between Townsville and the mountains near Brisbane, the slopes of the Great Dividing Range and coastal hillsides once were overgrown with conifers and a thick matting of wet temperate rain forest. West of the divide a tremendous inland sea submerged Queensland from north to south. Water, in one form or another, had a dominant influence on central Queensland.

Eons have passed and time has created an entirely different landscape here. Today it is the scarcity of water that rules the center of the state. Generally, central Queensland is a vast expanse of eucalypts, brigalow, montane heath, and grasslands, a landscape often summarized as flat and monotonous. The great Queensland park of Carnarvon is the exception. It is a veritable oasis whose deep gorges and permanent water are home to a variety of plant and animal

One of the most historically impressive areas in Queensland, Carnarvon National Park is well known for Its Aboriginal rock paintings, especially for the stenciled-hand artwork

species. Carnarvon is also a place of incredible beauty. A visitor to Carnarvon Gorge in the 1920s wrote, "Before these sandstone walls of vermilion and ivory I fall speechless. This vision bankrupts the English language." Even today, bushwalkers return from the gorge in quiet awe, as if they had spent the day within the holy walls of some remote monastery.

Approaching Carnarvon Gorge from flat open expanses of scrub and dust, one begins to notice a greening of the landscape as if life was once again suffusing the parched country. At the entrance to the gorge, gums reach unusual heights for this arid climate, thriving in an environment nurtured by the ever-flowing Carnarvon Creek. Year-round, life-giving waters percolate through beds of sandstone and replenish underground supplies in the Great Artesian Basin. From its source, Carnarvon Creek flows eventually into the Pacific Ocean 250 mi/400 km away via the Comet and Fitzroy rivers.

GEOLOGY

The geologic evolution of Carnarvon Gorge began nearly 200 million years ago, when the entire region slumped below the level of the surrounding area. The broad depression filled with a variety of sediments as creeks and rivers diverted into this lowland. Layers of sand and mudstone were sealed by volcanic activity, which deposited over them a cap of basaltic earth.

Over the past millions of years, the landscape has experienced numerous uplifts and tiltings, the result of this activity being clearly evident in the sloping layers of Clematis Ridge. Finally, the eroding action of Carnarvon Creek and its tributaries successfully carved deep into the soft basalt and sandstone, exposing the geology of the past and creating magnificent land forms. Carnarvon Creek now runs atop relatively impervious shale underlying the Kooramindangie Plain, on which the campground rests.

Along its initial 19 mi/30 km, Carnarvon Creek has cut deep into the Consuelo Tableland. The resultant formation is a complex network of serpentine gorges and side gorges comprising the Carnarvon Gorge section of the park. In some places, such as the confluence of Kooraminya and Carnarvon creeks, the gorge walls may rise several hundred feet and stand only 160 ft/50 m apart.

WILDLIFE AND VEGETATION

The floor of Carnarvon Gorge is green and very fertile, unexpected in this dry region. Lining the main creeks and upper moist banks are casuarinas, or she-oaks, lofty Sydney blue gums, and weeping red bottlebrush. When in bloom, the brilliant red flowers of the bottlebrush are an irresistible lure to yellow-tufted honey eaters.

The constantly flowing creeks and the open eucalypt forests with grassy understory combine to provide food and shelter for a wide variety of birds, mammals, and reptiles. Several species of wading birds—ibises, spoonbills, and herons—and tree dwellers such as cockatoos and fairy wrens can be spotted throughout the day near the water. Green tree frogs and eastern water dragons also live along the water's edge.

Wards Canyon, 3 mi/4.8 km west along Carnarvon Creek, contains a narrow section locally called Angiopteris Ravine after the ancient king fern (*Angiopteris evecta*) growing there. King ferns are the largest and among the most magnificent ferns on earth. The fronds of mature individuals, mounted atop thick woody trunks, can reach 16 ft/6 m in length.

Mornings and evenings become very active in the gorge as most of the major mammals begin foraging about. Eastern gray kangaroos

Also called the "pretty-face wallaby," the whip-tailed wallaby is found from eastern Queensland south through northeastern Victoria. Often seen in large groups, the whip-tail is more active than other wallabies, resting only in the hottest part of the day.

are the largest residents of Carnarvon Gorge, although their more lightly built relative, the brush-tailed rock wallaby, draws far more attention. Like most rock wallabies, the brushtail has a limited habitat range throughout Australia, confined to drier regions of broken shale or rock scree. The beautiful whip-tailed wallaby also is seen with regularity in the gorge.

Nights here are active with the ramblings of the brush-tailed possum and the shyer greater and yellow-bellied gliders.

Splitting at right angles from the main creek are tributaries and their associated smaller gorges and ravines. These cool, narrow slots in the sandstone walls are magical green worlds adorned with delicate orchids, colonies of ferns, and mosses wet with trickling water. The plants line water-soaked overhangs and plummeting waterfalls. Days can be spent exploring the unbelievable variety of these secluded worlds.

The great majority of visitors to Carnarvon National Park spend their time discovering the wildlife and vegetation within the gorge. Few venture into the arid tablelands and other parts of the park,

The main gorge at Carnarvon was created by Carnarvon Creek over several million years. Surrounded by walls of white sandstone, the isolated area harbors many plant and animal species.

where low, open eucalypt forest dotted with picturesque grass trees lends a soft gray-green tint to the sandstone landscape.

Aborigines recognized the oasis quality of Carnarvon Gorge centuries before the area was discovered by white explorers. Exactly how long Aborigines inhabited the gorge is uncertain, since all that remains of their activities are some expansive and colorful rock paintings. The most dramatic and complex of these, at Cathedral Cave, indicates 3,600 years of occupancy. Evidence suggests, however, that the area of Consuelo Tableland and Clematis Ridge has been occupied for as long as 19,000 years.

The art is principally stencilwork in rich red ocher on the cream-colored sandstone. The objects depicted include adults' and children's hands, tools, animals, and weapons such as axes and boomerangs. In the view of some archaeologists, the size and development of the art at two sites—Cathedral Cave and The Art Gallery—imply that the area was of significant ceremonial importance to Aborigines of central Queensland. Other archaeologists have suggested, however, that the presence of children's prints is a strong indicator that these areas were not sacred, since most Aboriginal groups did not include children in such activities.

BUSHWALKING

Aijon Falls and Wards Canyon. A short, steep climb goes past Lower Aijon Falls to the small but beautiful Wards Canyon 3 mi/ 4.8 km from the camp, known for its flourishing growth of mosses and ferns. At the canyon's edge is a shaded pool fed by Upper Aijon Falls.

The Art Gallery. This is a major Aboriginal art site 3.5 mi/5.6 km from the camp. The rock surface on which these paintings are inscribed erodes easily. Remain on the boardwalk and do not touch the artwork.

Cathedral Cave. In the shelter of this large overhang, 6 mi/9.3 km along the main Carnarvon Gorge trail, Aborigines once spent time painting and feasting. The lower walls are blanketed with carvings and paintings. Stay on the boardwalks. Camping is not permitted in the cave. There are no well-defined walking tracks past Cathedral Cave, but Boowinda Gorge nearby (to the left), with its narrow passages and sculptured rock walls, is worth discovering.

Moss Garden. This unusual garden, 2.2 mi/3.6 km from the camping area, is situated in Violet Gorge, a side gorge in the Hellhole Gorge complex. A small waterfall cascades over a large rock overhang into an icy pool. The rock walls drip with water and support a prolific growth of mosses, ferns, liverworts, and hornworts. These small, delicate plants fall easily, and should be admired but not touched.

Battleship Spur. A series of steep, difficult climbs starting from Boowinda Gorge leads to Battleship Spur, where there are excellent views of Carnarvon Gorge. This hike is not a part of the walking trail system, has no signs, and is recommended only for expert bushwalkers. See the ranger for details before attempting it.

FRASER ISLAND

Fraser Island Recreation Board, c/o Queensland National Parks and Wildlife Service, Rainbow Beach Road, P.O. Box 30, Rainbow Beach, QLD 4570, or call (071) 86 3160.

Located 118 mi/190 km north of Brisbane, Fraser Island is accessible by several means of transportation.

Vehicle ferries run daily from Inskip Point near Rainbow Beach to the southern end of the island. Others run from the Urangan boat harbor and River Heads at Hervey Bay to various points on the western side of the island. A four-wheel-drive vehicle is the only practical means of transportation on the island, and all vehicles must have permits. Four-wheel drives can be rented on the mainland, but you must make a reservation well in advance.

Charter aircraft leave from Brisbane, Hervey Bay, Rainbow Beach, Maryborough, and the Sunshine Coast.

Launches depart daily from either Urangan boat harbor or River Heads at Hervey Bay.

There are plenty of accommodations to choose from, ranging from luxury resorts to camping areas. Campgrounds require permits unless they are privately owned. Be sure to make reservations well in advance.

Fraser Island is a beachcomber's paradise, with rolling white beaches, areas of rocky coastline, magnificent forests, and sparkling freshwater lakes. This is the world's largest sand island, and colored sand cliffs and natural sandflows are among its prominent features.

The sands are of two major types. The beach sands, typically, are white, while the sands of the island's cliffs and formations, called teewah sands, are in shades of yellow, red, and brown. The Cathedrals are permanent sculptures of teewah sands shaped by erosion into spires and cliffs. The range of colors in this area – reds, yellows, and oranges accented by rich black sand – might seem like the work of an impressionist painter. The colored sands stretch 29 mi/35 km north from Happy Valley.

Fraser Island has many freshwater lakes, the largest being Lake Boomanjin. Like most of the lakes on Fraser, it lies atop a peat base and so is called a "perched lake." Lake Boomanjin, at 494 acres/ 200 hectares, is the largest perched lake in the world. Picturesque and serene, it is an ideal place to stop for a relaxing swim. Many people come to Fraser for its excellent ocean fishing areas and its abundance of whiting, Taylor flathead, and bream.

HISTORY

Fraser Island is unusual in that it is one of the few islands off the Australian mainland that is neither continental in origin nor the result of a coral-reef formation. Instead, Fraser Island, 77 mi/27 km long and 14 mi/8.7 km wide at its widest point, was derived from the weathering of mountain ranges in what is now New South Wales. Rivers and ocean currents transported large quantities of sand northward. Much of the sand was deposited around rocky headlands, such as Indian Head, where it gradually accumulated, creating in time a huge sand island. Besieged by winds and tides, this fragile environment is subject to a continual process of buildup and erosion.

Fraser Island was first sighted by Captain Cook in 1770. Cook did not realize it was an island, taking it to be a huge promontory off the coast. He named its northernmost peak Sandy Point and called one of its four large outcrops of volcanic rock Indian Head because he sighted Aborigines there. It was not until 1822 that Captain William Edwardson discovered that Fraser was indeed an island.

The island was inhabited originally by a few thousand Aborigines from the Butchalla tribe. Among the tribe members there was resentment of the European settlers, and some, like the survivors of the wreck of the brig *Sterling Castle*, including Capt. James Fraser and his wife Eliza, suffered death or harsh treatment at their hands.

Fraser Island was declared a "native" reserve in 1860, but the Aboriginal population eventually dwindled to several hundred. The diseases they caught from the European settlers and the malnutrition they suffered as the land was cleared greatly reduced their numbers. Eventually they were moved to the mainland.

The island, with its huge pine forests and excellent fresh water supply, drew the attention of timber companies in the mid-1800s. It was soon dominated by the logging industry, which equipped it with large sawmills, a township, a school, and even an island train.

The dangerous waters of the Great Sandy Strait and the sections of the island that jut out into the sea have made Fraser Island the

Fraser Island's colored sand cliffs, known as The Cathedrals, are continually being eroded by the wind.

graveyard for a large number of ships. Two of these wrecks, the *Marloo* and the *Maheno*, are still present in the area. A lighthouse built in 1870 at Sandy Cape has helped reduce the occurrence of shipping disasters.

WILDLIFE

Most islands off the coast of Australia have varied wildlife populations due to the absence of the dingo, but on Fraser these wild dogs have had a suppressive influence. For their part, the dingoes of Fraser have benefited from their isolation from the mainland. They have avoided breeding with feral domestic dogs; indeed, they are believed to be the purest strain in existence.

Besides dingoes, Fraser's wildlife includes possums, echidnas, and wallabies, as well as native rodents and numerous reptiles and frogs. As a consequence of European settlement of the island, there is a large population of "brumbies," or feral horses, which often prove to be a nuisance.

The abundant supply of fresh water and the diversity of vegetation attract a profusion of bird life to the island. More than 240 species of birds have been recorded. There is suitable environment for both shorebirds and forest species. Among the shorebirds are dotterels, pelicans, pied oystercatchers, gulls, and terns. Forest birds include cockatoos, kingfishers, swallows, and wrens. The island also attracts jabirus, ospreys, and peregrine falcons. At any time of the day it is easy to identify at least twenty species of birds close by, and it is not unreasonable to aim at sighting forty different species in one day.

VEGETATION

One would not expect a sand island to support a large variety of vegetation, but that is precisely the case on Fraser Island. There is a forest of satinays, magnificent trees with rough bark, dark fleshy leaves, and straight trunks; some stand over 230 ft/70 m tall. Not too far from the satinays are forests of piccabeen palms and kauri pines. Each forest type alone is a distinctive and rewarding experience, but even more amazing is the large area of transition forest, where specimens from several forest types intermingle.

Other trees found on the island include blackbutt trees, the main timber on the island, and scribbly gums, so named for the scribble lines left on their bark by burrowing insects. On the mainland side are cypress and paperbark forests.

While Fraser is most famous for its trees, it also supports a rich array of flowers that bloom on the heathlands and low areas. In spring it is worth a trip just to see the wildflower display.

MORETON ISLAND NATIONAL PARK

The Ranger, Queensland National Parks and Wildlife Service, c/o Tangalooma Resort, Moreton Island, QLD 4004, or call (075) 48 2710.

Vehicle barges leave from Amity Point, Lytton, and Scarborough. Four-wheel-drive vehicles are necessary for island driving.

Passenger launches leave regularly for Tangalooma Resort from Hamilton, Redcliffe, and Bribie Island. A launch from Manly lands at Koorengal. There are aircraft landing strips at Cowan Cowan and Koorengal. Private boats can be hired on the western side of the island.

Campsites must be reserved, and a permit system operates. There are shops for food, fuel, and ice at Koorengal and Buling.

Moreton Island, 25 mi/40 km from Brisbane, forms the eastern side of Moreton Bay. About 24 mi/38 km long and 5.6 mi/9 km wide at its widest point, its chief geological feature is Mt. Tempest, one of the highest stable sand dunes in the world at 919 ft/280 m.

This sand island supports many different plant communities and habitats. There are beaches, dunes, rocky headlands, lakes, streams, sedge and paperbark swamps, open forest and woodland, mangrove swamp and salt marsh. There are human communities, too, including townships and a resort.

Whale watching is good here during migration season, as humpbacks make their way through Moreton Bay. Seabirds and shorebirds abound. Agile wallabies are common. So too are reptiles, and walkers should be alert for them. Of interest, though ecologically undesirable, are the feral pigs, goats, and horses, all introduced, that roam the island. Ocean fishing is a popular activity, in addition to viewing the island's many scenic features.

The glowing orange head of the Australian king parrot is hard to miss among the treetops in the coastal areas of eastern Australia. The bird is sometimes seen walking clumsily on the ground in search of fallen seeds, nuts, or fruit.

LAMINGTON NATIONAL PARK

The Ranger, Lamington National Park, Binna Burra section, Beechmont, via Nerang, QLD 4211, or call (075) 33 3584. The Ranger, Lamington National Park, Green Mountains section, via Canungra, QLD 4275, or call (075) 45 1734.

The camping area at Green Mountains has leveled sites, toilets, showers, and barbecues.

The landscape of Queensland's southeastern corner has experienced tremendous uplifts, volcanic activity, and weathering, and the result is a region of awesome topography. Within this terrain the visitor may feel an overwhelming sense of isolation. But one need only crest an escarpment or climb a peak and there will be the bright lights of Brisbane and the Gold Coast twinkling in the distance. Thousands of people visit the nearby coast and never realize that less than two hours away, in the hinterlands, await parklands of extraordinary beauty. One such place is Lamington National Park. Comprising 49,914 acres/20,200 hectares of rolling hills, valleys, ridges, and mountain tops, the park sits atop the Lamington Plateau, a mere 60 mi/100 km south of the state capital, Brisbane. With wildlife and plant communities as diverse as its topography, the park also contains the most significant remainder of subtropical rain forest and the most northerly area of Antarctic beech growth in Queensland.

GEOLOGY AND VEGETATION

Dense temperate rain forest once grew throughout Queensland during a geologic period when the Australian continent was positioned farther south in the hemisphere. During that period, forests with mammoth red cedars and exposed slopes of Antarctic beech covered the landscape of what is now Lamington National Park. A northerly shift in the continent's position brought an increase in temperature, and the rain forest began a subtle but steady change in appearance. Epiphytic ferns, orchids, mosses, and rope-like lianas took possession of the environment. The plateau and ranges of the Great Dividing Range became overgrown with jungle vegetation. The resulting combination of climates and terrain has created a complex mixture of vegetation types. This mingling of environments, known as the "McPherson overlap," makes Lamington National Park one of the most fascinating parks in Australia and botanically unique in the world.

En route to the Green Mountains-O'Reilly section of Lamington National Park, a narrow paved road enters the western side of the park through a cultivated valley and begins to climb through open scrub and a variety of eucalypt trees. On these western slopes rain clouds are scarce and the soils less fertile than on the eastern slopes. Fires are frequent; evidence of burning can be seen in areas of sparse undergrowth and in the abundance of burn-resistant grass trees. Near the crest, still on a westerly influence, tall gray gums and brush box growing in tight proximity prepare the visitor for the dense rain forest that exists inside the park boundary.

Entering Lamington National Park, the road winds through the dense trunks and buttresses of giant tulip oaks. Tallowwood, a

Elabana Falls is one of the almost 500 waterfalls that cascade into clear tranquil pools in Lamington National Park.

eucalypt species, grows here too. The temperature drops a few degrees, and the number and variety of epiphytes and vines increase remarkably.

Among the epiphytes, orchids are extremely numerous throughout the park, with more than 700 species identified. September through October is especially good for viewing these amazing flowers in bloom. Near O'Reilly's Guest House at Green Mountain, an orchid garden maintains a fine collection of native Australian species.

The walk from O'Reilly's Guest House to Elabana Falls along the Border Trail gives an excellent opportunity to wander through the many levels of rain-forest growth in the park. Approaching the falls, the trail passes beneath a massive garden of bird's-nest and staghorn ferns and a scattering of piccabeen palms. This area also contains one of the most impressive stands of smooth pink-barked brush box in the park.

Elabana Falls is only one of several hundred falls that cascade and tumble through the park. These falls line the headwaters of many major creeks and rivers flowing north through southeast Queensland.

WILDLIFE

Lamington National Park is ranked as one of the five best areas in Australia for seeing native wildlife species in their natural habitats. It has long been one of the great bird-watching areas of the continent. More than 120 species of birds have been spotted in the park, many quite special to the Lamington forests (for example, the Albert's lyrebird, which is a darker reddish brown than its southern cousin). Crimson rosellas and satin and regent bowerbirds are not unique to Lamington, but few locations offer such excellent close viewing of these beautiful birds.

For sheer numbers, the crimson rosellas deserve attention. Thousands of the flashing red and blue birds descend on the grass lawns and nearby trees in front of O'Reilly's Guest House. Seeking handouts of sunflower seed, the crimsons will literally eat out of your hand.

Fascinating and exquisitely feathered, the regent and satin bowerbirds alone are worth a visit to the park. Male bowerbirds are known for their ingeniously built, specially decorated courting chambers, or bowers. Other birds include the pied currawong, brush turkey,

BOWERBIRDS
Paradisaeidae

Male bowerbird.

Female bowerbird.

The bowerbird builds an elaborate structure solely for courting purposes and a separate nest for its eggs. It is surely one of the most ingenious architects of all the bird species.

During the mating season, the male constructs his bower out of branches, plants, and other materials. Each species of bowerbird has a unique way of decorating the bower, usually by adding objects that match the bird's particular color. The male regent bowerbird, a black bird with bright yellow markings, adds brightly colored shiny objects to his bower. The blue satin bowerbird actually paints the inside of his bower blue, using a piece of bark mixed with charcoal and fruit fragments and saliva. Some bowerbirds, however, do not add any adornments.

Once the bower is completed, the male bird stands inside it and performs a complex mating dance, stiffening his legs, spreading his wings, and making hissing and wheezing noises until he attracts a responsive female.

wompoo pigeon, king parrot, bell bird, spine-tailed log runner, and (by night) the boobook owl.

Mammals are equally plentiful. Platypuses show themselves at Blue Pool, below Elabana Falls on West Canungra Creek, and the red-shouldered pademelon and potoroo frequent the campgrounds at dusk. But it is the brush-tailed and ring-tailed possums that steal the show nightly in the trees outside O'Reilly's. Just past dusk each evening, as many as a half-dozen possums, including the copper-colored version of the ringtail, perform their begging routine, hang-

Baby red-necked pademelons communicate by uttering high squeaks in response to their mother's repetitive clicking noises.

ing by prehensile tails with outstretched open paws and choosing only the best bread and jam and the sweetest fruits from among the offerings. It is an excellent opportunity to observe these round-eyed marsupials of the night at the very closest range.

Another unusual resident of these mountains is the Lamington spiny crayfish. Protected within the park, this crustacean lives in many of its creeks but is especially numerous in the Blue Pool area.

BUSHWALKING – GREEN MOUNTAINS SECTION

Blue Pool trail and Stairway Falls track. The trail to Blue Pool, 3 mi/4.9 km, veers off the Border Trail 273 yd/250 m from the park entrance and descends steadily, passing some large rain-forest trees, including several specimens of the red cedars once eagerly sought by lumbermen for their beautiful timber and now rather scarce. The Christmas orchid may be seen along this trail. In season, its fragile white flowers dot the rain-forest floor. The trail finally reaches Blue Pool on West Canungra Creek, where large eels and platypuses may be seen. Stairway Falls is 1 mi/1.7 km further along the same path.

Box Forest circuit. This circuit of 6.6 mi/0.6 km branches from the Border Trail 1 mi/1.6 km from the park entrance. It leads down through the rain forest, passing impressive stands of smooth pink-barked brush box before reaching Picnic Rock and Elabana Falls on Canungra Creek. There is a swimming hole below Sunshine Falls about 110 yd/100 m upstream from Picnic Rock. The trail continues down the valley, then climbs the opposite side.

Toolona Creek circuit. This is a fairly long trail of 10.9 mi/17.4 km. It branches from the Box Forest circuit near Elabana Falls, then follows Toolona Creek up a gorge and past its headwaters to emerge on the Border Trail near the Wanungra lookout. Waterfalls and cascades are viewed along the way. In the many pools along this trail you may discover the Lamington spiny crayfish. The return walk is via the Border Trail passing Toolona and Bithongabel lookouts. Many large clumps of Antarctic beech are seen near the lookouts.

Canungra Creek circuit. This 8.7-mi/13.9-km trail meets the Box Forest circuit and the Blue Pool trail to complete a loop. The trail follows the creek for most of its length, crossing it a number of times.

The common ringtail possum's usual diet consists of leaves, but it has also been known to eat flowers and fruits. Frequently found in suburban gardens, it especially enjoys nibbling rosebuds.

Bird life is plentiful, and species such as the spine-tailed log runner and Australian ground thrush may be seen hunting for insect meals in the leaf litter.

BUSHWALKING – BINNA BURRA SECTION

Bellbird Lookout circuit. Branching off the Ships Stern circuit, this 1.2-mi/2-km trail goes through rain forest (passing a giant tallow-wood in the eucalypt forest) before emerging at Bellbird lookout. This provides an excellent view of Ships Stern, Turtle Rock, Egg Rock, and the Numinbah Valley of the Nerang River.

Notice the hoop pines growing on the exposed northern slopes. The harvesting of hoop pine and red cedar led to the initial settlement and ultimate clearing of the Numinbah Valley for grazing.

Senses trail. Over a distance of either 437 yd/400 m or 765 yd/ 700 m, this unusual self-guided nature walk encourages visually impaired (or blindfolded) walkers to awaken their other senses in a forest environment. Walkers follow a guiding rope, while trailside markers in Braille point out many sensuous aspects of the forest experience. Brochures are available at the kiosk, Binna Burra Lodge, or from the box at the trail head.

Coomera circuit. A circuit of 10.9 mi/17.4 km, it branches right off the Border Trail after 1.2 mi/1.9 km and passes through rain forest and giant smooth pink-barked brush box before emerging at the Coomera Falls lookout 2.2 mi/3.5 km from the Border Trail entrance. The 210-ft/64-m falls drop from one narrow gorge into another, for a total gorge depth of 175 yd/160 m.

The circuit continues up the rain-forested Coomera River valley, crossing the river several times and passing many waterfalls before rejoining the Border Trail and returning to Binna Burra. Lamington spiny crayfish are common in this area.

Daves Creek circuit. This trail offers great botanical interest as it winds through a variety of vegetation types – from rain forest to open eucalypt forest and on to montane heath, home of the rare eastern bristle-bird. The nature of the soils derived from different volcanic rocks has affected the distribution of these vegetation types.

Creeping lianas (or vines) wrap themselves around trees for support, climbing until they reach sunlight, then spreading out their wide crown of leaves.

GREAT BARRIER REEF

Capricorn-Bunker Groups:
Heron Island, Lady Elliot Island,
Other Islands of the
Capricorn-Bunker Groups

Swain Reefs and Pompey Complex

Whitsunday Islands:
Lindeman Island, Hamilton Island

Hayman Island

Hinchinbrook Island

Dunk Island

Green Island

Michaelmas Cay
and Hastings Reef Complex

Lizard Island

Masthead Island is one of the largest coral cays in the Capricorn-Bunker Groups. It is
heavily forested and attracts many migratory birds.

Great Barrier Reef Marine Park Authority, P.O. Box 1379, Townsville, QLD 4810, or call (077) 71 2191.

Queensland National Parks and Wildlife Service, P.O. Box 190, North Quay, QLD 4000, or call (07) 244 0414.

Southern Regional Director, Capricorn-Bunker Groups, Queensland National Parks and Wildlife Service, State Government Building, Roseberry Street, P.O. Box 315, Gladstone, QLD 4680, or call (079) 761 621.

AUSTRALIA'S GREAT BARRIER REEF is the largest living organism in the world. Its southern boundary is south of the Tropic of Capricorn, off the shore of central Queensland, and it extends north for 1,200 mi/2,000 km to the Torres Strait, between Australia and Papua New Guinea. Like a huge serpent, it winds toward and away from the Queensland coastline, at some points only a few miles from the mainland, at others almost 200 mi/320 km away. Together, 2,600 coral reefs and about 320 coral islands make up the Great Barrier Reef.

Fringing, ribbon, and patch reefs, lagoons, cays, and continental islands combine to form the complex of the Great Barrier Reef. The diversity of fishes, corals, and other marine creatures in the fringing reefs along the mainland and around the continental islands is as great as anywhere else in the Great Barrier Reef. However, it is the lure of the outer reef that attracts most fishermen and divers.

The outer reef is really a maze of reefs on the edge of the continental shelf beyond which the seabed plunges into a deep-blue abyss. Through this maze swim the grand game fishes, such as marlin, swordfish, and tuna, in the company of great sharks and whales. Here the waters are usually transparent to more than 100 ft/30 m, and scuba divers claim that this visibility makes their dives breathtaking. Marine scientists say, however, that although the aesthetics of the outer reef may be alluring, the variety of creatures that live there is no greater than that of the inner reefs.

In 1975, the Australian government passed the Great Barrier Reef Marine Park Act, which seeks to allow enjoyment and reasonable use of the Great Barrier Reef while preserving its natural environment. More than 98 percent of the Great Barrier Reef Region has so far been declared a protected marine park.

Heron Island, an international mecca for sport divers, is the most built-up of the coral islands in the Capricorn-Bunker Groups.

ORIGINS OF A REEF

A coral reef is formed when tiny animals called coral polyps attach themselves to the shallow sea bottom and secrete a limestone skeleton, composed principally of calcium carbonate. A symbiotic relationship between the coral and tiny single-celled plants called Zooxanthellae, which live within the cells of the coral polyp, aids the coral in the production of limestone. The presence of sunlight is vitally important to those corals that rely on the Zooxanthellae to grow. This is why live corals are found only in waters that are clear, well-lit, and shallow (30 ft/10 m).

As the original coral polyp grows and divides, it creates a living coral colony. These colonies, plus the skeletons of old colonies whose corals have died, form the framework of the reef; broken-down coral fragments and skeletal material from other reef animals fill in the many gaps. In time this matter is cemented together by encrusting algae and sponges. It is this combination that forms the solid coral reef.

Coral reefs begin in shallow water when coral polyps attach themselves to the sea bottom and begin secreting a limestone skeleton. Sometimes the colonies grow high enough to break the surface of the water. This can be the beginning of a coral cay.

As a reef matures and reaches the ocean surface, it begins to flatten and expand horizontally. The resultant barrier interrupts wave action and water circulation, creating different environments on each side of the reef. The side protected from the full forces of the open sea, called the inner reef, is bathed by warmer, less turbulent waters, which consequently have a lower content of oxygen and nutrients. Corals and other creatures found there are delicately structured. The other, windward side of the reef is rife with hardier corals and myriad sea creatures that thrive in the harsher conditions of the open seas. This exposed side often develops a strong growth of algae.

Birth of a Barrier Reef Island

Reef islands are formed when coral reaches above sea level, even at low tide. The wind and waves bring sediments and pound the deposits and dead coral into sand. Before long, the deposits can withstand the daily pressures of tidal exchange. When even very high waves can no longer crest the newly created sand island, a cay is formed.

The cay is an ideal nesting habitat for turtles and numerous sea birds, such as noddies, terns, and gannets. Nesting sea birds bring foreign materials to the cay, including plant seeds that become accidentally trapped in their feathers as they forage for nesting material and food. Many of these seeds take root on the cay. The growth and development of vegetation binds the shifting sands and stabilizes the cay.

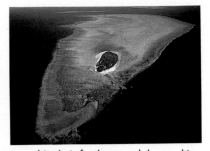

Birds inadvertently bring seeds to the cay trapped in their feathers, and the resulting small plants help stabilize the island sand. When rainwater solidifies beach rock and dense vegetation takes root, the cay has become a coral reef island.

Rain water plays an important role in stabilizing the cay. Calcium carbonate is released by the sediments and coral fragments as fresh water filters down through them, cementing the sediments and forming beach rock. Once the cay has grown to at least four or five acres, it is capable of maintaining a fresh-water lens (a small sub-surface fresh-water pond). Fresh water is less dense than salt water, hence it floats under the cay. Larger plants, such as the pisonia tree, can now tap into this slightly brackish water supply.

ORIGINS OF THE GREAT BARRIER REEF

Because most corals can grow only in shallow water, the most important influence on the pattern and development of the Great Barrier Reef's growth has been the intermittent fluctuations in sea level caused by the alternating advance and retreat of glaciers in the polar regions. When the sea level dropped, the exposed corals died. As the sea level again rose, the old reefs acted like a bench on which new corals could begin to grow.

Because the Great Barrier Reef is affected by many other climatic and oceanic conditions, its coral species and its rate of growth vary immensely. The reef is also influenced by sediments and fresh-water runoff from the mainland. No two portions of the Great Barrier Reef are the same, although there are some regional patterns of coral growth and reef development.

The type of coral reef most people hear about is the fringing reef. Fringing reefs are widely distributed and occur as far south as Lord Howe Island, in the Tasman Sea; indeed, they are the southernmost

reefs in the world. Many of these reefs have grown offshore from the Great Barrier Reef's more than 600 continental islands. Fringing reefs also exist along some parts of the mainland coast. But because they are so close to land, the fringing reefs suffer during the wet season. Fresh-water runoff lowers the salinity, thus slowing the growth of corals. The floodwaters also transport excessive amounts of silt and debris, which have a severe and often devastating effect on corals. Sediments not only smother the delicate corals as they settle, but they also drastically reduce the amount of sunlight available to the Zooxanthellae, which is necessary for the plants' survival. Thus, on some fringing reefs, exploring at low tide may prove disappointing during the wet season.

Ribbon reefs, which begin north of Townsville, are usually less than 150 ft/45 m wide, but they can be 20 mi/32 km long. Because the water there has more nutrients than in any other region of the Great Barrier Reef, the marine life is more colorful and spectacular than it is anywhere else on the reef. It has been suggested that ribbons formed on top of the fringing reefs of coastlines that existed 6,000 to 15,000 years ago when the sea level was approximately 150 ft/45 m lower than at present.

CORALS

The dominant creatures of the reef are, of course, the corals themselves. First-time visitors to the reef are often surprised to learn how diverse this group of animals really is. The word *coral* describes similarly structured creatures that boast a variety of colors, shapes, and sizes, in much the same way that *bird* is the generic term for any member of an enormous group of feathered creatures. Corals may be described as either *hard* (*stony*, or *true*) corals or *soft* corals.

The hard corals are associated with the construction of the reef itself. The appearance of a specific type of coral has to do with the way its individual polyps lay down their skeletons and give rise to new polyps. Brain coral polyps divide without forming completely separate walls, resulting in a series of convoluted channels and folds

The brightly colored gorgonian corals, commonly called fan corals, spread their tentacles at right angles to the current to collect passing plankton.

in the colony's surface that resemble the convolutions of the lobes. Staghorn coral polyps grow out from the parents' skeleton to form a branch-like structure that looks like antlers. But coral colonies are also molded by their environment, with underwater currents, low tides, and wave action sculpting them, so shape cannot be taken as a guide in species identification.

If the hard corals are the architects and builders of the reef, then the soft corals can be regarded as the decorators. The major difference between the two types is that soft corals lack hard calcium-carbonate outer walls. That soft corals may appear pliable, even structureless, belies the fact that they have an internal skeleton of sclerites, hard miniature crystalline structures. In many soft corals, sclerites are so loosely assembled that the animal appears to have no skeleton at all. In others, the sclerites collect just densely enough to form flesh-like stalks from which the polyps extend.

Most species of soft coral grow on the exposed reefs and current-swept walls of the outer reef where the turbulent sea keeps suspended plankton in motion. The soft corals depend on currents to push plankton into their polyps, which capture the plankton with stinging cells on their tentacles. Soft corals rarely colonize the calm inner reef, although two species, the lobophytons and the sarcophytons, have adapted to inner-reef life.

Soft, gorgonian corals grow into gorgeous fans and whips of red, yellow, soft blue, gray, black, and orange. Many gorgonians have developed a different sort of protective skeleton formed from sclerites, proteins, and minerals. Famous among this collection are the precious jewelry corals of black, red, and pink, whose hard, dense skeletons are cut and polished into rings, beads, and tiny sculptures.

Infamous among the Great Barrier Reef's soft corals is fire coral. Divers and snorkelers quickly become acquainted with the shape, color, and sting of this delicate but potent branching coral. The burning sensation left as a reminder of contact with fire coral is akin to that felt after an encounter with a stinging jellyfish.

During the day, coral polyps are retracted and the structures appear a mottled combination of pale browns, greens, and creams. But at night, the nocturnal polyps emerge, their exposed tissues presenting a multicolored palette.

Clockwise from top left: three soft corals and three hard corals. Despite their range of shapes and colors, corals are classified into genera and species by the shape of their internal skeleton.

INVERTEBRATES

Few marine environments can boast the clarity of the Great Barrier Reef. Because nutrients and plankton do not cloud its waters as they do temperate waters, the sea around the reef is often assumed to be nutrient-poor and barren. But one reef walk at low tide or snorkel trip along the reef edge will disprove that theory. Each reef animal is constantly straining, filtering, and catching almost every particle that passes by: that is why the water is so clear.

FILTERERS

Coral reef creatures have developed many ways to compete or to cooperate with one another in their struggle for food. Filterers constitute the largest group of animals living on the reef. Among those are the sponges, one of the oldest and most primitive of all life forms. Sponges add a rainbow of colors to the landscape of the reef, but they are also a key component in the reef environment. Filtering sea water is the sponge's specialty. A sponge the size of a soccer ball, for example, can in a day filter an amazing 5,000 gal/19,000 l of water through its body. In addition, their numerous surface openings and complex network of channels and passages provide ideal living space for thousands of tiny creatures such as shrimp, crabs, and fishes.

MOLLUSKS

A walk on the reef flat at low tide will reveal dozens of kinds of mollusks. This group includes bivalves, or clam-like creatures; snails; shell-less snails called sea slugs, or nudibranchs; squids; and octopuses. Unique to this tropical world is the giant clam, which can grow to more than 2 ft/0.6 m in diameter. They grow so large that they cannot even close their shells completely. The mantle, or exposed fleshy portion between the shell halves, is decorated with hues of green, blue, purple, and beige, making the giant clam one of the more attractive bivalves on the reef.

Shell collectors prize the plentiful and diverse gastropod, or snail, shells more than other molluscan shells. Cowries are among the most numerous and beautifully patterned gastropods on the Great Barrier Reef, with over 200 species gliding about on the reef top

Top: Colonial ascidians take in water through one opening, filter it for food, and then expel it through a second opening. Bottom: The flatworm's bright colors warn potential predators of their bad-tasting flesh, which is lethal to some fish.

The daisy coral's brilliant tentacles are dotted with stinging cells that catch its prey. At night or when the coral is alarmed, its tentacles close up into light pink structures.

and grazing on the thin layer of algae growing on rocks and dead coral heads. It would be rare for someone examining shells on a reef walk not to see at least two or three kinds of cowries. Unlike many other mollusks, cowries retain their glossy coatings even after being removed from the sea. Many of the islands and reef areas are restricted or off-limits to shell collectors, however, and those caught disobeying the law must pay stiff fines. It is best to check with marine park authorities about collecting any marine creatures before visiting a specific area of the reef.

Cones and volutes are the only major species of gastropod that are carnivorous hunters. The beautiful cone shells, in particular, can be extremely venomous; at least twenty-two people have died world-wide as a result of a cone-shell sting. Cones, usually 2 to 4 in/5 to 10 cm long and variously colored, thrust into their prey a hollowed-out barb, through which a highly toxic venom is pumped. Cone shells usually feed on small marine worms and other mollusks, but a few extremely specialized ones feed on small fishes. Never pick up a cone.

Nudibranchs, or sea slugs, are often referred to as the clowns of the sea because of their festive ornamentation and bright coloration. Unique among the mollusks for having lost their shells totally, nudi-branchs have evolved an assortment of defense mechanisms, such as bold colors, pungent odors, and a distinctly bad taste. Some, such as aeolids, take advantage of the defense systems of the prey they eat. As aeolids bite off copious amounts of corals and sea anemones, they ingest stinging cells without releasing their toxic charge. The stinging cells are stored in the feathery cerata lining the aeolids' backs. Any predator attempting to bite into them is stung by the stinging cells.

CEPHALOPODS
The cephalopods, which include octopuses, squids, cuttlefish, and the elegant chambered nautilus, form one of the strangest groups of mollusks. They are all capable of either crawling or jet-propelling at a very rapid speed and have highly developed eyes that can distinguish basic form and movement. Only the nautilus has retained an external shell, shaped in the classic coil and used as a flotation device, the animal occupying only the outermost part. Other cephalopods, such as the cuttlefish and squid, have either an internal sheath or pen; the octopus has no shell at all. Cuttlebones are familiar to most people as the whitish bones used to keep the beaks of pet birds in trim.

Legendary on the Great Barrier Reef is the tiny blue-ringed octo-pus. Scarcely longer than 5 in/12.5 cm, this miniature cephalopod possesses a venomous bite strong enough to kill a human. When alarmed, it displays its showy electric-blue rings, which cover its body and eight legs. Reef walkers generally discover blue rings while turning over coral debris and rocks at low tide. If blue rings are common in the area you are exploring, it is wise to be cautious.

CRUSTACEANS

Many of the most easily recognizable reef inhabitants are the crustaceans: shrimp, crabs, lobsters, and crayfish. Crustaceans must be nocturnal in order to survive. Fish can be blamed for their general daytime absence. Like many humans, fish find most crustaceans too tasty to resist.

In a world as overcrowded as a coral reef, sharing a living space can be a very effective method of survival. A cleverly camouflaging costume allows many shrimp and crabs to hide in the branches of coral or on the surface of a brightly colored sponge. Other crustaceans develop a symbiotic relationship with a host. Shrimp, in particular, have established fascinating symbiotic relationships with other reef dwellers. Divers on the reef often see "cleaning stations" established by the banded coral shrimp. These cleaner shrimp usually are found in pairs of adults, males slighter than females. Perched atop a coral outcrop or just inside a rock overhang, the banded coral shrimp wave their antennae to attract the attention of passing fish that are suffering from microscopic parasites or dead skin. As a troubled fish approaches the cleaning station, the shrimp jump onto their temporary host and begin searching for areas to clean. It is not uncommon to see several fish lined up at one of these cleaning stations in anticipation of service.

Other shrimp, species of the genus *Periclimenes*, have found safety and comfort within the venomous tentacles of sea anemones. Found throughout the Great Barrier Reef, these little shrimp are among the most beautiful on the reef. Measuring just in excess of 1 in/2.5 cm, they nestle in and around the tentacles of their host, removing debris and eating leftovers from the sea anemone's meal. It has been suggested that *Periclimenes* may function as a lure. Unsuspecting predators attempt to dart in and snatch the shrimp and instead become ensnared in the anemone's tentacles.

A number of crab species inhabit the beaches and exposed reef flats of coral cays and continental islands. Mysterious burrows left on the beach at sunrise are the signs of ghost crabs, which, with their pointed eyestalks extended, have become infamous on islands in the Capricorn–Bunker Groups because they attack hatchling sea

Fiddler crabs are found only during low tide when they emerge from their burrows to feed on the organic matter in the muddy areas of shores.

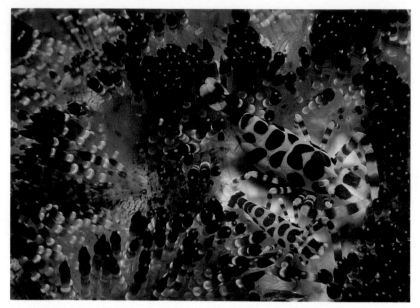

The coloring of the banded coral shrimp camouflages it against an anemone. Called cleaner shrimp, they relieve their host of microscopic parasites and dead skin.

turtles as they emerge from the sand. A few species of hermit crab have established themselves successfully as true islanders. These crabs hatch from eggs deposited in the sea and spend months maturing before they venture onto land. As adults, they scavenge through the litter left by high tides and visiting sea birds.

ECHINODERMS

Echinoderms are the very conspicuous, five-parted animals that include the brittle stars, sea stars, sea cucumbers, sand dollars, and crinoid, or feather, stars. Many types, such as the sea stars and sea urchins, possess highly sophisticated designs, with ultra-light and super-strong skeletons. All the members of the group have the ability to self-repair: some sea stars, for example, can suffer the loss of all but one arm and still regenerate back to their original appearance. Although these animals look very different from one another, there are three consistent features. In addition to the five-part body and the thin, strong skeleton of calcium-containing plates (from which the group gets its name), echinoderms possess rows of tube

Feather stars, or crinoids, usually live in clusters near the top of the reef. Their many arms act as an effective filtering system.

feet that operate on a hydraulic-pressure system. The feet get longer as fluid is pumped into them. They extend and attach to the ground by means of suckers. Fluid is then pumped out of the tube feet so that they shorten, pulling the animal forward.

The most familiar echinoderms are the starfish, of which the fire-armed cobalt-blue, little brown, and horned (or chocolate-chip) sea stars are very numerous. The basket (or feather) stars have arms subdivided so many times that the five-point structure is completely obscured by what looks like a woven basket. The brittle stars resemble the sea stars in shape, but they also use their pencil-thin arms to make their way across the sea floor.

The crown-of-thorns starfish, which feeds almost exclusively on coral polyps, is infamous. So voracious is its appetite that some areas of reef, such as that around Green Island off Cairns, have nearly been wiped out by excessive populations. No one is certain why these population booms occur.

Pages 360 and 361: Red sea stars, like most other starfish, have thousands of tiny feet on their underside that move them along.

FISHES

Much of the lure of the Great Barrier Reef has to do with its fishes. A square acre of reef may be home to 150 species, totaling nearly 100,000 fish. No other habitat on earth, including the tropical rain forest, can boast such a variety of vertebrate inhabitants.

Reef fishes have evolved a wide range of sizes and a variety of body forms. The largest, the whale shark, reaches nearly 50 ft/15 m and weighs over 30,000 lbs/15,000 kg. On a nearby coral head, a miniature goby weighs less than 0.04 oz/1 g, yet has a very similar basic structure.

The way they are distributed demonstrates a great deal about fishes and their lives. Directly above and in the reef, the vast majority of the fishes are small and weigh less than 1 lb/0.5 kg. They include small wrasses, butterfly fish, angel-, clown-, and damselfish, gobies, and puffers–all of which are either delicately colored in order to camouflage or brightly painted in order to warn. Among them are some of the most cleverly designed of all fishes. For exam ple, the long-nose butterfly uses its elongated snout, which is two-thirds its body length, to pick at difficult-to-reach bits of food among the corals.

A boldly colored fish is usually a sign of danger to other fishes on the reef. It is often covered with poisonous spines and so is fairly free from predators. Members of the family Scorpaenidae, such as the butterfly cod, or lionfish, demonstrate this feature, as does the stonefish, which belongs to a related family. Contact with the venom-filled dorsal spines of these fishes can cause severe pain and swelling and, with the stonefish, even death. For this reason it is important to wear strong-soled shoes for reef walking.

One of the more common methods of defense on the reef is mimicry. Many fishes look alike and use this resemblance to their advantage. For example, the cleaner wrasse is not preyed on by other fish because it offers the valuable service of removing parasites and loose skin. The cleaner blenny resembles the wrasse so closely that other fishes cannot distinguish between the two. As a consequence, the blenny not only avoids being eaten, but also may exploit an

Coral cod live on the reef edge and eat almost anything small enough to fit into their mouths. Their relative, the coral trout, has similar coloring.

Clockwise from top: striped perch; long-nose butterfly fish; lion fish; blue eel.

CLOWNFISH
Amphiprion pericleraion

Clownfish, or anemone fish, have adapted to reef life with their symbiotic relationship with the flower-like sea anemones. Normally, the tentacles of the sea anemone would be deadly to a fish the size of a 4-in/120-cm clownfish. But clownfish have evolved a mucous coating similar to that of the anemone's own tentacles, allowing the little fish to frolic in complete immunity. They use the anemones for protection, and get food by cleaning scraps and debris out of the anemone's tentacles. It is theorized that the anemone uses the

clownfish to lure other fishes into its clutches. The nature of their relationship is still a mystery.

unsuspecting fish that is hoping to be cleaned but instead gets bitten. Fortunately, the blenny, a mere 2 in/5 cm long, can inflict little more than a small nip.

Larger fishes, and fewer of them, live farther from the reef edge. Securing safety in their size and aggressiveness, these fishes often lack the intricacy of pattern, design, and color generally seen in smaller ones. The more common large reef fishes include sharks, manta and eagle rays, cods, and groupers. Rarely seen near the reef are tuna, marlin, and other deep-sea game fishes.

Reef fishes can be divided into the bony and the cartilaginous kinds, this latter being principally the sharks. While most of the bony fish dwelling on the reef are small, a few, such as the potato cod, can reach enormous size. Despite their mass–300 to 400 lbs/150 to 200 kg is not unusual–giant cods are curious and friendly. Because of their rarity, many of the potato cods along the reef have acquired local nicknames.

One of the most awe-inspiring sights for the diver or snorkeler is the approach of a harmless giant manta ray. With their mouth flaps funneling plankton, the 10- to 14-ft/3- to 4-m rays swim effortlessly into the current, slowly coming into view from the distant blue. Occasionally, they can be seen leaping from the sea and then crashing back with an echoing slap. This behavior is thought to be an attempt to dislodge parasites or a territorial or sexual display. Manta rays frequent the waters around many of the southern reef islands, such as Heron Island. It is not uncommon for a returning dive boat to be filled with excited chatter about swimming with a giant manta.

Few people come to the Great Barrier Reef without the hope of encountering the reef's most infamous resident—the shark. No matter how clear the waters are, there is always a point where the blue becomes too deep and the diver's imagination may take over. This is where one might expect to find the deadliest predator in the sea. But divers and snorkelers on the reef have little to fear from sharks. Indeed, for those interested in seeing a shark, the search may be frustrating and long. Sharks are not easily found.

SHARKS

Sharks are among the most feared yet awe-inspiring creatures of the sea. Visitors to the Great Barrier Reef often dread encountering them, but are disappointed if they do not.

Great white sharks are not very prevalent in the waters of the Great Barrier Reef. They are more likely to be found near the coast of South Australia, where seals offer tasty and satisfying meals.

Tiger sharks inhabit the Great Barrier Reef area. Second only to the great white shark in ferocity, the tiger shark is recognized by the vertical bands across its upper body. These bands fade as the sharks mature. Its large mouth and sharp teeth allow the tiger shark to eat marine creatures as large as young sawsharks and hammerhead sharks.

Sharks are particularly adept at sensing food within their reach. They have acute sensitivity to electric fields and are capable of picking up electric impulses from animals buried beneath the ocean floor. They are also highly sensitive to the smell of blood.

SEA TURTLES

Sea turtles are different from most turtles because they have flippers instead of toed feet and they cannot retract their heads completely under their shells. They have strong limbs and a bony, well-developed shell covered with plates laid side to side or overlapping.

Males spend their entire lives at sea, whereas females return to the beach where they were born in order to lay their eggs. It may take decades before females are able to lay eggs. They may come ashore to nest every two, three, or more years but often nest several times during that year.

Eggs are laid during high tide on the highest point of the beach. The young are born approximately forty-eight to ninety-four days later, during the next high tide, when the water is closest to them. Although this increases their chances of survival, very few are not caught and eaten by ever-watchful birds, crabs, and fishes at sea.

Major research into the activities and life cycles of sea turtles is currently being conducted on Heron Island. Scientists record the movements of female turtles, weigh and count their eggs, watch the migration of the babies to the sea, and try to gather as much information as possible about these mysterious creatures. Adult sea turtles are known to swim in hundreds, even thousands, of miles before migrating back to the nesting beaches, but their life during the years between hatching and maturity is largely a mystery.

Reptiles

There are two main reptile types on the reef, sea turtles and sea snakes. Turtles are the more common of the two. Loggerhead and green turtles often swim over the reef in the shallower waters and are frequently seen by visitors. Turtles also nest on several of the coral cays and islands and on a few mainland beaches. Those found nesting usually create considerable interest among both scientists and the public. For many years, sea turtles were under siege, and great numbers were taken by hunters who hoped to profit from the high prices paid for turtle meat and eggs.

Sea snakes have attained a fearsome reputation for their nasty and aggressive behavior when caught and hauled aboard boats, a situation in which–understandably–they will lash out in self-defense.

The huge loggerhead turtle returns to sea after spending the night laying anywhere from 100 to 150 eggs on a small offshore island.

Some of them, like the olive sea snake, are curious and often find themselves in contact with divers. During mating season the olive can be very aggressive, which has probably added to the snakes' reputation for belligerence.

For the most part, though, sea snakes are shy and unaggressive. They tend to inhabit the outer reef areas where few visitors venture, such as the Swain Reefs and the Coral Sea. Most sea snakes pack poisons in their fangs and feed on fishes. An exception is the beautiful turtle-headed sea snake, with its pale-yellow and black bands, which feeds almost exclusively on fish eggs and has no need for fangs and venom-filled glands.

WHALES AND DOLPHINS

Marine mammals have always evoked special emotions in humans. Along the Great Barrier Reef, they are infrequently seen but always generate tremendous excitement when spotted. Dolphins can be found throughout the channels and passageways of the reef. Occasionally, their playfulness and acrobatics can be witnessed as they swim beside the bow of a speeding dive or fishing boat on its way to the reef. Dolphins must surface periodically to breathe, and this usually affords the only view of them that people get. On rare occasions, dolphins have approached divers around the reef. The spinner and the bottle-nosed dolphins are the kinds most likely to be seen.

In the past several years, the southern humpback whale has drawn ever-increasing attention on the Great Barrier Reef in the vicinity of the Whitsunday Islands and the Capricorn–Bunker Groups. After several decades of commercial whaling along the east coast of Australia south of the reef, the great whales—in particular, the humpback—had all but disappeared. Fortunately, whaling activities in Australian waters ceased in time for the whales to begin a recovery. The Marine Parks staff, interested in the migration and behavior of southern humpbacks, has begun to add immensely to the growing body of knowledge about these whales. Between late July and early October, humpbacks are seen passing through the waters around Heron Island and north to the outer passages of the Whitsunday Islands.

Now the nesting site for many birds, the Protector was sunk deliberately on Heron Reef in 1945 to serve as a warning for the island's resort boats.

CAPRICORN–BUNKER GROUPS

Southernmost region of the Great Barrier Reef, the Capricorn–Bunker Groups expose more visitors to the reef than does any other section. The groups, encompassing 11 coral islands and more than 22 reefs and associated shoals and sand banks, lie within 50 mi/ 80 km of the mainland.

The Bunker group owes its name to the American whaler Ebor Bunker, who first charted it in 1803. Long before, however, thousands of sea birds and sea turtles began migrating to the assemblage of cays and islands for breeding and nesting.

The Capricorn–Bunker Groups have not always enjoyed protection. In the 1920s, Lady Elliot Island, at the southern end of the chain, was ravaged by guano mining and the grazing of feral goats. Vigorous attempts are being made to reverse the damage. The reintroduction of native plants has been effective in stabilizing the soils and in encouraging sea birds to nest on the island, which they had essentially abandoned for more livable conditions.

Large breeding colonies of sooty terns are found nesting on coral islands. Approximately 20,000 nest on Michaelmas Cay alone.

As part of the Great Barrier Reef Region, the groups fall within marine park jurisdiction, and strict regulations may apply to activities on the islands or in the water, including shell collecting, scuba diving, fishing, anchorage by unauthorized vessels, and camping. If you have questions about regulations, it's best to contact the ranger station in Gladstone or on Heron Island or the regional headquarters in Rockhampton.

HERON ISLAND

Heron Island, the best-known island of the Capricorn–Bunker Groups, has long been the mecca for those searching for a reasonably priced and fairly accessible way to discover the beauty and mystery of the Great Barrier Reef. The island is only 50 mi/80 km off the south-central Queensland coastline. Unlike many of the continental resort islands to the north, Heron is a coral cay formed from the very coral reef that visitors come to see. One has only to step out the door, and a morning reef walk is only a few feet away.

The island is at the northwestern corner of a large lagoon–reef complex. About 10 ft/3 m at its highest level, the island is one of the most densely vegetated of the Capricorn–Bunker Groups. Pisonias, broad-leafed trees that reach a height of 50 ft/15 m, grow in a thick forest over much of the heart of Heron. Encircling the pisonias along the broken sand and coral shore are casuarinas and slender-stemmed pandanus. The trees provide shade from the hot tropical sun and help to secure the soil.

Every visitor to Heron expects to see coral, fishes, turtles, or, possibly, a humpback whale, but more often than not it is the birds that are the surprise. They seem to be everywhere you look. Thousands of noddy terns nest on the branches of the pisonias. Flying out to sea and back again, they put on a never-ending aerial display. Sand flies below your feet from the burrow-digging efforts of the sooty shearwater, or muttonbird. Its nighttime crying will make you think of ill-tempered babies. By the second day, the crying becomes tolerable, even ignored. Birds seem to have taken over the island. In the Heron Island Resort dining room, scarcely a meal passes without the begging antics of a resident white reef heron at tableside, while banded land rails race about under the table, picking up breadcrumbs.

Heron Island is one of the few regular breeding sites for green turtles. The activity of the turtles each summer draws considerable attention. Female turtles, after spending several years at sea maturing and breeding, return to Heron to renew the cycle.

For a snorkeling and diving vacation, the experience on Heron is unsurpassed. Since spear fishing and shell collecting on the reefs are strictly prohibited, the marine life not only is rich and diverse, but also is generally unafraid of humans. The reefs surrounding the island have never suffered the adverse effects of boat anchors or the depredations of the crown-of-thorns starfish.

On Heron, you are seldom more than 15 minutes from any of a dozen prime dive spots. The 35-acre reef around the island offers a variety of dives in both deep and shallow water. One of the best dive spots for hand feeding and photographing fish is at the Bommies,

Although they have a fearsome reputation because of their rows of backward-curving teeth, some of the larger tesselated moray eels have become reef island "pets" that allow divers to touch and feed them.

home of two popular moray eels named Harry and Fang. The Bommies are giant coral heads ranging in depth from 10 to 60 ft/3 to 18 m. They attract a wide variety of reef fishes, such as barramundi cod, spangled emperors, golden trevallies, and coral trout, along with a few resident reef sharks at the Bommies' base. The 5-ft/1.5-m sharks are shy and virtually harmless.

Another popular dive spot is around the tip of Heron Reef to the north side at Gorgonia Hole. A shallow dive area, it features a small wall running parallel to the reef edge that is divided by an interrupted series of gutters, holes, and swim-throughs. Many soft corals are found here as well as octopuses, crabs, and angelfish.

A third location is known as Blue Pools, which gets its name from its relative closeness in size to an Olympic-size swimming pool. This region features many brightly colored small fishes, such as the colorful parrotfish, which pick up and grind down coral rubble for food along the sandy ocean floor. Occasionally, white-tip reef sharks can be found resting on the bottom under ledges. Green turtles may also be seen under many of these ledges.

There is no camping on Heron Island, and all arrangements for staying on the island must be made through the Heron Island Lodge. A set fee covers rooms and meals. All other activities are additional. Access to the island is either by launch each morning from the Gladstone docks or by helicopter flight from Gladstone Airport. Several flights a day connect with domestic carriers.

LADY ELLIOT ISLAND

The 100-acre Lady Elliot Island marks the southern boundary of the Great Barrier Reef. It has over recent years become a more popular destination for visitors to the reef. With virtually no reef flat surrounding the island, the reef edge is just beyond the beach, making diving even better than it is off many of the more popular islands to the north. The absence of a reef flat also ensures that water surrounding the reef is clear and sediment-free at low tide. Manta rays are an added highlight to many dives, since the giant winged fish seem to have a particular liking for the reefs near Lady Elliot.

Both campgrounds and cabins are available on the island, with

North Reef Cay is a small but important island for nesting birds. Colonies of more than 6,000 common noddies have been sighted there.

special bookings and tours arranged through Australian Wildlife Tours in Brisbane, Queensland. Air service to the island is available from Brisbane, Hervey Bay, and Bundaberg. Charter boats also run from Bundaberg.

OTHER ISLANDS OF THE CAPRICORN–BUNKER GROUPS

Self-contained camping is permitted on Lady Musgrave, Hoskyn, and Masthead islands. Campers must provide for all their needs, including fresh drinking water. Length of stay and activities on the islands are limited, and transportation to and from the islands is up to the visitor. For complete information, contact the Ranger-in-Charge, Queensland National Park and Wildlife Service, State Government Building, Roseberry Street, P.O. Box 315, Gladstone, QLD 4680.

SWAIN REEFS AND POMPEY COMPLEX

The Swain Reefs and Pompey Complex are more remote than the Capricorn–Bunker Groups. Extending for 1,400 mi/2,300 km from the Capricorn Channel to opposite the Whitsunday Islands, this portion of the reef is considered to be the most spectacular, yet because of its remoteness and inaccessibility from the mainland, it is rarely visited. It can be reached only by private boat or by charter boat (out of Rockhampton).

In the southern Swain Reefs section, the reef complex is over 200 mi/320 km wide; it narrows rapidly to approximately half that width in the Pompey Complex area. Viewed from the air, the Swain–Pompey region forms the most intricate network of coral reefs in the world. An underwater maze of rich blue channels winds its way through individual reef complexes that stretch over an area of 60 sq mi/156 sq km. This central reef system has developed its own microenvironment of tide fluctuations, highest in the world for a reef system, and deep internal channels with currents in excess of 12 knots. Some channels have been deepened to exceed 200 ft/60 m, considerably deeper than the surrounding outer-reef waters.

WHITSUNDAY ISLANDS

The Whitsunday Islands have impressed almost every visitor since their discovery by James Cook in 1770. "Shores rise in a very steep slope, with occasional precipices to a height of several hundred feet and are completely covered by a magnificent forest," wrote botanist Joseph B. Jukes aboard the British survey ship H.M.S. *Fly*. Jukes was so impressed with the beauty and quality of the islands for a possible port site that he went on to suggest that should the newly founded colony in New South Wales deem it necessary to move north, there could be no finer spot on the entire coast.

Thousands venture into the Whitsundays each year to escape the rush of the cities, spend lazy afternoons sailing or scuba diving in one of the hundreds of fringing reefs that line the islands, or sit on a secluded beach to watch the sun rise from across the Pacific. Fringed

Black noddy tern.

by coral reefs and brightly colored tropical marine creatures, the islands appear to fulfill every expectation of what a reef should be.

The Whitsundays are the remnants of two drowned coastal mountain ranges. As the polar glaciers retreated and the sea level rose, the valleys between these mountaintops and the adjacent mainland were submerged. Over the past several thousand years, corals have thrived in favorable sites along the rocky islands, creating fringing reefs. The islands are classified as "continental" because their geologic make-up, wildlife, and vegetation are essentially identical to those of the adjacent mainland.

The Whitsundays lie at the southern extreme of the central section of the Great Barrier Reef Marine Park. Now protected by park laws, the islands earlier suffered at the hand of progress, and some of the old scars are still visible. Where luxurious resorts dot many of the major islands, small logging camps used to operate. During the early nineteenth century, loggers cut down many of the tall native hoop pines for housing construction on the mainland.

The history of the Whitsundays before the arrival of Europeans is a considerable mystery. It is known that Aboriginal tribes utilized

Seen from above, the Whitsunday Islands are revealed to be a submerged mountain range. A fringing reef has grown around them, making their coves ideal for snorkeling, sailing, and fishing.

the islands, and their settlements may have been some of the first along the Queensland coast. Extensive archaeological sites have been found in some places, particularly on the Keppel Islands. To many who either live on the islands or frequently return to the relaxed life among the thousands of bays, coves, and beaches, there is only one way to truly see and experience the Whitsundays: you must climb aboard one of the many bare-boat charters and sail off in search of your own secluded tropical paradise. Bare-boat chartering means renting a boat without a crew. You determine where you will sail. It is the best way to appreciate the islands.

The Whitsundays offer a holiday experience on practically any level. Five-star resorts on Hamilton and Hayman islands cater to hedonistic tropical indulgences; islands in the southern Cumberland Group, such as Brampton Island, feature cozy resort atmospheres in the setting of native bush; still others, such as Whitsunday, Thomas, and Goldsmith islands, lure the adventurous into roughing it on their own.

Camping is available on several of the islands throughout the Whitsundays and the Cumberland Group; however, it often requires a bit of planning and initiative.

Many of the islands are reachable only by private boat or charter arranged weeks in advance. Permits are necessary throughout the marine park for any overnight visit. For specific information, contact the ranger at Conway National Park via Arlie Beach. In making plans to visit the islands, it is important to make note of local festivals and holidays when securing any kind of accommodation. It may be necessary to make reservations as early as ten weeks in advance.

LINDEMAN ISLAND

Lindeman Island lies about 40 mi/64 km northeast of Mackay and lays claim to the oldest resort on the reef isles. This continental island, which features a great variety of bird life and flora, also offers more than 12 mi/19 km of great bush-walking trails along its rugged coastline and through its inland bush. Because of the isle's prime location between the Whitsunday and the Cumberland Group islands, visitors can enjoy many good views of the other islands.

Although Lindeman Island is far from any coral formations, its resort features boat and airplane trips to the reef, snorkeling, fishing, and day trips to other islands—for example, to nearby Hook Island, to visit its underwater observatory. This larger underwater fishbowl allows visitors to observe coral gardens and colorful fish without getting their feet wet.

Visitors reach Lindeman by plane from Mackay or Proserpine, or by boat (day trips or charters) from Shute Harbour, Mackay, or Proserpine. The resort is small and moderately priced, with meals included. No camping is permitted on the island.

HAMILTON ISLAND

Hamilton Island, a 1,500-acre continental island, lies about 10 mi/ 16 km southeast of Shute Harbour and is recognized by many as the country's largest offshore resort complex. Although named in the mid-nineteenth century, the island remained uninhabited until the mid-1940s. It has now been developed very extensively.

In addition to first-class accommodation, the island features scuba-diving facilities, daily flights to the reef, fishing charters, and a fauna park that includes many Australian favorites, such as kangaroos, koalas, wallabies, and emus.

Hamilton is reached by air from Proserpine, Shute Harbour, Mackay, and most major Australian cities.

HAYMAN ISLAND

Hayman Island recently reopened after a $200 million face-lift by its owner, Ansett Airlines of Australia. Although the "creator" of the resort, Sir Reginald Ansett, began it as a way for the airline to compensate for the slow winter season, Hayman is now considered to be the most exclusive of all Great Barrier Reef resort isles.

Set in the middle of the beautiful Whitsunday Passage, 21 mi/ 34 km off the coast, Hayman looks like a tropical emerald isle. While some walking trails are available, Hayman's strength lies in its five-star accommodations, *haute cuisine*, and personalized service. Even though the resort can be reached by helicopter, most guests make the short ferry ride aboard the luxurious *Sun Goddess* cruise ship.

HINCHINBROOK ISLAND

Near the northern border of the Central Section of the Great Barrier Reef Marine Park is one of Australia's most spectacular national parks, Hinchinbrook Island. The highest and largest of the islands on the Queensland coast—more than 20 mi/32 km long and 13 mi/ 21 km at its widest point—Hinchinbrook has existed in almost complete anonymity. Hinchinbrook's great blessing may simply be that it is in a bad location. There are no flights to the island; only a few charter boats make the trip; and Cardwell, the town on the adjacent mainland, has no airport for large domestic or international flights. It is far enough out of the way that most visitors to northern Queensland cannot justify the trip. For those willing to spend the time and go through the difficulties of getting to Hinchinbrook, the experience will repay them tenfold.

Hinchinbrook Island is like few places on earth. Excluding the tiny, unpretentious cabin-resort that has been cut out of the forest on the far northern tip of the island on Cape Richards, all else is unspoiled. No other island on the coast has such a strong Robinson Crusoe atmosphere. There are two bush-camping areas, reachable by boat only, at Zoe Bay and Scraggy Point. The most popular, though primitive, campground is at Macushla Point. Arriving there, the charter boat backs as close to the beach as it can without running aground, and then all belongings must be waded ashore. As the boat departs, the sense of true isolation sets in. On the beach the greeting party consists of a pair of 5-ft/1.5-m sand goanna lizards and a few smaller varieties, along with a half-dozen curious feathered locals. Fringing much of the shoreline is rich and diverse tropical mangrove forest. An elevated walkway at Missionary Bay, built for scientists from the Australian Institute of Marine Science who are studying the forest, offers visitors a unique view of mangrove life.

The island has several high rocky peaks, the tallest of which is Mount Bowen, at 3,650 ft/1,095 m. Mantling the slopes of these peaks are lush tropical rain forests and forests of pine and hardwood. Cool streams, rushing waterfalls, and crystal-clear pools await the bush walker who explores these forests. At most times, there is the feeling that no one else has been here before. For the visitor seeking a more open landscape, Hinchinbrook offers its secluded beaches and isolated coves. You can spend your days luxuriating on what feels like your own private beach, known only to the sea birds and curious beach creatures.

The island's main wildlife attractions are its dugongs and sea turtles. Dugongs are large sea mammals—8 to 10 ft/2.5 to 3 m long and almost 1,200 lbs/600 kg—that look like a cross between a pig and an elephant. In fact, although they live in the sea, they are distant cousins of the elephant. They are most often seen at night, foraging in shallow water for aquatic plants.

Dugongs were almost hunted to extinction for their delicious meat and because it was wrongly believed that their oil (one dugong can yield 5 gal/19 l) cured lung and rheumatic illnesses. Now their main predators are the sharks, which particularly enjoy stealing young nursing dugongs away from their mothers.

Dugongs shed tears when wounded. Aborigines attributed mystical powers to these tears, and some tribes even forbade women to go near a dugong unless it was cooked and ready to be eaten.

Sea turtles are the other popular attractions at Hinchinbrook. Giant female sea turtles make their way to high ground at night in order to lay their eggs. They are determined and are rarely thwarted by a visitor's curious gaze. Four species of sea turtles have been sighted on Hinchinbrook: luth, green, hawkbill, and loggerhead.

DUNK ISLAND

Dunk Island is one of the most popular resort islands off the northern coast of Queensland. It lies 16 mi/26 km from Tully. Named by Captain Cook after George Montagu Dunk, earl of Halifax, Dunk Island is known for its magnificent rain forests, splendid scenery, and abundance of wildlife and vegetation. More than ninety species of birds have been sighted on the island, which also attracts a large variety of butterflies. The island is also known for its display of wild orchids.

What made Dunk Island famous, though, were the books of E. J. Banfield, who published *Confessions of a Beachcomber* in 1908 and then wrote three more books (one published posthumously) detailing life on Dunk Island. He likened his existence to the timeless

SEABIRDS

Most seabirds, or pelagic birds, spend most of their lives at sea. It is only during the breeding season that the birds seek out isolated islands and sandbanks on which to lay their eggs and raise their young.

Seabirds are generally colonial nesters. The larger groups of birds afford greater protection to the chicks. Nesting areas are always rife with activity and noise. Aerial and ground courtship displays are common. The young are recognized by their smell and their distinct calls, and they are constantly crying out for more food.

Coral cays are excellent breeding sites for such seabirds as shearwaters, petrels, boobies, tropic birds, and terns. Shearwaters usually rely on cliffs of coastal islands to support their nests. Unable to maneuver well on land because of their webbed feet, they simply fall off the cliffs to give them momentum in flight. On coral cays they take advantage of low flat winds to gain momentum in flight.

Three species of boobies may nest on the same island, but they occupy different habitats. Red-footed boobies prefer trees and bushes; brown boobies seek out cliffs or small clearings near bushes; and masked boobies need large clearings of up to 50 sq yd/42 sq m.

Crested terns are by far the most regimented of all the nesters. Although thousands of them may be nesting in the same location, a precise distance is maintained between the nests. They are close together, but out of pecking distance of one another. What is remarkable is that each bird sitting on its nest faces in the same direction.

The female brown booby nests in the coral sand, safely camouflaging her coral-white chick.

dream of living on a secluded desert island, free from disturbances and the trials and tribulations of city life.

Dunk Island retains much of this splendor, although the Aborigines who used to share the island with Banfield (they called it Coonanglebar) have long since been removed and placed on a reservation on the mainland. A small resort accommodates the limited number of tourists who visit. It is on a small beach on the landward side of the island and does not interfere with the island's beauty.

Access is available from a launch at Clump Point or by air from Townsville or Cairns. Facilities are available for campers, who may stay for a maximum of three nights. A permit (obtained from the Cardwell office) is required.

GREEN ISLAND

Like Heron Island, Green Island is one of the few coral islands on the Great Barrier Reef that has tourist accommodation. Only 15 mi/ 24 km northeast of Cairns, 30-acre Green Island is composed of pristine white coral and covered by lush green vegetation. It is accessible by launch from Cairns, and because of its closeness to the mainland, day trips are possible.

Heron Island is one of the few places in the world where the two color phases of the reef heron can be seen at once.
Facing page, clockwise from top left: silverback gull; brown booby chick; masked plover, or lapwing.

Another island discovered by Captain Cook, Green Island is extremely accommodating to the tourist, especially the one who does not snorkel or scuba dive. It boasts the first theater built on a coral island. At the Castaway Theatre, visitors can see excellent and highly informative films about the Great Barrier Reef.

For those who want to experience the reef first-hand without getting wet, there are two options. Green Island has an excellent underwater observatory. Glass-bottom boats also allow nondivers to observe and study the corals on the outskirts of the island. At low tide, these coral gardens are most visible. Unfortunately, they are not as spectacular as they used to be. Over the past few decades, the crown-of-thorns starfish, which feeds almost exclusively on coral polyps, has destroyed much of the coral population around Green Island.

MICHAELMAS CAY AND HASTINGS REEF COMPLEX

Both Michaelmas Cay and the Hastings Reef complex are famous for the thousands of sea birds that flock there. Lying only 20 to 30 mi/32 to 48 km from Cairns, these islands are small coral sand

cays. Michaelmas Cay is only 200 sq yd/160 sq m. Rising only 10 ft/3 m above sea level, the cays support low-growing and colorful vegetation.

Visitors arriving by launch from Cairns cannot help being astonished at the amount of avian activity occurring in such a small location. There are birds on the wing, fish being carried to waiting nestlings, occasional squabbles, and incessant chatter. Everywhere one looks or ventures, there are birds. Walking is precarious because many young birds are underfoot. The birds display almost no fear of humans; on the contrary, they are extremely curious about the visitors.

The most popular birds on the islands include several species of tern, most notably sooty and crested terns, and white-capped and brown noddies. Amazingly, with all the action going on, the young do not get mixed together. They manage to stay clustered together by species. Small patches of brown, white, and striped hatchlings can be seen dotting the tiny landscape.

Because the islands are national parks, movement is severely limited in order to protect the nesting birds. On Michaelmas Cay, which has been nicknamed Isle of Terns, visitors are allowed on only the western shore.

LIZARD ISLAND

Lizard Island is the most northerly of the Great Barrier Reef resort islands. Lying 47 mi/75 km north of Cookstown and only 10 mi/16 km from the mainland at Point Lookout, it is a 50-minute flight from Cairns.

Lizard Island is the perfect place to vacation for those interested in an extremely quiet, intimate hideaway. The one resort on the island can accommodate only a few dozen guests, who have 5 sq mi/13 sq km of beach and lightly timbered slopes to wander on and explore.

Besides attracting the visitor who seeks privacy, Lizard Island appeals to the avid deep-sea fisherman who is tempted and challenged by the abundant marlin and tuna off the outer reef. Deep-sea fishing as well as scuba diving and snorkeling are extremely rewarding here.

Sooty tern.

Lizard Island was named by Captain Cook in 1770 after the large monitor lizards he found on the island. Cook's Look is the point from which Captain Cook surveyed the Great Barrier Reef and plotted a course for the open seas. Lizard Island gained its notoriety, however, from the sad story of one of its former inhabitants, Mary Watson. When a mainland tribe invaded her secluded island home, Mary, her infant son, and a servant escaped in a 4-sq-ft/.36 sq m barrel, her husband having taken their only boat with him when he left to start a new fishing depot on another island. Mary never found fresh water, despite landing on several nearby islands, and was found dead with her baby in her arms, the servant lying dead close by. She left a journal of her trials and has become a symbol of martyrdom and motherhood. A dry fountain was built in her honor in Cookstown.

The Great Barrier Reef is attracting more and more visitors to enjoy the natural beauty of its islands and reefs. New services are constantly being developed for these visitors. High-speed catamarans now take visitors in a few hours to spots that used to be a two-day sail away. A floating hotel is being built at John Brewer Reef off Townsville. Semisubmersible craft with glass sides give even non-divers the experience of underwater exploration.

Before visiting the Great Barrier Reef, be sure to find out about the newest services from a branch of the Australian Tourist Commission.

I N D E X

The type in this book was set in Century Expanded by Arkotype Inc., New York, New York. The book was printed and bound by Toppan Printing Company, Ltd., Tokyo, Japan.